Better Homes and Gardens®

Fast Fix
family food

MORE THAN 400 EASY RECIPES YOUR FAMILY WILL LOVE

D1413575

Meredith® BOOKS

Better Homes and Gardens® Fast Fix Family Food
Editor: Jessica Saari
Graphic Designer: Renee E. McAtee
Design Coordinator: Diana Van Winkle
Copy Chief: Terri Fredrickson
Copy Editor: Kevin Cox
Publishing Operations Manager: Karen Schirm
Senior Editor, Asset and Information Management: Phillip Morgan
Edit and Design Production Coordinator: Mary Lee Gavin
Editorial Assistant: Cheryl Eckert
Book Production Managers: Pam Kvitne, Marjorie J. Schenkelberg,
    Mark Weaver
Imaging Center Operator: Mitchell Barlow
Photographers: Jason Donnelly, Scott Little, Blaine Moats, Jay Wilde
Contributing Proofreaders: Karen Fraley, Stacie Gaylor,
    Donna Segal
Contributing Indexer: Elizabeth T. Parson
Test Kitchen Director: Lynn Blanchard
Test Kitchen Product Supervisor: Colleen Weeden
Test Kitchen Home Economists: Elizabeth Burt, R.D., L.D.;
    Marilyn Cornelius; Juliana Hale; Laura Harms, R.D.;
    Maryellyn Krantz; Greg Luna; Jill Moberly; Dianna Nolin;
    Lori Wilson

Meredith® Books
Editor in Chief: Gregory H. Kayko
Executive Director, Design: Matt Strelecki
Managing Editor: Amy Tincher-Durik
Executive Editor: Jennifer Darling
Senior Editor/Group Manager: Jan Miller
Marketing Product Manager: Toye Guinn Cody

Executive Director, Marketing and New Business: Kevin Kacere
Director, Marketing and Publicity: Amy Nichols
Executive Director, Sales: Ken Zagor
Director, Operations: George A. Susral
Director, Production: Douglas M. Johnston
Business Director: Jim Leonard

Senior Vice President: Karla Jeffries
Vice President and General Manager: Douglas J. Guendel

Better Homes and Gardens® Special Interest Media/Food & Health
Creative Director: Bridget Sandquist
Editors: Rachel Martin, Lois White
Deputy Art Director: Stephanie Hunter
Associate Art Director: Stacey Willey

Better Homes and Gardens® Magazine
Editor in Chief: Gayle Goodson Butler
Deputy Editor, Food and Entertaining: Nancy Wall Hopkins

Meredith Publishing Group
President: Jack Griffin
Executive Vice President: Doug Olson

Meredith Corporation
Chairman of the Board: William T. Kerr
President and Chief Executive Officer: Stephen M. Lacy

In Memoriam: E. T. Meredith III (1933–2003)

All of us at Meredith® Books are dedicated to providing
you with the information and ideas you need to create
delicious foods. We welcome your comments and
suggestions. Write to us at: Meredith Books, Cookbook
Editorial Department, 1716 Locust St., Des Moines, IA
50309-3023.

Pictured on front cover: Bean & Beef Enchilada Casserole,
    page 107

Our seal assures you that every
recipe in *Fast Fix Family Food* has
been tested in the Better Homes
and Gardens® Test Kitchen. This
means that each recipe is practical
and reliable, and meets our high
standards of taste appeal. We
guarantee your satisfaction with
this book for as long as you own it.

Dinner is back!

Who has time to cook??? Between Monday night soccer practice and Wednesday night music lessons, family life can be very hectic—sometimes even a little frantic! And after working all day, driving the kids around town, and running all your errands, finding the time to whip together a homecooked meal may seem like a daunting task. But stop … and take a deep breath.

Meals at home are possible. No matter how much or how little time you have to put good food on the table for yourself and your family, there's a recipe in here for you. Whether it's 10 minutes or 30 minutes until suppertime, you can find a soup, salad, sandwich, or entree that quiets your family's I'm-hungry-right-now demands. There are also comforting favorites that you can load into the slow cooker in the morning and not think about again until you get home at night. Breakfast and lunch have their place in the day as well. Get the morning off to a bright start with lazy Saturday favorites like pancakes and waffles or last-minute grab-and-go gulpers like breakfast wraps and smoothies. For lunch? Bag it up and bring it to work or school with these quick-fix sandwiches and salads.

And that's just for starters. You'll also find chapters that re-create all of Mom's best recipes (only easier to prepare), dinner menus that are ideal for Sunday together as a family, and foods that will keep even the pickiest eaters happy and well-fed. And finally, indulge your sweet tooth after dinner with some simple desserts or make it grand with your pick of an outstanding celebration cake.

Fast Fix Family Food **was created just for you**—the time-crunched grown-ups who are juggling everything but also know the importance of homecooked meals for themselves and their families. For that reason, these recipes were designed to be not only irresistible but also easy-to-prepare and fast-to-the-table. So go ahead—enjoy food again!

good-to-know tips

handy-dandy PB

Did you know peanut butter is an excellent cleaning agent? Use it to remove sticker goo and ink from your kids' toys. Simply swipe on, let sit for a few minutes, and wipe clean. Voilà!

flip tip

Honey never goes bad, but if it crystallizes in the jar, put the honey in a microwave-safe container and heat.

the
well-stocked
pantry

Fill your cupboard with these staples and you'll have a wealth of options.

flip tip

For a yummy soy-sesame vinaigrette recipe, turn to page 110.

thank you, vanilla

Next time you have a stomachache, reach for a bottle of pure vanilla extract. Add a few drops to a glass of mineral water for a stomach-soothing elixir.

good to know

Cocoa powder keeps for 2 years if stored in a cool, dark place.

is it still good?

CANNED GOODS Beware of dented or punctured cans. Check the "use by" date on the can and store in a cool, dry place. If you can't remember when you bought it, toss it.
SPICES Use your nose. Seasonings lose their strength over time. If the scent isn't strong, neither is the flavor. Ground spices keep for 1–2 years if stored in a cool, dry place.
BAKING SUPPLIES Throw out any ingredient that smells bad. Storage in a cool, dry place is key for flour, sugar, etc. Flour keeps for 8 months; sugars keep indefinitely.

smart idea
Store chocolate chips in a flip-top container for easy scooping access.

fun idea
Make your own flavored sugar: Store a vanilla bean with 1 to 2 cups of sugar. Sprinkle on oatmeal or in your coffee.

goodbye, clumps
Sick of annoying brown sugar lumps? Seal a slice of bread in with the brown sugar for several hours; then remove. The bread will regulate the moisture level and get rid of hard clumps.

food safety 101

keep it chilled

Keep your food cold and your energy costs low—shut the fridge door.

Without refrigerators, it would be hard to enjoy such a wide variety of deliciously fresh food.

But even the fresh stuff will eventually go bad, and that's certainly the case with storing food in the fridge. The best way to make sure all is fresh is by keeping a close eye on the refrigerator thermometer. Have one? Probably not. Most home cooks don't. But it's important to have such a gadget, which costs as little as $5 at hardware and grocery stores.

Make sure the refrigerator temperature never goes above 40°F. Place the thermometer in the middle of the fridge, toward the back, for an accurate reading. While you're at it, buy a separate thermometer for the freezer and check to make sure it stays 0°F or colder.

MORE HANDY TIPS FOR REFRIGERATING FOOD:

✳ Chuck leftovers after four days. Most people store them too long. Certain foods last only a day or two, including stuffing, greens, and fish.

✳ Don't store eggs and milk in the door. Everytime you open the door, the temperature will fluctuate. Keep eggs in their original carton—they stay fresher that way.

✳ Defrost meat and chicken in a sealed bag on the bottom shelf of the fridge. It's tempting to leave it on the counter, but that's a great way to breed bacteria. The sealed bag keeps raw juices from dripping onto produce.

✳ Don't crowd food together since air needs to circulate to keep everything cool. If a packed fridge is a continual problem (or preference) for you, consider buying a second refrigerator or buy smaller amounts more frequently.

✳ After making soup or chili, divide the food into small containers before storing in the refrigerator. A hot pot raises the temperature inside and endangers other foods.

✳ Clean your fridge regularly, checking expiration dates each time. When in doubt, throw it out.

food safety 101
the produce aisle

Use these tips to select and properly prepare fruits and vegetables.

Safe Handling

* While you're at the grocery store, keep fresh produce separate from household chemicals and raw meat in your shopping cart. Bag produce and raw meat separately. At home, place them apart in the refrigerator.

* Wash your hands with soap andwarm water before and after handling produce and raw meat.

* Clean everything that touches the produce before and after food preparation with soap and water. This includes knives, work surfaces, cutting boards, and utensils.

Cleaning Tips

Fruits and Vegetables:
* Gently rub firm-skinned fruits and vegetables, such as tomatoes, zucchini, and grapes, under running tap water. Dry the produce with a clean cloth or paper towel.

* Produce with inedible skins or rinds, such as cantaloupes and avocados, must still be rinsed.

* If a package is labeled "ready to eat," "washed," or "triple washed," you do not need to wash the produce.

Mushrooms:
* To clean fresh mushrooms, wipe them with a clean, damp cloth or rinse them lightly and dry them with paper towels.

* Do not soak mushrooms; it ruins their texture.

Salad Greens:
* To prepare heads of lettuce, remove any outer leaves that are wilted or discolored. Remove the core. Rinse the lettuce, core side up, under cold running water. Invert the head and allow that water to run out.

* To prepare loose salad greens, submerse in cold water and drain in a colander.

* Pat all salad greens dry with a cloth or paper towel or spin them in a salad spinner.

Potatoes and Carrots:
* If you do not plan to peel the vegetable, use a stiff-bristle scrub brush to remove any dirt.

* For potatoes, use a vegetable peeler to remove any eyes, blemishes, or green spots. If more than half of the potato is green, discard it. The green portion creates a bitter flavor and contains solanine, which is slightly toxic.

Buying Guide

LOOK FOR plump, crisp, bright-colored vegetables that are heavy for their size.

AVOID produce that is bruised, discolored, shriveled, or cracked.

PURCHASE fresh-cut vegetables, such as packaged salads, relish trays, or precut fruit, only if they're refrigerated. Then you know they're fresh and safe to eat.

grilling

Summer provides all the ingredients for a get-together around the grill. It would be a real bummer to blow it with a bout of food poisoning. Before you serve it, make sure your food is properly cooked.

Don't forget: Use a clean meat thermometer each time you check the internal temperature.

meat	size	time	doneness
Chicken/Turkey			
breast half	4–5 oz.	12–15 min.	170°F
thigh	4–5 oz.	12–15 min.	190°F
Beef			
boneless steak	1 in. thick	14–18 min.	160°F
steak with bone	1 in. thick	13–16 min.	160°F
hamburger	½ in. thick	10–13 min.	160°F
Pork			
chop with bone	¾ to 1 in. thick	11–14 min.	160°F
chop without bone	¾ to 1 in. thick	12–15 min.	160°F
brats, hot dogs		3–7 min.	heat through
Seafood			
whole fish	½ to 1½ lbs.	6–9 min. per ½ lb.	flakes
fillets, steaks	½ to 1 in. thick	4–6 min. per ½ in.	flakes
kabobs	½ to 1 in. thick	4–6 min. per ½ in.	flakes
shrimp (medium)	20 per lb.	5–8 min.	opaque
shrimp (jumbo)	12–15 per lb.	7–9 min.	opaque

rise and shine

Sausage & Egg Alfredo Skillet

Start to Finish: 25 minutes

Nonstick cooking spray
1   7-ounce package light cooked sausage links (10)
¼   cup sliced green onion (2)
6   eggs, lightly beaten
½   cup purchased light Alfredo sauce or Homemade Alfredo Sauce (page 117)
1½   teaspoons yellow mustard
½   cup shredded American cheese (2 ounces)
Cooked potato wedges, hash brown potatoes, and/or toast (optional)

1. Coat a large skillet with cooking spray. Cook sausage and green onion over medium heat until sausage is brown. Pour eggs over sausage mixture in skillet. As mixture sets, run a spatula around edge of skillet, lifting egg mixture so uncooked portion flows underneath. Continue cooking and lifting edges until egg mixture is almost set (surface will be moist). Remove from heat; cover and set aside.

2. In a saucepan, stir together the Alfredo sauce and mustard. Heat over medium heat until bubbly. Stir in the cheese. Stir until melted. Cut egg mixture into wedges and serve with sauce. If desired, serve with potatoes and/or toast. Makes 4 to 6 servings.

Per serving: 271 calories, 16 g fat (7 g sat. fat), 365 mg cholesterol, 814 mg sodium, 5 g carbo, 0 g fiber, 23 g pro.

Sun-Up Wrap-Ups

Start to Finish: 10 minutes

1　teaspoon butter
1　egg
1　slice American cheese
　　(1 ounce)
1　ounce thinly sliced
　　honey-roasted ham or
　　Canadian-style bacon
1　5- to 6-inch flour tortilla

1. In a small nonstick skillet, melt butter over medium heat. Lightly beat egg and add to skillet; spread egg to size of the tortilla. Cook for 2 to 3 minutes, or until golden on the bottom. With a large spatula, turn egg over. Cook for 1 to 2 minutes more or until set. Top with cheese and ham.

2. Carefully transfer layered egg, cheese, and ham to tortilla. Roll up tortilla to enclose filling. Wrap filled tortilla in a napkin or waxed paper. Serve immediately. Makes 1 serving.

Per serving: 347 cal., 21 g fat (10 g sat. fat), 261 mg chol., 1,029 mg sodium, 20 g carbo., 1 g fiber, 19 g pro.

{omelet ideas}

Whether
it's morning,
noon, or night,
your family will
come eagerly to the
table for these
fun takes on omelets.
They're so good
and so easy—and you'll
see how perfectly eggs
adapt to flavors
from around
the world. Time to
get crackin'!

Easy Omelets

4 eggs
¼ cup water
1 tablespoon butter
Desired filling
(recipes, pages
16 and 17)

Start to Finish: 10 minutes Makes: 2 omelets

1 In a medium bowl, whisk together eggs and water until completely blended. Meanwhile, in a 10-inch nonstick skillet, melt half of the butter over medium-high heat until hot enough to sizzle when a drop of water is added. Pour in half of the egg mixture (about ½ cup).

2 Using a heat-resistant rubber scraper, carefully push cooked portions at edges toward center so the uncooked portions can reach hot pan surface, tilting pan and moving cooked portions as necessary.

3 When top is thickened and no visible liquid egg remains, top half of the omelet with about ¼ cup of the desired filling.

4 Using a heat-resistant rubber scraper, fold omelet in half over filling. Invert omelet onto a plate. Repeat.

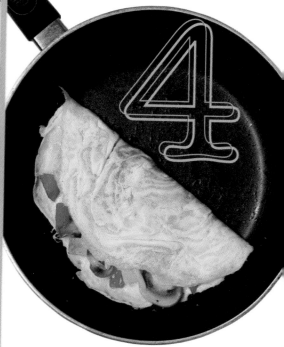

American Filling:

Combine ¼ cup sliced mushrooms, ½ cup chopped tomato, ¼ cup chopped ham, and ¼ cup shredded cheddar or American cheese.

Per omelet: 294 cal., 22 g fat (10 g sat. fat), 463 mg chol., 492 mg sodium, 4 g carbo., 1 g fiber, 20 g pro.

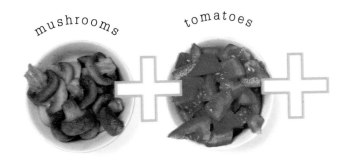

Greek Filling:

Combine ¼ cup chopped fresh spinach, ¼ cup chopped canned artichokes, ¼ cup sliced pitted ripe olives, and ½ cup crumbled feta cheese.

Per omelet: 301 cal., 24 g fat (11 g sat. fat), 463 mg chol., 748 mg sodium, 5 g carbo., 2 g fiber, 17 g pro.

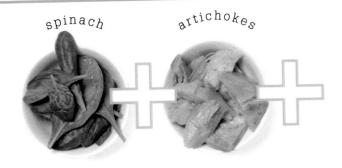

Mexican Filling:

Combine ¼ cup avocado slices, ¼ cup cooked and drained chorizo sausage, 2 tablespoons snipped fresh cilantro, and ½ cup shredded Monterey Jack cheese with jalapeño peppers.

Per omelet: 453 cal., 37 g fat (16 g sat. fat), 482 mg chol., 602 mg sodium, 4 g carbo., 0 g fiber, 20 g pro.

Italian Filling:

Combine ¼ cup cut-up roasted red sweet pepper, ¼ cup snipped fresh basil, ¼ cup sliced, cooked and drained Italian sausage, and 1 ounce sliced fresh mozzarella.

Per omelet: 320 cal., 25 g fat (11 g sat. fat), 462 mg chol., 528 mg sodium, 3 g carbo., 1 g fiber, 20 g pro.

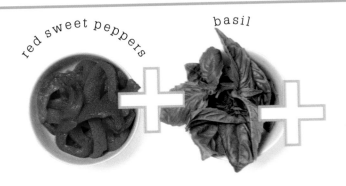

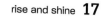

ham + cheddar cheese =

black olives + feta cheese =

cilantro + Monterey Jack cheese =

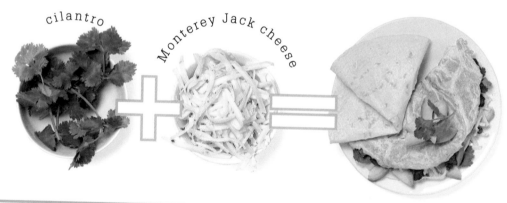

Italian sausage + mozzarella cheese =

ALL THE FIXINS:
There isn't much you can do wrong with a sausage link or patty. It's delicious no matter what you serve with it or what time you eat it. Below are some yummy accompaniments, but feel free to combine sausage with what you like. Here are some ideas to get you started: ● Jalapeño peppers and salsa ● Hash browns and ketchup ● Mozzarella cheese and pasta sauce ● Tomatoes and onions ● Pancakes and maple syrup ● Toast and jam

↑ CAN YOU TELL?
These sausage links and patty are actually vegetarian and made of soy products.

Egg & Sausage Sandwiches

Start to Finish: 30 minutes

4   cooked light sausage patties
2   tablespoons fat-free mayonnaise
1   tablespoon honey mustard
3   eggs
2   tablespoons water
⅛   teaspoon salt
    Dash ground black pepper
    Nonstick cooking spray
4   English muffins, split and toasted
4   slices Colby and Monterey
    Jack cheese (4 ounces)

1. Preheat oven to 350°F. Place sausage patties on a shallow baking pan. Bake about 10 minutes or until heated through.
2. In a bowl, stir together mayonnaise and mustard; set aside. In another bowl, beat together eggs, water, salt, and pepper. Heat a skillet over medium-high heat until hot.
3. Coat skillet with cooking spray and add egg mixture; reduce heat to medium. Gently stir egg mixture with a spatula until small pieces of cooked egg are surrounded by liquid egg. Stop stirring. Cook 1 minute more or until mixture is set but shiny.
4. Use the spatula to divide egg sheet into 4 portions. Spread bottoms of muffins with mayonnaise mixture. Top with egg portion, sausage patty, and cheese slice. Place sandwiches on a baking sheet and return to oven for 2 to 3 minutes or until cheese melts. Add muffin tops. Makes 4 sandwiches.

Per sandwich: 336 cal., 15 g fat (8 g sat fat), 195 mg chol., 782 mg sodium, 29 g carbo., 2 g fiber, 18 g pro.

Polenta with Sausage & Eggs

Start to Finish: 30 minutes

½   of a 16-ounce tube refrigerated
    cooked polenta
    Nonstick cooking spray
1   7-ounce package (10 links)
    cooked light sausage links,
    halved crosswise
1   medium red sweet pepper,
    cut into bite-size strips
4   eggs
1   to 2 teaspoons water
¼   cup purchased basil pesto or
    Homemade Pesto (recipe, page 117)

1. Mash polenta and cook according to package directions.
2. Coat a large skillet with cooking spray. Cook sausage and sweet pepper over medium-high heat for 4 minutes or until pepper is tender. Remove and keep warm.
3. Break eggs into skillet. Cook over medium heat. When whites are set, add the water to skillet. Cover skillet and cook eggs for 3 to 4 minutes or until yolks begin to thicken but are not hard. Remove eggs to serving platter. Return sausage mixture to skillet. Stir in pesto and heat through. Serve eggs with sausage mixture and polenta. Makes 4 servings.

Per serving: 304 cal., 17 g fat (2 g sat. fat), 238 mg chol., 698 mg sodium, 16 g carbo., 2 g fiber, 17 g pro.

waffles

Any day that begins with waffles is a good day.
It doesn't matter whether they come from the
freezer or a sizzling griddle—
they're always tasty!

Basic Waffles

Start to Finish: 20 minutes

1¾	cups all-purpose flour
2	tablespoons sugar
1	tablespoon baking powder
¼	teaspoon salt
2	eggs
1¾	cups milk
½	cup cooking oil or butter, melted
1	teaspoon vanilla

1. In a large bowl, stir together flour, sugar, baking powder, and salt. Make a well in the center of the flour mixture; set aside.
2. In a medium bowl, beat eggs lightly; stir in milk, oil, and vanilla. Add egg mixture all at once to the flour mixture. Stir just until moistened (batter should be slightly lumpy).
3. Preheat waffle baker according to manufacturer's directions. Grease lightly; add batter. Close lid quickly; do not open until done. Bake according to manufacturer's directions. When done, use a fork to lift waffle off grid. Repeat with remaining batter. Serve warm.* Makes about twelve 4-inch regular waffles or about six 7-inch Belgian waffles.
***Tip:** Keep prepared waffles warm in a 300°F oven while baking the other waffles.

Per basic waffle: 180 cal., 11 g fat (2 g sat. fat), 38 mg chol., 135 mg sodium, 17 g carbo., 0 g fiber, 4 g pro.

Buttermilk Waffles: Prepare as above, except reduce baking powder to 1 teaspoon and add ½ teaspoon baking soda. Substitute 2 cups buttermilk or sour milk for the milk.

Per buttermilk waffle: 179 cal., 10 g fat (2 g sat. fat), 37 mg chol., 188 mg sodium, 17 g carbo., 0 g fiber, 4 g pro.

Did you know?

✳ Waffle House restaurants have served more than 495 million waffles since opening in 1955. That's enough waffles to circle the Earth 1¼ times!

✳ International Waffle Day is March 25 and originated in Sweden. It's now associated with the start of spring too.

Ham Wafflewich
Start to Finish: 5 minutes

2   **frozen plain or apple-cinnamon
      waffles**
1   **tablespoon tub-style cream cheese**
1   **tablespoon apricot preserves**
1   **ounce thinly sliced cooked ham**
      Maple syrup (optional)

1. Toast the waffles in the toaster until golden. Spread one waffle with cream cheese and the other with preserves; set aside. Place the ham on a microwave-safe plate. Microwave ham on 100-percent power (high) for 10 seconds. Using hot pads, remove the plate from the microwave oven. Use a fork to put the ham on top of one waffle, spread side up. Top with remaining waffle, spread side down. If desired, serve with syrup. Makes 1 serving.

Per wafflewich: 134 cal., 4 g fat (1 g sat. fat), 16 mg chol., 606 mg sodium, 17 g carbo., 1 g fiber, 8 g pro.

Waffle Casserole
Prep: 10 minutes   **Chill:** 4 hours
Bake: 50 minutes

1   **pound bulk pork sausage**
6   **frozen waffles, toasted and cubed**
1   **cup shredded cheddar cheese
      (4 ounces)**
6   **eggs**
2   **cups fat-free milk**
1   **teaspoon dry mustard**
⅛ **teaspoon ground black pepper**
      Frozen waffles, toasted (optional)
      **Maple-flavor syrup or pure maple
      syrup (optional)**

1. In a large skillet, cook sausage over medium heat until browned. Drain off fat.
2. Arrange half of the waffle cubes in a 2-quart rectangular baking dish. Top with half of the sausage and about ⅓ cup of the cheese. Repeat layers.
3. In a large bowl, beat eggs with a fork; stir in milk, mustard, and pepper. Pour over layers in dish. Cover and chill for at least 4 hours or up to 24 hours.
4. Preheat oven to 350°F. Uncover and bake for 50 to 60 minutes or until a knife inserted near center comes out clean. Sprinkle with the remaining ⅓ cup cheese. Let stand for 10 minutes. If desired, serve on toasted waffles and drizzle with maple syrup. Makes 8 servings.

Per serving: 353 cal., 22 g fat (9 g sat. fat), 221 mg chol., 55 mg sodium, 15 g carbo., 1 g fiber, 21 g pro.

Banana-Pecan Waffles

Prep: 20 minutes   **Cook:** 3 minutes per waffle

1¾   cups all-purpose flour
2   tablespoons sugar
1   tablespoon baking powder
½   teaspoon ground cinnamon
¼   teaspoon salt
2   small bananas, mashed (¾ cup)
2   eggs
1   cup milk
¼   cup cooking oil or melted butter
1   teaspoon vanilla
½   cup finely chopped pecans, toasted
     and cooled
     Butter, maple syrup, and/or caramel ice
     cream topping (optional)

1. In a large bowl, stir together flour, sugar, baking powder, cinnamon, and salt.

2. In a medium bowl, beat together bananas and eggs. Stir in milk, oil, and vanilla. Add banana mixture all at once to the flour mixture. Stir just until moistened (batter should be slightly lumpy). Stir in pecans.

3. Add batter to a preheated, lightly greased waffle baker according to manufacturer's directions. Close lid quickly; do not open until done. Bake according to manufacturer's directions. When done, use a fork to lift waffle off grid. Repeat with remaining batter. Serve warm with desired toppings.* Makes about 9 waffles.

*Tip: Keep prepared waffles warm in a 300°F oven while baking the other waffles.

Per waffle: 241 cal., 12 g fat (2 g sat. fat), 49 mg chol., 172 mg sodium, 28 g carbo., 2 g fiber, 5 g pro.

Peanut Butter Waffle Bites

Start to Finish: 5 minutes

¼ cup peanut butter
2 frozen waffles, toasted
2 tablespoons honey
2 tablespoons raisins

1. Spread peanut butter on one of the toasted waffles. Drizzle with honey and sprinkle with raisins. Top with remaining waffle. If desired, cut into quarters. Makes 2 servings.

Per serving: 367 cal., 19 g fat (4 g sat. fat), 11 mg chol., 411 mg sodium, 44 g carbo., 3 g fiber, 10 g pro.

Pear-Walnut Muffins

Brown sugar and walnuts make a crunchy
stir-together topping for these muffins.
Prep: 15 minutes   **Bake:** 20 minutes

1½   cups all-purpose flour
½   cup packed brown sugar
2   teaspoons baking powder
1½   teaspoons apple pie spice or
       pumpkin pie spice
⅛   teaspoon salt
1   egg
½   cup cooking oil
½   cup plain low-fat yogurt
1   pear, cored and finely chopped
3   tablespoons finely chopped walnuts
2   tablespoons packed brown sugar

1. Preheat oven to 400°F. Line 12 muffin cups with paper bake cups; set aside. In a mixing bowl, stir together flour, ½ cup brown sugar, baking powder, apple pie spice, and salt. Make a well in the center of the flour mixture. In a bowl, beat egg; stir in oil and yogurt. Add all at once to the flour mixture; stir just until moistened. Stir in pear.

2. Fill prepared muffin cups two-thirds full. For topping, combine walnuts and 2 tablespoons brown sugar; sprinkle onto batter in cups. Bake about 20 minutes or until golden. Serve warm. Makes 12 muffins.

Per muffin: 210 cal., 11 g fat (2 g sat. fat), 18 mg chol., 82 mg sodium, 26 g carbo., 1 g fiber, 3 g pro.

flipping over flapjacks

Few foods make children
flock to the table faster
than a piping hot stack
of pancakes.
Spruce up this basic
flapjack recipe with
whole grains,
fruits and nuts, sausage,
and other yummies.

Buttermilk Pancakes

Pancakes are fun-to-eat favorites with endless variations. Here are some ideas sure to please the whole family.

Prep: 15 minutes **Cook:** 4 minutes per batch

3½   cups all-purpose flour
¼   cup granulated sugar
4   teaspoons baking powder
1   teaspoon baking soda
½   teaspoon salt
2   eggs, lightly beaten
4   cups buttermilk
⅓   cup cooking oil
    Desired fruit options (optional)
    Desired syrup (optional)

1. In a large bowl, stir together flour, sugar, baking powder, baking soda, and salt. In bowl, use a fork to combine eggs, buttermilk, and oil. Add egg mixture all at once to flour mixture. Stir just until moistened (batter should be slightly lumpy).

2. For a standard-size pancake, pour ⅓ cup batter onto a hot, lightly greased griddle. For dollar-size pancakes, use 1 tablespoon batter.

3. Cook over medium heat for 2 to 3 minutes on each side or until pancakes are golden brown, turning to second sides when pancakes have bubbly surfaces and edges are slightly dry. Serve warm. Makes 20 to 24 standard-size pancakes or 120 dollar-size pancakes.

Per standard-size pancake: 141 cal., 5 g fat (1 g sat. fat), 23 mg chol., 228 mg sodium, 20 g carbo., 1 g fiber, 4 g pro.

TIP: If you don't have buttermilk, prepare Buttermilk Pancakes as above, except pour ¼ cup vinegar into a 4-cup glass measuring cup; add milk to equal 4 cups. Let stand for 5 minutes and proceed as above.

simple sauteed fruit topping

In a large skillet, melt 2 tablespoons butter over medium heat. Add 2 cups thinly sliced fresh fruit (peeled, if desired) or frozen fruit and ¼ cup packed brown sugar to skillet. Cook and stir until sugar is dissolved and fruit is tender. Some fruit options are apples, bananas, peaches, or pears. Feeling extra creative? Pair two fruits for extra zip.

even simpler fruit topping

In a microwave-safe medium bowl, stir together a 21-ounce can of cherry or blueberry pie filling and 2 tablespoons orange juice. If desired, microwave, covered, on 100-percent power (high) for 2 to 2½ minutes or until heated through, stirring twice. Makes 2 cups.

WHOLE WHEAT PANCAKES:

Prepare Buttermilk Pancakes as suggested, except substitute whole wheat flour for all-purpose flour and packed brown sugar for granulated sugar. Optional: Stir in ½ cup miniature milk chocolate baking pieces or chopped nuts.

OATMEAL PANCAKES:

Prepare Buttermilk Pancakes as suggested, except reduce all-purpose flour to 2 cups and add 1½ cups quick-cooking oats. Increase the buttermilk to 4½ cups.

CORNMEAL PANCAKES:

Prepare Buttermilk Pancakes as suggested, except use 2½ cups all-purpose flour and add 1 cup cornmeal.

SAUSAGE ROLLS:

Prepare Buttermilk Pancakes as suggested. Roll finished pancakes around browned link sausages; secure with wooden toothpicks. Serve with warm applesauce or syrup for dipping.

whole wheat pancakes

sausage rolls

cornmeal pancakes

oatmeal pancakes

freezing pancakes

Layer pancakes between sheets of plastic wrap, place in a resealable plastic bag, and freeze up to 3 months. To reheat, remove 2 regular-size or 6 dollar-size frozen pancakes and heat in microwave, uncovered, for 1 to 1½ minutes for regular-size pancakes or 30 to 45 seconds for dollar-size pancakes. Turn pancakes halfway through heating time.

warm start

Piping-hot oatmeal is ready in a moment thanks to the miracle of the microwave. These yummy stir-ins will have you jumping out of bed to get a bite.

Bananas Foster Oatmeal
Start to Finish: 10 minutes

- **2** 1-ounce envelopes instant oatmeal (plain)
- **1** medium banana, peeled and sliced
- **2** tablespoons chopped toasted pecans
- **2** to 3 teaspoons caramel-flavor ice cream topping
  Half-and-half or milk (optional)

1. In two microwave-safe bowls, prepare oatmeal according to package directions. Top each serving with banana and pecans; drizzle with ice cream topping. If desired, microwave on 100-percent power (high) for 30 seconds. If desired, serve with half-and-half. Makes 2 servings.

Per serving: 230 cal., 7 g fat (1 g sat. fat), 0 mg chol., 17 mg sodium, 38 g carbo., 5 g fiber, 6 g pro.

{ Extra ideas for mix-ins, see opposite page. }

RASPBERRIES & YOGURT

PINEAPPLE & BROWN SUGAR

CHUNKY APPLESAUCE & CINNAMON

ALMONDS

FRESH APPLES

TEST YOUR HEALTHY-EATING IQ:
You know oatmeal is good for you, but did you know
it might also help save your life? Studies have shown
that oatmeal lowers bad LDL cholesterol and boosts
good HDL cholesterol to keep your ticker in top shape.

Peanut Butter Breakfast Bars

Prep: 20 minutes **Bake:** 28 minutes

Nonstick cooking spray
4   cups sweetened oat cereal flakes
     with raisins
¾   cup quick-cooking rolled oats
½   cup all-purpose flour
½   cup snipped dried apple
2   eggs, lightly beaten
½   cup honey
½   cup chunky peanut butter
⅓   cup butter, melted

1. Preheat oven to 325°F. Line a 9×9×2-inch baking pan with foil. Lightly coat foil with nonstick cooking spray. In a large bowl, combine cereal, rolled oats, flour, and dried apple. Set aside.

2. In a bowl, stir together eggs, honey, peanut butter, and melted butter. Pour over cereal mixture in bowl. Mix well. Transfer to pan. Press mixture firmly into pan. Bake 28 to 30 minutes or until edges are browned. Cool completely. Cut into bars. Makes 16 bars.

Note: To refrigerate, individually wrap bars in plastic wrap and store up to 3 days. To freeze, place individually wrapped bars in a freezer container or resealable plastic bag up to 3 months.

Per bar: 208 cal., 9 g fat (3 g sat. fat), 37 mg chol., 131 mg sodium, 29 g carbo., 2 g fiber, 5 g pro.

Cinnamon Bagel Fries

These hearty, sweet fries taste great dipped in strawberry-jam "ketchup."

Start to Finish: 10 minutes

1   4-inch plain, cinnamon-raisin, egg,
     or poppy seed bagel, split
1   tablespoon butter, melted
1   tablespoon sugar
½   teaspoon ground cinnamon

1. Toast bagel halves. Place warm bagel halves on a cutting board. Using a serrated knife, slice halves into ¼- to ½-inch-wide strips. In a large resealable plastic bag, place bagel slices; drizzle with melted butter. Seal bag and shake to coat. Add sugar and cinnamon; seal bag and shake to coat again. Serve immediately. Makes 2 servings.

Per serving: 198 cal., 6 g fat (4 g sat. fat), 15 mg chol., 279 mg sodium, 30 g carbo., 1 g fiber, 5 g pro.

PB & Strawberry Pockets

Fresh strawberries provide a twist to the PB&J classic.

Start to Finish: 15 minutes

2 large white or whole wheat pita bread rounds, halved crosswise
½ cup chunky peanut butter
¼ cup raisins
1 cup sliced or chopped fresh strawberries
2 tablespoons dry-roasted sunflower kernels

1. Open pita bread halves to make pockets. In a bowl, combine peanut butter and raisins.

2. Spread peanut butter mixture inside pita pockets. Divide strawberries and sunflower kernels among pockets. Serve immediately or wrap and chill for up to 6 hours. Makes 4 servings.

Per serving: 333 cal., 18 g fat (3 g sat. fat), 0 mg chol., 318 mg sodium, 35 g carbo., 5 g fiber, 12 g pro.

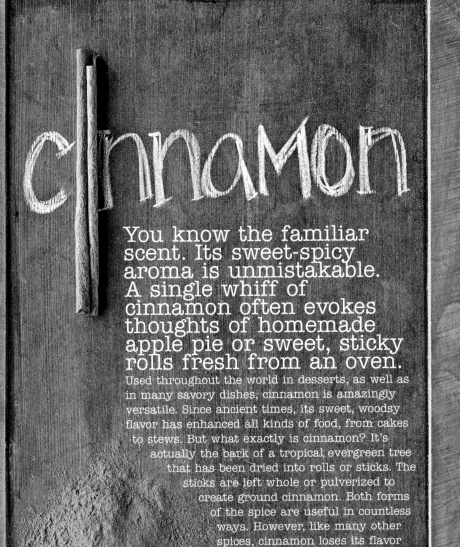

cinnamon

You know the familiar scent. Its sweet-spicy aroma is unmistakable. A single whiff of cinnamon often evokes thoughts of homemade apple pie or sweet, sticky rolls fresh from an oven. Used throughout the world in desserts, as well as in many savory dishes, cinnamon is amazingly versatile. Since ancient times, its sweet, woodsy flavor has enhanced all kinds of food, from cakes to stews. But what exactly is cinnamon? It's actually the bark of a tropical evergreen tree that has been dried into rolls or sticks. The sticks are left whole or pulverized to create ground cinnamon. Both forms of the spice are useful in countless ways. However, like many other spices, cinnamon loses its flavor quickly. Purchase cinnamon in small quantities and keep it away from light in airtight containers. Here are some sweet morning recipes that showcase the seasoning.

Easy Cinnamon Rolls

If you think cinnamon rolls are too much work, think again. These little gems are on the table in a snap.

Start to Finish: 25 minutes

1   8-ounce package (8) refrigerated
    crescent-roll dough
1   tablespoon butter, melted
1   teaspoon ground cinnamon
2   tablespoons granulated sugar
½   cup powdered sugar
¼   teaspoon vanilla
1   to 2 teaspoons orange juice
    or milk

1. Preheat oven to 375°F. Grease an 8×1½- or 9×1½-inch round baking pan; set aside. Unroll dough (do not separate); press perforations to seal. Brush dough with melted butter. In a small bowl, stir together the cinnamon and granulated sugar; sprinkle over dough. Starting from a long side, roll up dough. Using a sharp knife, slice dough into eight 1½-inch pieces. Arrange pieces, cut sides up, in prepared pan, flattening each roll slightly.

2. Bake for 15 to 18 minutes or until golden. Remove and cool rolls slightly in pan on a wire rack. Remove from pan. In a small bowl, stir together powdered sugar, vanilla, and enough orange juice to make an icing of drizzling consistency. Drizzle over warm rolls. Serve warm. Makes 8 rolls.

Per serving: 155 cal., 7 g fat (2 g sat. fat), 4 mg chol., 241 mg sodium, 22 g carbo., 0 g fiber, 2 g pro.

Get the homemade taste without the from-scratch hassle.

Cinnamon Granola Loaf

Prep: 20 minutes   **Rise:** 45 minutes
Bake: 25 minutes

3   tablespoons sugar
1   teaspoon ground cinnamon
1   1-pound loaf frozen sweet or white
     bread dough, thawed
2   tablespoons butter, softened
½   cup granola cereal (plain or with
     raisins), crushed
½   cup chopped almonds or pecans,
     toasted

1. Grease an 8×4×2-inch loaf pan. In a bowl, stir together sugar and cinnamon; set aside.
2. On a lightly floured surface, roll the thawed bread dough to a 10×8-inch rectangle. Spread with 1 tablespoon of the softened butter. Sprinkle with 2 tablespoons of the sugar mixture. Sprinkle with crushed granola and nuts to within ½ inch of the edges. Roll up tightly, starting from a short side. Pinch seam to seal. Place, seam side down, in prepared pan.
3. Cover and let rise in a warm place until nearly double in size (45 to 60 minutes).
4. Preheat oven to 350°F. Bake about 25 minutes or until bread sounds hollow when lightly tapped. Remove loaf from pan to a wire rack. Spread loaf with remaining 1 tablespoon butter; sprinkle with remaining 1 tablespoon sugar mixture. Makes 12 servings.

Per serving: 172 cal., 6 g fat (2 g sat. fat), 5 mg chol., 208 mg sodium, 25 g carbo., 1 g fiber, 4 g pro.

GROUND CINNAMON goes a long way, giving a nice spicy-sweet bite to this frozen bread dough.

Monkey Bread Rolls

Prep: 20 minutes **Bake:** 40 minutes
Cool: 15 minutes **Chill:** Overnight

1   **34.5-ounce package frozen cinnamon sweet roll dough or frozen orange sweet roll dough (12 rolls)**
⅔   **cup coarsely chopped pecans**
⅓   **cup butter or margarine, melted**
1   **cup sugar**
⅓   **cup caramel ice cream topping**
1   **tablespoon maple-flavor syrup**

1. Place frozen rolls about 2 inches apart on a large greased baking sheet. Cover with plastic wrap. Refrigerate overnight to let dough thaw and begin to rise. Frosting packets, if present, can be set aside for another use.

2. Preheat oven to 350°F. Generously grease a 10-inch fluted tube pan. Sprinkle ⅓ cup of the pecans over the bottom of the tube pan.

3. Cut each roll into quarters. Dip pieces in melted butter, then roll in sugar. Layer pieces in prepared pan. (Or dip and roll whole rolls; arrange rolls on their sides in the tube pan.) Drizzle with any remaining butter; sprinkle with any remaining sugar. Sprinkle remaining ⅓ cup pecans on top.

4. Combine ice cream topping and syrup; drizzle over tops of rolls in pan. Bake for 40 to 45 minutes or until golden brown. Let pan stand on wire rack for 1 minute. Invert rolls onto a large serving platter. Spoon any topping and nuts that remain in pan onto rolls. Cool slightly. Serve warm. Makes 12 servings.

Per serving: 382 cal., 14 g fat (4 g sat. fat), 13 mg chol., 302 mg sodium, 60 g carbo., 2 g fiber, 5 g pro.

Orange-Berry Smoothies

Strawberries give this smoothie a pretty peach color, bananas add extra body, and the creamy yogurt lends an extra kick of calcium.

Start to Finish: 15 minutes

3   medium oranges, peeled, seeded, and cut up
2   6-ounce containers low-fat vanilla yogurt
1   cup fresh strawberries, stems removed
1   medium banana, peeled and cut up
2   cups ice cubes

1. In a blender, combine oranges, yogurt, strawberries, and banana. Cover and blend until smooth. With blender running, gradually add ice cubes through hole in the top and blend until frothy. Pour into glasses. Makes 4 servings.

Per smoothie: 156 cal., 1 g fat (1 g sat. fat), 4 mg chol., 58 mg sodium, 33 g carbo., 4 g fiber, 6 g pro.

Peach-Cherry Smoothies

Mix and match other frozen fruits and fruit-flavor yogurts in these smoothies.
Start to Finish: 10 minutes

1 8-ounce carton low-fat peach
     or vanilla yogurt
1 cup fat-free milk
1 cup frozen unsweetened peach slices
½ cup frozen unsweetened pitted dark
     sweet cherries
¼ teaspoon vanilla
3 fresh sweet cherries (optional)

1. In a blender, combine yogurt, milk, peach slices, cherries, and vanilla. Cover and blend until smooth. If desired, top each serving with a fresh cherry. Makes 3 servings.

Per serving: 135 cal., 1 g fat (1 g sat. fat), 4 mg chol., 74 mg sodium, 27 g carbo., 3 g fiber, 6 g pro.

5-Minutes-to-Spare Smoothies

Prep: 5 minutes

2 cups peeled and cut-up fruit of your
     choice*
1 cup juice or low-fat milk
1 cup low-fat yogurt (plain, flavored,
     or frozen)

1. Combine all ingredients in a blender and process until smooth. Makes 2 servings.
***Note:** Frozen fruit makes thicker, slushier smoothies. If you are using fresh fruit but want the texture of frozen fruit, add a few ice cubes to the blender.

Per serving: 189 cal., 2 g fat (1 g sat. fat), 7 mg chol., 88 mg sodium, 36 g carbo., 3 g fiber, 8 g pro.

Fruit & Yogurt Smoothies
Start to Finish: 10 minutes

1½ cups cut-up fresh fruit (strawberries, raspberries, cantaloupe, honeydew melon, papaya, or kiwifruit)
1 medium banana, cut into chunks
1 6- or 8-ounce carton vanilla low-fat yogurt
¾ cup milk
   Honey (optional)
   Fruit slices (optional)

1. Place cut-up fruit, banana, yogurt, and milk in a blender or food processor. Cover; blend or process until mixture is smooth, scraping down sides as needed. Pour into tall glasses. If desired, stir in some honey and garnish with additional fruit slices. Makes 4 servings.

Per serving: 103 cal., 2 g fat (1 g sat. fat), 6 mg chol., 48 mg sodium, 19 g carbo., 2 g fiber, 4 g pro.

Blend 'n' Go
Start to Finish: 10 minutes

1 cup sliced fresh or frozen fruit (such as peaches, berries, bananas, and/or orange sections)
1 6- to 8-ounce carton low-fat vanilla yogurt
½ cup reduced-fat milk
1 tablespoon honey

1. In a blender, combine fruit, yogurt, milk, and honey; cover and blend well. Makes 1 serving.

Per serving: 342 cal., 5 g fat (3 g sat. fat), 18 mg chol., 163 mg sodium, 66 g carbo., 3 g fiber, 13 g pro.

brown baggin' it

how to pack a safe to-go lunch

Ever worry about the time that passes between making a sack lunch and eating it? Follow these tips to keep your noontime meal free of foodborne bacteria.

Let's be honest: Most sack lunches sit awhile before they're eaten. The best way to keep bacteria from growing is to remember these rules from the Partnership for Food Safety Education: Clean, separate, cook, and chill. Clean your hands, work surface, and food. Separate produce from meat products, using separate cutting boards for each. Keep cooked foods hot, and keep cold foods chilled. Below are three quick ways to protect you and your kids from foodborne illnesses.

✳ Wash your hands with warm, soapy water for 20 seconds before and after handling food or eating. Teach your kids to do the same. Wash all fruits and vegetables before packing them in a sack lunch.

✳ Buy a lunch bag that's insulated. Use an insulated bottle for hot food, and use an ice pack or freezer gel pack for cold food. Throw away any perishable items not eaten at lunch. This includes sandwiches made with beef, tuna, turkey, chicken, egg, or ham, as well as mayonnaise-based salad spreads and dressings.

✳ Store lunches in the refrigerator—not on the kitchen counter—if you pack them the night before. Throw away cold foods left unrefrigerated for more than two hours. Check to make sure your refrigerator is 40°F or below at all times.

Inside-Out Turkey Tempters
Start to Finish: 15 minutes

12	thin slices cooked turkey breast
2	purchased soft breadsticks (6 to 8 inches long), halved lengthwise
½	cup flavored reduced-fat cream cheese (½ of an 8-ounce container)
½	cup packaged fresh julienned carrots
4	bread-and-butter or dill pickle spears Leaf lettuce (optional)

1. Overlap 3 turkey slices so meat is the same length as breadstick halves. Spread turkey meat with 2 tablespoons of the cream cheese. Place 2 tablespoons of the carrots, one pickle spear, and one breadstick half on edge of turkey. Roll up so meat is wrapped around breadstick. If desired, roll one or two lettuce leaves around outside of sandwich. Repeat with remaining ingredients. Makes 4 servings.
2. For individual lunches, wrap rolls; chill.

Per serving: 194 cal., 5 g fat (3 g sat. fat), 49 mg chol., 395 mg sodium, 19 g carbo., 1 g fiber, 18 g pro.

Crunchy PB&A Wraps
Start to Finish: 5 minutes

⅓	cup peanut butter
4	7- to 8-inch flour tortillas
1	cup chopped apple
¼	cup low-fat granola

1. Spread peanut butter over each tortilla. Sprinkle evenly with apple and granola. Tightly roll up tortillas. Cut in half.
2. For individual lunches, wrap tortillas and chill. Makes 4 servings.

Per serving: 254 cal., 14 g fat (3 g sat. fat), 0 mg chol., 234 mg sodium, 28 g carbo., 3 g fiber, 8 g pro.

Tomato-Turkey Wraps

Prep: 20 minutes

1   7-ounce container prepared hummus
    (plain or desired flavor)
3   9- to 10-inch tomato-basil-flavor flour
    tortillas or plain flour tortillas
8   ounces thinly sliced, cooked
    peppered turkey breast
6   romaine lettuce leaves, ribs removed
3   small tomatoes, thinly sliced
3   thin slices red onion, separated
    into rings

1. Spread hummus evenly over tortillas. Layer turkey breast, romaine, tomatoes, and red onion on top of hummus. Roll up each tortilla into a spiral. Cut each tortilla in half. Wrap each half with plastic wrap. Serve immediately or chill for up to 4 hours.* Makes 6 wraps.

*Tip: Wrapping and chilling rolled tortillas helps them keep their shape when unwrapped, making them easier to eat.

Per wrap: 221 cal., 6 g fat (1 g sat. fat), 16 mg chol., 926 mg sodium, 29 g carbo., 3 g fiber, 14 g pro.

GREAT SIDES FOR KIDS

✻ Banana ✻ Grapes ✻ Unsweetened applesauce pack ✻ Small bag of pretzels ✻ Raisin boxes ✻ Reduced-calorie pudding snacks ✻ White or chocolate milk

GREAT SIDES FOR YOU

✻ Apple ✻ Pear ✻ Hard-cooked eggs ✻ Soy chips or baked chips ✻ 100-calorie snack packs of cookies ✻ Unsweetened iced tea or low-calorie soda ✻ Veggies

Car-Hoppin' Chicken Cups

Start to Finish: 15 minutes

¼   cup plain low-fat yogurt
¼   cup bottled reduced-fat ranch
     salad dressing
1½   cups chopped cooked chicken or turkey
½   cup chopped broccoli
¼   cup shredded carrot
¼   cup chopped pecans or walnuts
     (optional)

1. In a small bowl, stir together the yogurt and salad dressing.
2. In a medium bowl, combine chicken, broccoli, carrot, and, if desired, nuts. Pour yogurt mixture over chicken mixture; toss to coat. Divide chicken mixture among 4 plastic cups. Cover and chill up to 24 hours. Makes 4 servings.

Per serving: 146 cal., 7 g fat (1 g sat. fat), 53 mg chol., 225 mg sodium, 4 g carbo., 0 g fiber, 16 g pro.

Ham & Pickle Wrap

This wrap actually improves after a short time in the refrigerator. The flavors blend and the tortilla softens as it sits.

Prep: 5 minutes

1	tablespoon bottled ranch salad dressing
1	7- to 8-inch whole wheat or plain flour tortilla
2	thin slices cooked ham (about 1½ ounces)
1	to 2 thin lengthwise slices bread-and-butter pickles

1. Spread salad dressing over tortilla. Top with ham and pickle. Roll up. Wrap in plastic wrap. If desired, chill for up to 6 hours. If desired, cut wrap into halves or thirds and secure with toothpicks. Makes 1 wrap.

Per serving: 284 cal., 13 g fat (3 g sat. fat), 29 mg chol., 1,103 mg sodium, 30 g carbo., 3 g fiber, 11 g pro.

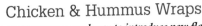

Chicken & Hummus Wraps

These wraps are a good way to introduce new flavors to your kids. Look for hummus in the deli or health-food section of your local grocery store.

Prep: 15 minutes

1	7-ounce carton desired-flavor hummus or one 8-ounce tub cream cheese spread with garden vegetables
4	10-inch flour tortillas
⅓	cup plain low-fat yogurt or dairy sour cream
1	6-ounce package refrigerated cooked chicken breast strips
¾	cup coarsely chopped roma tomato (2 large)
¾	cup thinly sliced cucumber

1. Spread hummus evenly over tortillas; spread yogurt over top of hummus. Top with chicken, tomatoes, and cucumber. Roll tortillas up tightly. Makes 4 servings.

Per wrap: 288 cal., 9 g fat (2 g sat. fat), 31 mg chol., 713 mg sodium, 36 g carbo., 3 g fiber, 16 g pro.

Dizzy Sandwich Rolls

Pack rolls with fresh fruit (peeled orange, grapes, or banana) and a plastic storage bag with whole-grain chips.

Start to Finish: 15 minutes

2 tablespoons whipped cream cheese spread*
1 8- or 9-inch tortilla (any flavor)
¼ cup shredded carrot
1 tablespoon dried tart cherries or raisins
1 ounce thinly sliced cooked ham or turkey

1. Spread the cream cheese evenly over tortilla. Top with carrot and cherries. Top evenly with ham. Roll up; cut into quarters. Wrap tightly in plastic wrap. Makes 1 serving.

* **Note:** If desired, substitute cream cheese spread with garden vegetables or with chives and onion for plain cream cheese.

Per serving: 334 cal., 11 g fat (5 g sat. fat), 32 mg chol., 796 mg sodium, 45 g carbo., 4 g fiber, 12 g pro.

Ham Focaccia Sandwich

Start to Finish: 10 minutes

1   individual Italian flatbread (focaccia)
    or ciabatta roll
1   tablespoon bottled creamy garlic
    or ranch salad dressing
1   romaine lettuce leaf
1   slice leftover cooked ham or deli
    sliced cooked ham
1   slice provolone cheese
2   cherry tomatoes, thinly sliced
1   tablespoon chopped roasted red
    sweet pepper

1. Slice the bread in half horizontally. Spread salad dressing on the cut side of the bottom half. On the bottom half, layer romaine lettuce, ham, provolone, tomatoes, and sweet peppers. Cover with top half of roll; wrap. If desired, chill for up to 24 hours. Makes 1 sandwich.

Per serving: 461 cal., 19 g fat (7 g sat. fat), 45 mg chol., 1,235 mg sodium, 54 g carbo., 4 g fiber, 22 g pro.

Curried Pasta & Chicken Salad

Prep: 25 minutes

- 8 ounces dried radiatore or rotini pasta (2 cups)
- 2 cups cubed cooked chicken
- 1½ cups seedless green grapes, halved
- 1½ cups cubed cantaloupe
- ¾ cup sliced celery
- ½ cup sliced green onion (4)
- 1 8-ounce carton plain low-fat yogurt
- 3 tablespoons mango chutney or orange marmalade
- 1½ teaspoons curry powder
- ¼ teaspoon salt

1. Cook pasta according to package directions; drain. Rinse with cold water; drain again. In a large bowl, stir together pasta, chicken, grapes, cantaloupe, celery, and green onion.
2. In a small bowl, stir together yogurt, chutney, curry powder, and salt. Add to pasta mixture. Toss to coat; cover. If desired, chill up to 4 hours.
3. For lunches, spoon salad into 6 covered containers; chill. Makes 6 servings.

Per serving: 314 cal., 5 g fat (2 g sat. fat), 44 mg chol., 204 mg sodium, 46 g carbo., 3 g fiber, 21 g pro.

Ham & Cheese Calzones

Prep: 15 minutes **Bake:** 15 minutes
Cool: 30 minutes

- 1 10-ounce package refrigerated pizza dough
- ¼ cup coarse-grain mustard
- 6 ounces sliced Swiss or provolone cheese
- 1½ cups cubed cooked ham (8 ounces)
- ½ teaspoon caraway seeds

1. Preheat oven to 400°F. Line baking sheet with foil; lightly grease foil. Unroll dough. On a lightly floured surface, roll dough into a 15×10-inch rectangle. Cut into 4 equal rectangles.
2. Spread mustard over rectangles. Divide 3 ounces cheese among rectangles, placing slices on half of each. Top cheese with ham and caraway seeds. Top with remaining cheese. Brush edges of dough with water. Fold dough over filling to opposite edge, stretching if necessary. Seal edges.
3. Place calzones on baking sheet. Prick tops with a fork. Bake about 15 minutes or until golden. Cool on wire rack 30 minutes.
4. For individual lunches, wrap each sandwich and chill. Makes 4 servings.

Per serving: 421 cal., 21 g fat (10 g sat. fat), 72 mg chol., 1,390 mg sodium, 28 g carbo., 1 g fiber, 30 g pro.

Thai-Style Beef Salad

Make a roast beef and save the leftovers for this irresistible lunchtime salad.

Start to Finish: 15 minutes

- 2 tablespoons bottled Italian salad dressing
- 2 to 3 teaspoons lime juice
- 1½ teaspoons soy sauce
- 1 teaspoon snipped fresh cilantro
- 2 cups fresh spinach leaves or torn mixed salad greens
- ¼ cup purchased shredded carrot
- ½ cup shredded cooked roast beef
- 1 tablespoon chopped peanuts

1. For dressing, in a small container with a tight-fitting lid, combine dressing, lime juice, soy sauce, and cilantro; cover and shake well. If desired, chill for up to 24 hours.

2. In a container with a lid, combine spinach, carrot, beef, and peanuts. Cover. If desired, chill up to 24 hours.

3. To serve, shake dressing; add dressing to spinach mixture and toss to coat. Makes 1 serving.

Per serving: 328 cal., 22 g fat (5 g sat. fat), 56 mg chol., 1,095 mg sodium, 10 g carbo., 3 g fiber, 25 g pro.

Barbecue Beef Wrap

Do your kids turn up their noses at leftovers?
Completely reinvent beef from last night
with this delicious wrap.
Prep: 10 minutes

⅓   cup shredded cooked roast beef
1   7- to 8-inch flour tortilla
1   tablespoon bottled barbecue sauce
2   tablespoons shredded Monterey
    Jack cheese
2   tablespoons packaged shredded
    broccoli (broccoli slaw mix)

1. Arrange beef on tortilla. Drizzle with barbecue sauce and top with cheese and broccoli. Roll up. Wrap tightly in plastic wrap. If desired, chill up to 24 hours. Makes 1 serving.

Per serving: 280 cal., 13 g fat (6 g sat. fat), 57 mg chol., 367 mg sodium, 17 g carbo., 1 g fiber, 21 g pro.

Antipasto Tortellini Salad

*Pack this salad in an individual-size
airtight container and toss in the office fridge.*

Prep: 25 minutes **Chill:** 2 hours

- 1   9-ounce package refrigerated
     cheese tortellini
- ½   cup chopped bottled roasted
     red sweet pepper
- 1   6-ounce jar marinated quartered
     artichoke hearts, drained
- ¼   cup sliced pitted ripe olives
- 1   ounce Genoa salami, cut into thin strips
- 1   ounce provolone cheese, cubed
- ¼   cup bottled vinaigrette salad dressing

1. Cook tortellini according to package directions. Drain; place in a large bowl. Stir in sweet pepper, artichoke hearts, olives, salami, and cheese. Add dressing; toss to coat. Cover and refrigerate for 2 hours or overnight. Toss before serving. If necessary, toss with additional dressing to moisten. Makes 4 (1-cup) servings.

Per serving: 340 cal., 17 g fat (4 g sat. fat), 41 mg chol., 869 mg sodium, 36 g carbo., 1 g fiber, 14 g pro.

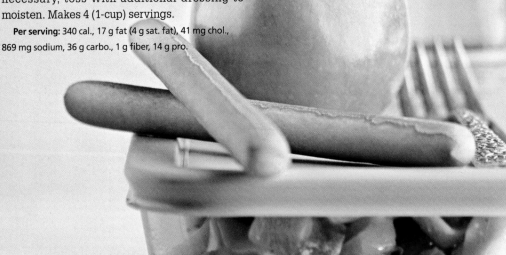

snack attack

Veggie Mix with Ranch Dip

Fussy eaters? Here's a great way to get in their daily dose of veggies! Feel free to use any assortment of veggie favorites.

Start to Finish: 10 minutes

½ of a medium red or yellow sweet pepper, cut into sticks

1 stalk celery, cut into slices

4 cherry tomatoes, halved

4 packaged peeled fresh baby carrots

½ cup ranch salad dressing or cottage cheese

¼ cup coarsely shredded cucumber

⅛ teaspoon dried dillweed

1. In a medium bowl, combine pepper sticks, celery slices, cherry tomatoes, and carrots. In a small bowl, stir together ranch dressing, cucumber, and dillweed. Serve dressing mixture as dip for vegetables. Makes 4 servings.

Per serving: 159 cal., 16 g fat (3 g sat. fat), 5 mg chol., 349 mg sodium, 4 g carbo., 1 g fiber, 0 g pro.

Veggies-on-the-Go

Being busy is no excuse for not eating right! Take this veggie cup on the road when you or the kids need a quick nutrient fix after school or before soccer practice.

Start to Finish: 10 minutes

¼ cup low-fat dill vegetable dip
  Finely shredded lemon peel
½ cup vegetable sticks* (carrots, zucchini, red sweet pepper, celery, jicama, blanched green beans)

1. In a small bowl, stir together vegetable dip and lemon peel to taste. Spoon dip into the bottom of a plastic drinking cup. Insert vegetable sticks into dip in cup. Cover cup and tote with an ice pack. Makes 1 serving.

* Note: Look for precut vegetable sticks in the produce aisle of your supermarket.

Per serving: 145 cal., 10 g fat (2 g sat. fat), 10 mg chol., 502 mg sodium, 10 g carbo., 2 g fiber, 1 g pro.

Carrots with Dried Fruit Dip

Prep: 15 minutes **Chill:** 1 hour

1 8-ounce tub cream cheese spread with honey and nuts or with brown sugar and cinnamon
2 to 3 teaspoons milk
1 cup dried tropical fruit bits, finely snipped
3 medium carrots, cut into sticks
3 stalks celery, cut into sticks

1. In a medium bowl, stir together cream cheese and milk. Stir in fruit bits. Serve dip with carrot and celery sticks. Makes 12 snack servings.

Per serving: 114 cal., 5 g fat (3 g sat. fat), 18 mg chol., 95 mg sodium, 15 g carbo., 1 g fiber, 1 g pro.

Top 3 Reasons To Love Yogurt

Health experts are buzzing about the many benefits of yogurt. Here are three great reasons to try it:

1. "Good" bacteria. Also called "probiotics." Yogurt is full of them. These bacteria aid your digestive tract and help prevent yeast infections.

2. Calcium. Vital for bone health and growth. Calcium is packed into yogurt, providing about 30 percent of the amount you need each day.

3. Protein. Essential for gaining strength (and necessary for growing kids). Yogurt is a great low-fat protein provider.

❋ **But watch for sugar.** Check the label before you buy. Some yogurt brands contain as much sugar as a candy bar or soda.

Summer Fruits with Creamy Yogurt Dip

Be creative and substitute different flavored yogurts in this recipe.

Start to Finish: 10 minutes

- ⅓ cup low-fat ricotta cheese
- 1 tablespoon sugar
- 1 teaspoon finely shredded orange peel
- 1 tablespoon orange juice
- ⅓ cup low-fat vanilla yogurt
- 2 cups sliced nectarines, cubed cantaloupe, cubed honeydew melon, cut-up kiwifruits, and/or fresh pineapple chunks

1. For dip, in a blender or food processor, combine ricotta cheese, sugar, orange peel, and orange juice. Cover and blend or process until smooth. Stir cheese mixture into yogurt.

2. If desired, cover and chill up to 24 hours. Serve with fresh fruit. Makes 4 servings.

Per serving: 88 cal., 2 g fat (1 g sat. fat), 6 mg chol., 34 mg sodium, 16 g carbo., 1 g fiber, 3 g pro.

Bag O' Teddies
Start to Finish: 5 minutes

1   single-serving-size bag bear-shape
    graham snack cookies or
    animal crackers
½   cup vanilla or fruit-flavor low-fat
    yogurt*
¼   cup sliced fresh fruit or berries
    (strawberries, mandarin orange
    segments, blueberries, or bananas)

1. Use scissors to cut open bag of cookies along one of the short ends. Spoon some yogurt over cookies in bag. Top with desired amount of fruit. Serve from the bag with a spoon. Makes 1 serving.
***Note:** If desired, use vanilla or chocolate low-fat pudding instead of yogurt.

Per serving: 266 cal., 6 g fat (2 g sat. fat), 6 mg chol., 251 mg sodium, 46 g carbo., 2 g fiber, 8 g pro.

Down-to-Earth Granola
Prep: 15 minutes   **Bake:** 45 minutes

4   cups regular rolled oats
1½   cups sliced almonds
½   cup packed brown sugar
½   teaspoon salt
½   teaspoon ground cinnamon
¼   cup cooking oil
¼   cup honey
1   teaspoon vanilla
1½   cups raisins or dried cranberries

1. Preheat oven to 300°F. In a large bowl, combine oats, almonds, brown sugar, salt, and cinnamon. In a saucepan, heat oil and honey just until warm. Stir in vanilla. Carefully pour over oat mixture. Stir gently until combined.
2. Spread mixture in a 15 × 10 × 1-inch baking pan. Bake 45 minutes, stirring carefully every 15 minutes. Remove from heat; stir in raisins. Cool completely. Transfer to resealable plastic bags. Store at room temperature 1 week or freeze up to 3 months. Makes 24 servings.

Per serving: 174 cal., 8 g fat (1 g sat. fat), 0 mg chol., 51 mg sodium, 25 g carbo., 3 g fiber, 4 g pro.

CHILI powder

This spice is a village in a jar.

This aromatic reddish-brown dust is ground from a diverse crowd of herbs and spices. Together they create a colorful, multiethnic neighborhood of flavor.

Mixtures vary, but most begin with the friendly warmth of ancho chiles and the sweet smokiness of paprika. Assertive garlic and pungent oregano join in, followed by nutty cumin, fruity coriander, and a smidgen of peppery cloves.

Folks disagree about who invented chili powder, but everyone agrees this spice hails from deep in the heart of Texas. It's essential to Texas' famous Bowl o' Red (aka chili). Its spicy richness also enhances guacamole, enchiladas, and barbecue rubs.

The heat of chili powders varies greatly. The calmer ones offer a pleasing bite. The powerful ones can really burn. To get the flavor you desire, add slowly and taste as you go.

Chili powder is semiperishable and is most flavorful when used within a year of purchase. In hot climates, it benefits from refrigeration.

Chili Mixed Nuts

Don't expect chili powder to play a supporting role—its flavor usually dominates, making it perfect for unflavored mixed nuts.

Prep: 10 minutes **Bake:** 15 minutes

2 tablespoons butter, melted
1 tablespoon chili powder
1 tablespoon lime juice
1 teaspoon garlic salt
3 cups mixed nuts or peanuts

1. Preheat oven to 325°F. In a small bowl, combine melted butter, chili powder, lime juice, and garlic salt. In a 15×10×1-inch baking pan, combine butter mixture and nuts. Toss to coat.

2. Bake for 15 minutes, stirring twice. Spread nuts on a piece of foil to cool. Store in an airtight container at room temperature for up to 2 weeks or freeze up to 3 months. Makes 3 cups.

Per ¼ cup: 223 cal., 20 g fat (4 g sat. fat), 5 mg chol., 104 mg sodium, 9 g carbo., 3 g fiber, 6 g pro.

Spicy Snack Mix

Start to Finish: 30 minutes

4 cups bite-size shredded wheat biscuits
1½ cups broken bagel chips or mini bagel chips
1 cup peanuts
1 cup cashews
1 cup whole almonds
¼ cup butter, melted
2 tablespoons lime juice
1 teaspoon garlic salt
½ to 1 teaspoon chili powder
½ teaspoon onion salt

1. Preheat oven to 300°F. In a bowl, combine shredded wheat biscuits, bagel chips, peanuts, cashews, and almonds. Set aside.

2. In a bowl, combine melted butter, lime juice, garlic salt, chili powder, and onion salt. Pour over cereal mixture; toss to coat. Pour cereal mixture into a roasting pan.

3. Bake for 20 minutes, stirring twice. Remove from oven. Spread mixture on foil to cool. Store in an airtight container at room temperature for up to 2 weeks. Makes about 9 cups.

Per ½ cup: 204 cal., 15 g fat (3 g sat. fat), 7 mg chol., 175 mg sodium, 15 g carbo., 3 g fiber, 6 g pro.

Cherry Caramel Corn

*Dried cherries are a colorful and chewy substitute
for nuts in this simple caramel corn.*

Prep: 10 minutes   **Bake:** 15 minutes

3	tablespoons butter or margarine
¼	cup light-color corn syrup
1	tablespoon molasses
½	teaspoon baking soda
15	cups popped popcorn
1	cup dried tart red cherries

1. Preheat oven to 325°F. In a saucepan, melt the
butter over medium-low heat. Remove from heat;
stir in corn syrup, molasses, and baking soda until
soda is dissolved. Place popcorn in a large roasting
pan; drizzle molasses mixture over popcorn,
tossing to coat.
2. Bake for 15 minutes, stirring twice. Transfer
mixture to a very large serving bowl. Stir in
cherries. Cool. Serve the same day. Makes twenty
½-cup servings.

Per serving: 74 cal., 2 g fat (1 g sat. fat), 5 mg chol.,
49 mg sodium, 14 g carbo., 1 g fiber, 1 g pro.

Rocky Road Popcorn

Prep: 20 minutes **Stand:** 20 minutes

	Nonstick cooking spray
1	package (6- to 7-cup yield) plain microwave popcorn
12	ounces chocolate-flavor candy coating, chopped
2	tablespoons peanut butter
2	cups peanuts
1	cup crisp rice cereal
1	cup tiny marshmallows

1. Line a large baking sheet with foil. Lightly coat
foil with cooking spray; set aside. Pop popcorn
according to package directions. Pour popcorn
into a very large bowl; set aside.
2. In a medium saucepan, melt the candy coating
and peanut butter over low heat until smooth,
stirring frequently.
3. Meanwhile, add peanuts, cereal, and
marshmallows to popcorn; stir to combine. Pour
warm chocolate mixture over popcorn mixture;
toss until well-coated. Spread popcorn mixture
onto prepared baking sheet. Cool; break apart into
clusters. Store in a tightly covered container up to
2 days. Makes about 12 cups.

Per 1 cup: 360 cal., 25 g fat (11 g sat. fat), 0 mg chol.,
147 mg sodium, 30 g carbo., 3 g fiber, 8 g pro.

Caramel-Coated Spiced Snack Mix

Prep: 15 minutes **Bake:** 30 minutes

1	12-ounce box crispy corn and rice cereal (about 10 cups)
1½	cups mixed nuts
½	cup packed brown sugar
½	cup light-color corn syrup
½	cup butter
1	teaspoon ground cinnamon
½	teaspoon ground ginger
1½	cups chocolate-covered raisins
1½	cups semisweet or milk chocolate pieces

1. Preheat oven to 300°F. In a large roasting pan, stir together cereal and nuts; set aside.

2. In a small saucepan, stir together brown sugar, corn syrup, butter, cinnamon, and ginger. Cook and stir over medium heat until butter is melted and mixture is smooth. Pour over cereal mixture; stir gently to coat.

3. Bake for 30 minutes, stirring twice. Remove from oven. Spread mixture on a large piece of buttered foil to cool. Break into pieces. Stir in chocolate-covered raisins and the chocolate pieces. Store in an airtight container for up to 1 week. Makes 16 cups (32 servings).

Per serving: 216 cal., 10 g fat (5 g sat. fat), 10 mg chol., 129 mg sodium, 30 g carbo., 1 g fiber, 2 g pro.

Fruit & Chip Cookies

Prep: 25 minutes **Bake:** 10 minutes per batch

1   cup butter, softened
¾   cup packed brown sugar
½   cup granulated sugar
1   teaspoon baking soda
2   eggs
1   teaspoon vanilla
2   cups all-purpose flour
2   cups granola cereal
1   6-ounce package mixed
       dried fruit bits (1½ cups)
1   cup white baking pieces

1. Preheat oven to 350°F. In a bowl, beat butter for 30 seconds. Beat in brown sugar, granulated sugar, baking soda, eggs, vanilla, and some of the flour until combined. Stir in remaining flour, granola, dried fruit bits, and baking pieces.

2. Drop dough by rounded teaspoons 2 inches apart onto an ungreased cookie sheet. Flatten slightly. Bake about 10 minutes or until edges are golden. Cool 1 minute. Remove from sheet and cool completely. Makes about 60 cookies.

Note: To store, place cookies in layers separated by waxed paper in an airtight container; cover. Store at room temperature for up to 3 days or freeze for up to 3 months.

Per serving: 109 cal., 5 g fat (3 g sat. fat), 15 mg chol., 54 mg sodium, 15 g carbo., 1 g fiber, 2 g pro.

Banana-Raisin Trail Mix

Start to Finish: 10 minutes

2   cups raisins
2   cups dried banana chips
2   cups unsalted dry-roasted
       peanuts
1   6-ounce package mixed dried fruit
       (cut up any large pieces)
    Purchased ice cream cones dipped
       in chocolate (optional)

1. In a storage container, combine all ingredients. Cover and shake to mix. Store in a cool, dry place for up to 1 week. If desired, serve in ice cream cones. Makes about 7 cups.

Per ½ cup: 172 cal., 9 g fat (4 g sat. fat), 0 mg chol., 6 mg sodium, 22 g carbo., 1 g fiber, 3 g pro.

Fruit & Granola Parfait

Granola adds just the right amount of chew and crunch within the layers of these pretty parfaits.

Start to Finish: 15 minutes

1½   cups frozen vanilla or fruit-flavor
       yogurt
½   cup granola cereal
1   cup desired fruit, such as sliced
       bananas; peeled, sliced kiwifruit;
       refrigerated sliced peaches or
       mangoes; and/or cut-up pineapple
6   tablespoons strawberry ice
       cream topping
¼   cup frozen light whipped dessert
       topping, thawed (optional)
2   maraschino cherries with stems
       (optional)

1. Chill 2 tall parfait glasses.
2. Place ¼ cup frozen yogurt in the bottom of each chilled glass. Top each with 2 tablespoons of the granola, ¼ cup fruit, and 1 tablespoon strawberry topping. Repeat layers. Top each with ¼ cup frozen yogurt. Drizzle with remaining strawberry topping. If desired, top with whipped topping and garnish with maraschino cherries. Serve with long-handled spoons. Makes 2 servings.

Per serving: 375 cal., 9 g fat (4 g sat. fat), 15 mg chol., 138 mg sodium, 70 g carbo., 2 g fiber, 4 g pro.

Chewy Granola Goodies

These chewy dessert bars are a hearty, satisfying take on the classic crisp rice treats.

Start to Finish: 15 minutes

Nonstick cooking spray
1   10-ounce bag marshmallows
¼   cup butter or margarine
4   cups granola with raisins
1½   cups crisp rice cereal
½   cup shelled sunflower seeds

1. Line a 13×9×2-inch pan with foil. Lightly coat the foil with cooking spray; set aside. In a large saucepan, combine the marshmallows and butter. Cook and stir until the marshmallows are melted. Stir in granola, cereal, and sunflower seeds. Press mixture into the prepared pan. Chill for 5 minutes. Remove foil lining with uncut bars from pan. Cut into bars. Makes 24 bars.

Per bar: 154 cal., 7 g fat (3 g sat. fat), 6 mg chol., 50 mg sodium, 23 g carbo., 1 g fiber, 3 g pro.

Fruit & Cereal Drops

Vanilla-flavor candy coating acts as a sweet binder and balances the tartness of the dried fruit.

Start to Finish: 15 minutes

2   cups rice and wheat cereal flakes
¾   cup mixed dried fruit bits
½   cup whole almonds, toasted and
        coarsely chopped
6   ounces vanilla-flavor candy
        coating, chopped
1   tablespoon shortening

1. In a bowl, stir together cereal flakes, fruit bits, and almonds; set aside. In a saucepan, melt candy coating and shortening over low heat. Pour coating mixture over fruit mixture; toss gently to coat.

2. Working quickly, drop the cereal mixture from teaspoons onto a cookie sheet lined with waxed paper. Freeze for 5 minutes or until set. Makes about 24 drops.

Note: To store, place drops in layers separated by waxed paper in an airtight container; cover. Store at room temperature for up to 3 days. Do not store in freezer.

Per serving: 81 cal., 4 g fat (2 g sat. fat), 0 mg chol., 21 mg sodium, 10 g carbo., 0 g fiber, 1 g pro.

Fruit Muesli

The German word muesli (MEWS-lee) means
mixture. This version contains cereal, nuts,
and dried fruits.

Start to Finish: 10 minutes

- 4 cups multigrain cereal with rolled rye, oats, barley, and wheat
- 1 cup regular rolled oats
- ¾ cup coarsely chopped almonds and/or pecans, toasted
- 1 cup toasted wheat germ
- 1 6-ounce package dried cranberries
- ½ cup sunflower seeds
- ½ cup dried banana chips, crushed
  Nonfat yogurt

1. Stir together multigrain cereal, rolled oats, nuts, wheat germ, dried cranberries, sunflower seeds, and banana chips. Cover tightly and refrigerate for up to 4 weeks. Serve with yogurt. Makes 8 cups.

Per ⅔ cup: 346 cal., 12 g fat (3 g sat. fat), 1 mg chol., 48 mg sodium, 48 g carbo., 4 g fiber, 14 g pro.

Chocolate Cereal Bars

Try a new twist on cookies and milk. Cut these bars into small squares and dip them into milk using wooden picks.

Start to Finish: 15 minutes

Nonstick cooking spray
½ cup packed brown sugar
½ cup light-colored corn syrup
1 tablespoon margarine or butter
½ cup chocolate-hazelnut spread
3 cups crisp rice cereal
½ cup snipped pitted dates
½ cup chopped peanuts

1. Line an 8×8×2-inch pan with foil; lightly coat with cooking spray. In a saucepan, bring brown sugar, corn syrup, and margarine to boiling, stirring constantly. Remove from heat; stir in chocolate-hazelnut spread.
2. In a mixing bowl, combine cereal, dates, and peanuts. Pour brown sugar mixture over cereal mixture; stir until coated. Firmly press mixture into prepared pan. Chill for 5 minutes in the refrigerator. Store, tightly covered, at room temperature or in the refrigerator for up to 2 days. Do not freeze. Makes 20 to 24 bars.

Per bar: 161 cal., 6 g fat (1 g sat. fat), 2 mg chol., 83 mg sodium, 28 g carbo., 1 g fiber, 2 g pro.

Haystack Snacks

Start to Finish: 15 minutes

1 3-ounce can chow mein noodles
1 cup cornflakes
½ cup raisins and/or dried cherries
1 12-ounce package peanut butter-flavor pieces

1. In a bowl, stir together chow mein noodles, cornflakes, and raisins; set aside. Place the peanut butter-flavor pieces in a medium saucepan. Heat and stir over low heat until melted.
2. Pour melted peanut butter mixture over noodle mixture. Quickly stir until all of the mixture is coated.
3. Working quickly, drop the cereal mixture from teaspoons onto a cookie sheet lined with waxed paper. Freeze for 5 minutes or until set. Makes 15 snacks.
Note: To store, place snacks in layers separated by waxed paper in an airtight container; cover. Refrigerate for up to 5 days. Do not store in freezer.

Per serving: 163 cal., 9 g fat (3 g sat. fat), 0 mg chol., 101 mg sodium, 19 g carbo., 1 g fiber, 5 g pro.

No-Bake Butterscotch-Pretzel Treats

Prep: 25 minutes   **Chill:** 2 hours

Nonstick cooking spray
1½   cups powdered sugar
1   cup creamy peanut butter
6   tablespoons butter, melted
2   cups crushed pretzels (about 6½ ounces)
1   11-ounce package (about 2 cups) butterscotch-flavor pieces
¼   cup whipping cream
½   cup coarsely crushed pretzels
½   cup chopped peanuts

1. Line a 13×9×2-inch pan with foil. Lightly coat foil with cooking spray; set aside. In a bowl, mix powdered sugar, peanut butter, and melted butter. Stir in 2 cups crushed pretzels. Press mixture firmly into pan.

2. In a heavy medium saucepan, combine butterscotch pieces and whipping cream. Stir over low heat until pieces are just melted.

3. Carefully spoon and spread butterscotch mixture over crumb mixture in pan. Sprinkle ½ cup coarsely crushed pretzels and the peanuts evenly over butterscotch mixture; press gently.

4. Cover and chill for at least 2 hours. Cut into bars to serve. Store in refrigerator for up to 1 week. Makes about 36 bars.

Per bar: 166 cal., 10 g fat (5 g sat. fat), 7 mg chol., 154 mg sodium, 17 g carbo., 1 g fiber, 3 g pro.

Raspberry Cheesecake Shakes
Prep: 10 minutes

1   12-ounce package frozen unsweetened
    red raspberries, thawed
1   3-ounce package cream cheese,
    softened
¼   teaspoon almond extract
1   quart vanilla ice cream, softened
2   12-ounce cans or bottles cream soda
    Fresh raspberries (optional)

1. In a blender, combine raspberries, cream cheese, almond extract, half of the ice cream, and ½ cup cream soda. Cover and blend until smooth.

2. Divide blended mixture among six tall 16-ounce chilled glasses. Add a scoop of the remaining ice cream to each shake. Top each shake with remaining cream soda. If desired, garnish with fresh raspberries. Serve immediately. Makes 6 servings.

Per serving: 305 cal., 15 g fat (9 g sat. fat), 54 mg chol., 130 mg sodium, 36 g carbo., 2 g fiber, 4 g pro.

Soft Pretzels with Honey-Mustard Dip
Start to Finish: 10 minutes

6   frozen baked soft pretzels
1   8-ounce carton dairy sour cream and chive dip
1   tablespoon honey
1   tablespoon yellow mustard

1. Heat pretzels according to package directions. For dip, in a small bowl, stir together sour cream dip, honey, and mustard. Serve pretzels with dip. Makes 6 servings.

Per serving: 285 cal., 9 g fat (5 g sat.), 15 mg chol., 1,251 mg sodium, 46 g carbo., 2 g fiber, 8 g pro.

White Chocolate & Blackberry S'mores
Start to Finish: 10 minutes

4   chocolate graham crackers or regular graham crackers
1   4-ounce white chocolate bar
8   to 12 large marshmallows, toasted
8   to 12 tablespoons blackberry jam

1. Break crackers in half. Place 4 cracker halves on a foil-lined baking sheet. Layer 1 ounce of white chocolate and 2 to 3 large marshmallows on each cracker half. Broil 4 inches from heat 30 to 60 seconds. Remove; top with 2 to 3 tablespoons jam on each. Top with the remaining cracker halves. Makes 4 servings.

Per serving: 465 cal., 14 g fat (9 g sat. fat), 15 mg chol., 199 mg sodium, 80 g carbo., 1 g fiber, 4 g pro.

Peachy Keen Shakes

Whirl yogurt and frozen peaches in a blender for shakes chock-full of great summer flavor.

Prep: 10 minutes   **Freeze:** 1 hour

3   cups frozen sliced peaches
1   6-ounce container low-fat
    vanilla yogurt
1   cup fat-free milk
2   to 3 tablespoons honey
2   tablespoons creamy peanut butter
    Fresh peach slices, raspberries, and/or
    blueberries (optional)

1. In a blender, combine frozen peaches, yogurt, milk, honey, and peanut butter. Cover; blend until smooth. Pour into glasses. If desired, top with fresh fruit. Makes 3 servings.

Per serving: 417 cal., 6 g fat (2 g sat. fat), 5 mg chol., 137 mg sodium, 86 g carbo., 5 g fiber, 10 g pro.

Tropical Fruit Pops

Prep: 15 minutes **Freeze:** 4 hours

1 cup guava nectar
1 cup pineapple juice
1 cup fresh pineapple chunks
1 cup coarsely chopped or sliced fresh
   fruit (strawberries, kiwifruit,
   papaya, melon)

1. In a blender, combine nectar, juice, and pineapple chunks. Cover; blend until smooth. Divide fruit among 12 frozen ice pop molds or 4- or 6-ounce paper cups. Pour blended mixture over fruit.

2. Add sticks and cover molds. Or cover each cup with foil; make a small hole in the foil with a knife and insert a wooden stick into cups through hole. Freeze 4 hours or until firm. Makes 12 pops.

Per pop: 34 cal., 0 g fat, 0 mg chol., 1 mg sodium, 8 g carbo., 0 g fiber, 0 g pro.

Frozen Yogurt Pops

Make swirled yogurt pops by dividing yogurt in half and adding a different color of juice to each. Layer the colors in the paper cups.

Prep: 20 minutes   **Freeze:** overnight

2	cups low-fat vanilla yogurt
1	12-ounce can frozen juice concentrate, thawed
½	teaspoon vanilla
8	5-ounce paper cups
8	wooden frozen-dessert sticks

1. In a large bowl, combine yogurt, juice concentrate, and vanilla; divide among paper cups. Cover cups with foil; cut slits in the center of the foil and insert wooden sticks. Freeze overnight or until firm.

2. To serve, peel away the paper cup. Or peel away the side of the paper cup, leaving bottom intact for an instant dessert stand. Makes 8 pops.

Per serving: 165 cal., 1 g fat (0 g sat. fat), 3 mg chol., 63 mg sodium, 36 g carbo., 0 g fiber, 3 g pro.

Kid approved!

For sweeter pops, try a 12-ounce can of grape, raspberry, or fruit punch concentrate. For tart pops, use a 6-ounce can of lemonade or orange juice concentrate.

Very Berry Slushes

Start to Finish: 10 minutes

2	cups fresh strawberries or raspberries
1½	cups ice cubes
¼	cup honey
2	tablespoons lemon juice
1	pint vanilla ice cream (optional)

1. In a blender or food processor, combine berries, ice cubes, honey, and lemon juice. Cover and blend or process until pureed.

2. Pour mixture into glasses. If desired, top with vanilla ice cream. Makes 6 servings.

Per serving: 59 cal., 0 g fat, 0 mg chol., 1 mg sodium, 16 g carbo., 1 g fiber, 0 g pro.

Tutti-Fruity Slushes

Better than the store-bought kind, these cool drinks come in raspberry and peach flavors and are just right for sipping or slurping.

Start to Finish: 15 minutes

1	12-ounce package frozen lightly sweetened red raspberries or one 16-ounce package frozen unsweetened peach slices, thawed
1	cup apricot nectar
1	cup sifted powdered sugar
4	to 4½ cups ice cubes
	Fresh raspberries (optional)

1. Press thawed raspberries, if using, through a sieve to remove seeds.

2. Transfer pureed raspberries to a blender. Add apricot nectar and powdered sugar. Cover and blend until smooth.

3. Gradually add ice to mixture, blending until mixture is slushy. If desired, garnish servings with fresh raspberries. Makes 5 cups.

Per 1 cup: 160 cal., 0 g fat, 0 mg chol., 2 mg sodium, 40 g carbo., 3 g fiber, 1 g pro.

warm drinks

A soothing cup of hot cocoa goes far on a chilly fall day. Make it your way with one of these cocoa fix-ups.

Three-Way Cocoa

Prep: 5 minutes   **Cook:** 1 minute

$1^1/_2$ tablespoons sugar
1   tablespoon unsweetened
    cocoa powder
1   cup milk
$^1/_4$ teaspoon vanilla
    Marshmallows (optional)
    Ground cinnamon (optional)

1. In a large microwave-safe mug, combine sugar and cocoa powder. Add milk; stir to combine.
2. Microwave on 100-percent power (high) for 1 to $1^1/_2$ minutes, or until heated through, stirring once.
3. Stir in vanilla. If desired, top each serving with marshmallows and/or cinnamon. Serve immediately. Makes 1 serving.
Spicy Cocoa: Prepare as directed, except add $^1/_8$ teaspoon ground cinnamon with the cocoa powder. Top finished cocoa with a dash of ground nutmeg.
Mocha Cocoa: Prepare as directed, except add $^3/_4$ teaspoon instant coffee crystals to finished cocoa; stir.

Per serving: 175 cal., 4 g fat (2 g sat. fat), 15 mg chol., 98 mg sodium, 26 g carbo., 0 g fiber, 8 g pro.

weeknight solutions

Savory Chicken with Pasta

If this dish is too grown-up for younger taste buds, pan-fry a couple extra seasoned chicken breasts and serve them with pasta—minus the sauce and veggies.

Start to Finish: 35 minutes

8	ounces angel hair pasta
½	teaspoon dried thyme, crushed
½	teaspoon salt
¼	teaspoon ground black pepper
2	boneless, skinless chicken breast halves, halved horizontally (about 12 ounces total)
2	tablespoons olive oil
8	ounces presliced mushrooms (3 cups)
1	small red onion, halved and sliced (about 1 cup)
1½	teaspoons bottled minced garlic
1½	cups reduced-sodium chicken broth
1	tablespoon all-purpose flour
1	teaspoon Dijon-style mustard
4	plum tomatoes, cut into thin wedges
¼	cup chopped fresh flat-leaf (Italian) parsley

1. Cook pasta according to package directions; drain well.

2. Meanwhile, in a small bowl, combine thyme, ¼ teaspoon of the salt, and the pepper. Sprinkle over both sides of each chicken breast. In a very large skillet, heat 1 tablespoon of the oil over medium-high heat. Add chicken to skillet. Reduce heat to medium and cook until golden and cooked through (170°F), about 6 minutes, turning once. Remove chicken from skillet; cover and keep warm.

3. Add remaining 1 tablespoon oil to the skillet. Heat over medium-high heat. Stir in mushrooms, onion, and garlic; cook, stirring occasionally, until onion is tender, about 5 minutes. Whisk together broth, flour, mustard, and remaining ¼ teaspoon salt; add to skillet. Cook and stir until slightly thickened and bubbly. Stir in tomato and parsley; heat through. Serve chicken and sauce with pasta. Makes 4 servings.

Per serving: 426 cal., 9 g fat (2 g sat. fat), 49 mg chol., 604 mg sodium, 53 g carbo., 4 g fiber, 31 g pro.

Challenge: I need a chicken meal that has more grown-up flavors.

Chicken & Pasta Primavera

Boiling the vegetables with the pasta is a good way to piggyback kitchen tasks to save time. Make sure the vegetables are thinly sliced so they cook through.

Start to Finish: 25 minutes

1	9-ounce package refrigerated spinach or plain fettuccine
1	cup thinly sliced carrot (2 medium)
1	medium zucchini, halved lengthwise and thinly sliced (1¼ cups)
¾	cup frozen whole kernel corn
12	ounces deli-roasted chicken, cut into ½-inch strips (about 2½ cups)
1½	cups chicken broth
4	teaspoons cornstarch
2	teaspoons finely shredded lemon peel
1	teaspoon dried basil, crushed
½	cup dairy sour cream
2	tablespoons Dijon-style mustard
	Finely shredded Parmesan cheese

1. Cook pasta according to package directions, adding carrots, zucchini, and corn to the water with pasta. Drain pasta and vegetables. Return all to saucepan; add chicken. (If the chicken has been refrigerated, place it in a colander. Pour the pasta, vegetables, and cooking liquid over chicken to warm it; drain well.)

2. Meanwhile, in a medium saucepan, stir together broth, cornstarch, lemon peel, and basil. Cook and stir over medium heat until thickened and bubbly. Cook and stir for 2 minutes more. Remove from heat. Stir in sour cream and mustard. Pour over pasta mixture; toss gently to coat. Sprinkle with cheese. Serve immediately. Makes 6 servings.

Per serving: 334 cal., 10 g fat (4 g sat. fat), 98 mg chol., 547 mg sodium, 34 g carbo., 3 g fiber, 27 g pro.

Challenge: We're so busy! How can I get dinner on the table fast?

Challenge: How can I get my toddler to eat vegetables?

Kids' Favorite Pasta & Chicken

Coated in flavored cream cheese and Parmesan, your kids will barely notice the veggies in this dish.

Start to Finish: 25 minutes

1   12-ounce package frozen cooked breaded chicken nuggets
8   ounces dried wagon wheel pasta
4   cups sliced assorted vegetables (such as broccoli, summer squash, and sweet pepper)
½   of an 8-ounce tub cream cheese spread with chives and onion
½   cup milk
     Salt and ground black pepper
     Shredded Parmesan cheese

1. Heat chicken nuggets according to package directions.

2. Meanwhile, in a Dutch oven, heat a large amount of lightly salted water to boiling. Add pasta; cook for 4 minutes. Add vegetables; cook for 5 minutes more or until pasta is tender. Drain and return to pan.

3. Add cream cheese spread to pasta mixture. Heat through. Add enough milk to thin to desired consistency. Season to taste with salt and pepper. Sprinkle with Parmesan before serving. Serve with baked chicken nuggets. Makes 4 servings.

Per serving: 643 cal., 27 g fat (12 g sat. fat), 81 mg chol., 811 mg sodium, 72 g carbo., 4 g fiber, 25 g pro.

Challenge: How do I encourage my children to try new flavors?

Ginger Chicken Stir-Fry

Here's a low-stress way to get finicky eaters to branch out
with new tastes—such as ginger and stir-fry sauce.
The flavors are mild enough for picky palates.
Start to Finish: 25 minutes

- 1   **tablespoon cooking oil or peanut oil**
- 1   **medium zucchini, thinly sliced**
- 1   **medium carrot, thinly sliced**
- 1   **small onion, thinly sliced**
- 1   **small red sweet pepper, halved, seeded, and thinly sliced**
- ½   **head small green cabbage, shredded**
- 12   **ounces skinless, boneless chicken breast halves, cut into 1-inch pieces**
- ½   **cup bottled stir-fry sauce**
- ½   **teaspoon ground ginger**
-     **Hot cooked rice**
-     **Peanuts or cashews (optional)**

1. In a wok or extra-large skillet, heat oil over medium-high heat. Add half of the vegetables; stir-fry 2 minutes or until crisp-tender. Remove vegetables. Repeat with remaining vegetables; remove.

2. If necessary, add more oil to hot wok. Add chicken. Stir-fry for 3 to 5 minutes or until chicken is no longer pink. Push chicken from center of wok. Add sauce and ginger to center. Cook and stir until bubbly. Return cooked vegetables to wok. Cook and stir about 1 minute more or until vegetables are coated and heated through. Serve over hot cooked rice. If desired, sprinkle each serving with peanuts. Makes 6 servings.

Per serving, without rice: 130 cal., 3 g fat (1 g sat. fat), 34 mg chol., 540 mg sodium, 9 g carbo., 2 g fiber, 16 g pro.

Challenge: We love Asian food. How can I make our favorites at home?

Garlic Chicken

Homemade Asian-style food can be easier than you think to prepare. It's all in the sauce!

Prep: 20 minutes
Marinate: 30 minutes
Cook: 6 minutes

1	pound skinless, boneless chicken breasts
1	cup water
3	tablespoons reduced-sodium soy sauce
2	tablespoons chicken broth
1	tablespoon cornstarch
2	tablespoons cooking oil
10	green onions, bias-sliced
1	cup thinly sliced fresh mushrooms
12	cloves garlic, peeled and thinly sliced
½	cup sliced water chestnuts
	Hot cooked rice

1. Cut chicken into bite-size pieces and place in a resealable plastic bag. For marinade, mix water, soy sauce, and broth. Pour marinade over chicken in bag and seal. Marinate in the refrigerator for 30 minutes. Remove chicken; reserve the marinade. Stir cornstarch into marinade; set aside.

2. Heat oil over medium-high heat in a wok. Add green onion, mushrooms, and garlic; cook and stir 1 to 2 minutes or until tender. Remove vegetables from wok. Add chicken to wok; cook and stir 2 to 3 minutes or until no longer pink. Push chicken from center of wok. Stir marinade mixture; add to center of wok. Cook and stir until thickened and bubbly.

3. Return cooked vegetables to wok. Add water chestnuts. Cook and stir until combined. Serve with hot cooked rice. Makes 4 servings.

Per serving, with rice: 352 cal., 9 g fat (1 g sat. fat), 66 mg chol., 555 mg sodium, 34 g carbo., 3 g fiber, 32 g pro.

Cluck-Cluck BBQ Sandwiches

*This recipe also tastes great with leftover
cooked beef or pork.*

Prep: 15 minutes   **Cook:** 10 minutes

2   cups leftover cooked chicken breast
     cut into strips
1   medium carrot, shredded
½   cup bottled barbecue sauce
4   hamburger buns, split and toasted, or
     one 16-ounce loaf French bread,
     split and toasted
½   cup shredded Monterey Jack cheese
     (2 ounces) (optional)
     Pickle slices (optional)

1. In a medium saucepan, heat the chicken, carrot, and barbecue sauce over medium heat until bubbly.

2. Spoon chicken mixture onto bottom halves of buns. If desired, top with cheese. Place on a baking sheet. Broil 3 to 4 inches from heat for 1 to 2 minutes or until cheese melts. If desired, top with pickle slices. Cover with bun tops. Makes 4 servings.

Per serving: 269 cal., 6 g fat (2 g sat. fat), 53 mg chol., 520 mg sodium, 27 g carbo., 2 g fiber, 25 g pro.

Challenge: How can I make leftover chicken taste delicious?

Extra Saucy Chicken Sandwiches

The number of people sitting down to dinner can change on a daily basis. Here's a dish that can serve just two, but also easily doubles to serve four or more.

Start to Finish: 30 minutes

- 1 small onion, halved crosswise and thinly sliced
- 1 pound skinless, boneless chicken breast halves, cut into bite-size strips
- 1 tablespoon cooking oil
- ½ 14- to 16-ounce jar cheddar cheese pasta sauce (about ¾ cup)
- 1 tablespoon Worcestershire sauce
- 6 slices marbled rye bread, toasted
- 1 small tomato, sliced
- 6 slices bacon, crisp-cooked and drained (optional)

1. In a large skillet, cook onion and chicken in hot oil over medium-high heat for 4 to 5 minutes or until chicken is no longer pink. Add pasta sauce and Worcestershire sauce. Heat through.

2. To serve, spoon chicken and sauce mixture over half of the bread slices. Top with tomato and, if desired, bacon. Top with remaining bread slices. Makes 2 to 3 servings.

Note: This recipe easily doubles to serve 4 to 6 people. Multiply all the ingredients by two and prepare as directed.

Per serving: 491 cal., 18 g fat (5 g sat. fat), 114 mg chol., 1,084 mg sodium, 38 g carbo., 4 g fiber, 43 g pro.

Challenge: What can I make for two that will also easily double?

Chicken Tacos

Tweak your favorite tacos just a bit by substituting chicken for the more common beef. For grown-up tastes, top with extras like black olives, salsa, and hot sauce.

Start to Finish: 30 minutes

Nonstick cooking spray
1   cup chopped onion (1 large)
1   clove garlic, minced
2   cups chopped cooked chicken
1   8-ounce can tomato sauce
1   4-ounce can diced green chile
     peppers, drained
12 taco shells
2   cups shredded lettuce
½   cup chopped seeded tomato
     (1 medium)
½   cup finely shredded cheddar cheese
     and/or Monterey Jack cheese
     (2 ounces)

1. Spray an unheated large skillet with cooking spray. Heat skillet over medium heat. Add the onion and garlic; cook until onion is tender. Stir in the chicken, tomato sauce, and chile peppers. Heat through.

2. Divide chicken mixture among taco shells. Top with lettuce, tomato, and cheese. Makes 6 servings.

Per serving: 286 cal., 13 g fat (4 g sat. fat), 51 mg chol., 473 mg sodium, 25 g carbo., 4 g fiber, 19 g pro.

Challenge: I need a new twist on kid-friendly tacos!

Chili-Lime Chicken Salad

*This south-of-the-border salad has plenty of spunk
with the chili powder-spiked chicken, but also an
abundance of nutrition with lettuce, tomatoes,
and avocadoes.*

Prep: 25 minutes   **Roast:** 25 minutes
Stand: 15 minutes

Challenge: I need a nutritious meal that isn't boring or blah.

1	**pound chicken tenders**
2	**teaspoons chili powder**
	Salt and ground black pepper
1	**tablespoon olive oil**
1/4	**cup olive oil or salad oil**
3	**tablespoons lime juice**
2	**tablespoons snipped fresh cilantro**
1	**tablespoon white wine vinegar**
1/4	**teaspoon salt**
	Dash ground black pepper
6	**cups torn romaine lettuce**
8	**cherry tomatoes, halved or quartered**
1/2	**of a medium avocado, pitted, peeled, and coarsely chopped**

1. In a bowl, toss chicken tenders with chili powder and salt and pepper to taste. In a large skillet, heat 1 tablespoon oil over medium-high heat. Add chicken; reduce heat to medium. Cook 8 to 12 minutes or until chicken is no longer pink; turn once.

2. Meanwhile, for dressing, in a screw-top jar, combine 1/4 cup oil and the lime juice, cilantro, vinegar, 1/4 teaspoon salt, and dash pepper. Cover; shake well. Arrange lettuce on 4 salad plates. Top with chicken, tomato, and avocado. Drizzle with dressing. Makes 4 servings.

Per serving: 284 cal., 20 g fat (3 g sat. fat), 55 mg chol., 278 mg sodium, 8 g carbo., 4 g fiber, 20 g pro.

Chicken & Grape Pasta Salad

Chill this flavorful salad for up to 24 hours so every family member gets the chance to eat a homemade dinner.

Prep: 40 minutes   **Chill:** 4 hours

1	2- to 2½-pound deli-roasted chicken or 3 cups chopped cooked chicken
1½	cups dried radiatore, mostaccioli, and/or medium shell pasta
3	cups assorted fresh grapes, halved and seeded if desired
1½	cups halved small strawberries
1	cup chopped peeled jicama or one 8-ounce can sliced water chestnuts, drained
⅔	cup bottled cucumber ranch salad dressing
⅛	teaspoon cayenne pepper
1	to 2 tablespoons milk (optional)
	Leaf lettuce
	Purchased sugared sliced almonds (optional)

1. Remove skin and bones from chicken and discard. Tear chicken into bite-size pieces. Cook pasta according to package directions. Drain pasta. Rinse with cold water. Drain again.

2. In a large salad bowl, place chicken, pasta, grapes, strawberries, and jicama; toss to combine.

3. For dressing, in a small bowl, stir together dressing and cayenne pepper. Pour dressing over chicken mixture. Toss lightly to coat. Cover and chill for 4 to 24 hours.

4. Before serving, if necessary, stir in enough milk to moisten. Serve salad in lettuce-lined bowls and, if desired, sprinkle with almonds. Makes 6 servings.

Per serving: 455 cal., 20 g fat (3 g sat. fat), 67 mg chol., 269 mg sodium, 43 g carbo., 3 g fiber, 27 g pro.

Challenge: My husband works late. I need a dish that holds well.

Mediterranean Mostaccioli

Ground beef goes to the next level with this pull-out-the-stops pasta sauce. Say goodbye to burgers!

Start to Finish: 25 minutes

- 4 ounces dried mostaccioli or gemelli pasta
- 2 cups sliced zucchini
- 8 ounces lean ground beef
- ½ of a medium eggplant, peeled and cubed (about 2½ cups)
- 1 14½-ounce can diced tomatoes with basil, oregano, and garlic, undrained
- 2 tablespoons tomato paste
- ½ cup shredded carrot
- ¼ cup snipped fresh basil
- 2 tablespoons raisins (optional)
- ¼ teaspoon ground cinnamon
- 1 tablespoon balsamic vinegar (optional)
- ½ cup shredded mozzarella cheese (2 ounces)

1. Cook pasta according to package directions, adding zucchini during the last 2 minutes of cooking. Drain; cover with foil to keep warm.

2. Meanwhile, for sauce, in a large skillet, cook beef and eggplant over medium heat until meat is brown; drain off fat. Stir in undrained tomato, tomato paste, carrot, basil, raisins (if desired), and cinnamon. Bring to boiling; reduce heat. Simmer, uncovered, about 2 minutes or to desired consistency, stirring occasionally. Remove from heat. If desired, stir in vinegar.

3. Transfer pasta mixture to a serving dish. Spoon sauce over pasta mixture. Sprinkle with cheese. Makes 4 to 6 servings.

Per serving: 334 cal., 11 g fat (5 g sat. fat), 47 mg chol., 672 mg sodium, 38 g carbo., 4 g fiber, 21 g pro.

Taco Pizza

This quick-fix dinner is perfect for munching on while watching movies or playing games with the family.

Prep: 15 minutes   **Bake:** 20 minutes

8   ounces lean ground beef
1   medium green sweet pepper, chopped (¾ cup)
1   11½-ounce package refrigerated corn bread twists
½   cup purchased salsa
3   cups shredded taco cheese (12 ounces)
    Crushed tortilla chips (optional)
    Sour cream (optional)
    Chopped tomato (optional)
    Chopped green onion (optional)

1. Preheat oven to 400°F. In a skillet, cook beef and sweet pepper over medium heat until meat is browned; drain. Set aside.

2. Unroll corn bread dough (do not separate into strips). Press dough into the bottom and up the edges of a greased 12-inch pizza pan. Spread salsa on top of dough. Sprinkle with meat mixture and cheese. Bake about 20 minutes or until bottom of crust is golden when lifted slightly with a spatula. If desired, top with crushed tortilla chips, sour cream, tomato, and green onion. Cut into slices. Makes 6 slices.

Per slice: 451 cal., 30 g fat (15 g sat. fat), 73 mg chol., 901 mg sodium, 26 g carbo., 1 g fiber, 22 g pro.

Challenge: I need a fun meal for family movie time on Friday night!

Saucy Meatball Sandwiches

Cooking for big families can be difficult, but not with this easy mega-batch supper.

Start to Finish: 25 minutes

2	eggs
1½	cups soft whole wheat bread crumbs
½	cup finely chopped onion
½	teaspoon salt
½	teaspoon dried Italian seasoning, crushed
2	pounds lean ground beef
2	26- to 28-ounce jars red pasta sauce
12	hoagie or bratwurst buns
½	cup grated Parmesan cheese

1. Preheat oven to 350°F. In a large bowl, combine eggs, bread crumbs, onion, salt, and Italian seasoning. Add ground beef; mix well. Shape into 48 meatballs. Arrange meatballs in a large roasting pan or 15×10×1-inch baking pan. Bake for 15 to 20 minutes or until done (160°F). Drain well.

2. In a 4-quart Dutch oven, combine the pasta sauce and meatballs. Heat through. Split buns or hollow out tops of unsplit buns. Spoon hot meatball mixture into buns. Spoon any remaining sauce over the meatballs. Sprinkle cheese over the meatballs. Top with bun halves, if buns are split. Let stand 1 to 2 minutes before serving. Makes 12 servings.

Per serving: 599 cal., 18 g total fat (6 g sat. fat), 86 mg chol., 1,351 mg sodium, 83 g carbo., 6 g fiber, 29 g pro.

Challenge: How can I make plain spaghetti more exciting?

Contrary to popular belief, **size isn't important**. Fresh spears are tender, regardless of thickness.

Spaghetti with Shrimp, Asparagus & Tomatoes

Jazz up everyone's favorite pasta by tossing in some fresh ingredients—shrimp, asparagus, tomatoes, and basil.

Start to Finish: 30 minutes

4	ounces dried spaghetti
12	ounces fresh or frozen peeled and deveined shrimp
16	thin spears fresh asparagus
1	teaspoon olive oil
4	cloves garlic, minced
2	cups chopped seeded plum tomato (6 medium)
¼	cup chicken broth
¼	teaspoon salt
¼	teaspoon ground black pepper
1	tablespoon butter
¼	cup shredded fresh basil

1. Cook pasta according to package directions; drain and return to pan to keep warm.

2. Meanwhile, thaw shrimp, if frozen. Set aside. Snap off and discard woody bases from asparagus. If desired, scrape off scales. Remove tips; set aside. Bias-slice asparagus stalks into 1- to 1½-inch pieces; set aside.

3. In a skillet, heat oil over medium heat. Add garlic; cook and stir for 15 seconds. Add tomato; cook and stir for 2 minutes. Add asparagus stalks, broth, salt, and pepper. Cook, uncovered, for 3 minutes. Add asparagus tips and shrimp; cook, uncovered, for 2 to 3 minutes or until shrimp are opaque. Add butter; stir until melted.

4. Add asparagus mixture and basil to pasta in pan; toss to combine. Serve warm. Makes 4 servings.

Per serving: 274 cal., 6 g fat (2 g sat. fat), 137 mg chol., 362 mg sodium, 31 g carbo., 4 g fiber, 24 g pro.

Veggie Lasagna

Oozing with reduced-fat cheese and packed with fresh
vegetables, this dish gives you the best of both worlds—
gooey lasagna and healthful eating.

Prep: 30 minutes **Bake:** 50 minutes
Stand: 10 minutes

4	cups broccoli florets, chopped carrots, chopped zucchini, and/or chopped yellow summer squash
1	tablespoon olive oil
1	cup light ricotta cheese or low-fat cottage cheese
3	tablespoons grated Parmesan cheese
¼	teaspoon ground black pepper
2	cups purchased pasta sauce
4	dried no-boil lasagna noodles
1	cup shredded part-skim mozzarella cheese (4 ounces)
½	cup cherry tomato, quartered

1. Preheat oven to 375°F. In a large nonstick skillet, cook and stir vegetables in hot oil over medium-high heat about 10 minutes or until crisp-tender. Remove from heat and set aside. In a small bowl, stir together ricotta cheese, Parmesan cheese, and pepper.

2. To assemble, spoon about ½ cup of the pasta sauce into the bottom of a 2-quart square baking dish. Top with two of the lasagna noodles. Spread half of the ricotta cheese mixture evenly over the noodles. Top with half of the vegetable mixture, half of the remaining sauce, and half of the mozzarella cheese. Repeat layers.

3. Cover with foil. Bake for 45 minutes or until heated through and noodles are tender. Uncover; sprinkle with tomato. Bake, uncovered, 5 minutes more. Let stand for 10 minutes before serving. Makes 6 servings.

Test Kitchen Tip: If desired, add ½ cup chopped, cooked chicken on top of each vegetable mixture layer.

Per serving: 236 cal., 9 g fat (4 g sat. fat), 24 mg chol., 493 mg sodium, 25 g carbo., 4 g fiber, 13 g pro.

Challenge: We love lasagna. How can I make it more nutritious?

Vegetarian Gumbo

Bold flavors and hearty protein-packed black beans can satisfy a meat-eater's need for substance while still keeping a vegetarian's dietary restrictions in check.

Prep: 10 minutes   **Cook:** 6 hours (low) or
3 hours (high)

2 **15-ounce cans black beans, rinsed and drained**
1 **28-ounce can diced tomatoes, undrained**
1 **16-ounce package frozen loose-pack pepper stir-fry vegetables (yellow, green, and red sweet peppers, and onions)**
2 **cups frozen cut okra**
2 **to 3 teaspoons Cajun seasoning**
   Hot cooked white or brown rice (optional)
   Chopped green onion (optional)

1. In a $3\frac{1}{2}$- to $4\frac{1}{2}$-quart slow cooker, combine drained black beans, undrained tomato, frozen stir-fry vegetables, okra, and Cajun seasoning.

2. Cover and cook on low-heat setting for 6 to 8 hours or on high-heat setting for 3 to 4 hours. If desired, serve over hot cooked rice and garnish with green onion. Makes 6 servings.

Per serving: 153 cal., 0 g fat (0 g sat. fat), 0 mg chol., 639 mg sodium, 31 g carbo., 10 g fiber, 12 g pro.

Challenge: My husband loves meat—I don't. What can I serve?

Sweet Potato Soup

A major source of vitamins A and C, sweet potatoes
are an excellent ingredient to use in place of
regular potatoes. Also try them as a side dish in
this smooth, maple syrup sparked soup.

Prep: 20 minutes   **Cook:** 20 minutes

Challenge: Sweet potatoes are so healthful. How can I serve them?

½	cup chopped onion (1 medium)
½	cup chopped celery (1 stalk)
1	clove garlic, minced
1	tablespoon butter
1	sweet potato, peeled and cubed (about 2 cups)
2	cups reduced-sodium chicken broth
½	teaspoon ground nutmeg
1½	cups half-and-half or light cream
1	tablespoon maple syrup
	Dairy sour cream (optional)
	Ground nutmeg (optional)

1. In a Dutch oven, cook onion, celery, and garlic in hot butter over medium heat until onion is tender but not brown. Add sweet potato, broth, and nutmeg; bring to boiling. Reduce heat; simmer, covered, 20 minutes or until potato is tender. Remove from heat; cool slightly.

2. Transfer mixture to a blender or food processor. Cover and blend or process until smooth. Return all soup to the Dutch oven. Stir in half-and-half and maple syrup; heat through. If desired, top each serving with sour cream and additional nutmeg. Makes 4 servings.

Per serving: 233 cal., 13 g fat (8 g sat. fat), 41 mg chol., 392 mg sodium, 24 g carbo., 3 g fiber, 6 g pro.

Rice Pilaf with Oranges & Walnuts

For quick side dishes, rice mixes are always a good option. This sensational recipe incorporates unique ingredients to add life to meat, poultry, and seafood dishes.

Prep: 20 minutes   **Cook:** 25 minutes

1½ cups sliced button mushrooms
   (4 ounces)
 1 cup sliced celery (2 stalks)
 1 cup finely chopped onion (2 medium)
 1 tablespoon cooking oil
 1 14-ounce can chicken broth
⅔ cup water
 1 6-ounce package long grain and
   wild rice mix
 2 medium oranges, peeled and
   sectioned, or one 11-ounce can
   mandarin orange sections, drained
½ cup chopped toasted walnuts

1. In a large saucepan, cook mushrooms, celery, and onion in hot oil over medium heat about 5 minutes or until tender. Add broth and water; bring to boiling. Stir in wild rice mix and seasoning packet; reduce heat. Cover and simmer for 25 to 30 minutes or until rice is tender. Remove from heat. Gently stir in orange and walnuts. Makes 6 servings.

Per serving: 214 cal., 10 g fat (1 g sat. fat), 1 mg chol., 673 mg sodium, 29 g carbo., 3 g fiber, 6 g pro.

Challenge: Help! I need ideas for creative side dishes!

Basil & Tomato Pasta Salad

When the summer crop of vegetables and herbs starts ripening, here's a tasty dish to try. It makes use of green beans, tomatoes, and basil from the garden (or market).

Prep: 25 minutes   **Chill:** 4 hours

8   ounces dried pasta (such as rotini, cavatelli, or penne)
6   ounces fresh green beans, trimmed and cut into 1-inch pieces, or 1 cup frozen cut green beans
3   medium tomatoes, cut into thin wedges (about 1 pound)
1   cup desired-flavor bottled vinaigrette salad dressing
¾   cup finely shredded Parmesan cheese (3 ounces)
½   cup sliced pitted kalamata olives or ripe olives
½   cup finely shredded fresh basil
    Shaved Parmesan cheese (optional)

1. Cook pasta according to package directions, adding green beans the last 5 minutes of cooking; drain. Rinse with cold water; drain again.

2. In a very large bowl, toss together the pasta mixture, tomato, salad dressing, shredded cheese, olives, and basil. Cover and chill for 4 to 24 hours. Toss gently before serving. If desired, top with shaved Parmesan. Makes 12 to 16 side-dish servings.

Per serving: 170 cal., 8 g fat (2 g sat. fat), 4 mg chol., 384 mg sodium, 19 g carbo., 2 g fiber, 5 g pro.

Challenge: What can I do with the produce from my garden?

Garden Pasta

*This pasta toss is the perfect light meal for
hot summer nights on the deck. During late summer,
make use of garden-fresh veggies from the
farmer's market.*

Start to Finish: 25 minutes

4 ounces dried spaghetti, linguine,
fettuccine, or angel hair pasta
or one 9-ounce package
refrigerated pasta

1 medium zucchini or yellow
summer squash, halved
lengthwise and sliced

2 teaspoons olive oil

1 tomato, cut into thin wedges

3 to 4 tablespoons purchased
basil pesto

1. Prepare pasta according to package
directions; drain.

2. In a large skillet, cook the zucchini in
oil over medium heat until crisp-tender.
Place pasta in serving bowl. Add tomato,
pesto, and cooked zucchini. Toss gently
to mix. Makes 2 servings.

Per serving: 389 cal., 15 g fat (3 g sat. fat),
7 mg chol., 226 mg sodium, 51 g carbo., 4 g fiber,
12 g pro.

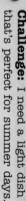

Challenge: I need a light dish
that's perfect for summer days.

Sugar Snap, Tomato & Feta Salad

Sauteed vegetables have outstanding flavor, without a lot of added fat or calories. Mix with mint and crumbled feta for added dimension.

Start to Finish: 15 minutes

½ **pound sugar snap peas or snow peas, strings removed (about 2 cups)**
1 **tablespoon extra virgin olive oil**
1 **cup grape tomatoes, halved**
¼ **cup fresh mint leaves, coarsely chopped**
  Salt and ground black pepper
½ **cup coarsely crumbled feta cheese**

1. In a large skillet, cook peas in hot oil over medium heat for 2 to 4 minutes over medium-high heat until crisp-tender. Stir in tomato, mint, and salt and pepper to taste. Heat through. Add cheese and toss to combine. Makes 4 to 6 servings.

Per serving: 111 cal., 8 g fat (3 g sat. fat), 17 mg chol., 359 mg sodium, 7 g carbo., 2 g fiber, 5 g pro.

Challenge: Steamed vegetables are dull. What else can I do?

Did you know?

❀ Tomatoes will ripen faster if they are stored in a brown paper bag, out of the sunlight, and at room temperature.

❀ Tomatoes are considered fruit, not vegetables, because the seeds are part of the edible plant.

a. Common Tomato

Has a sweet taste that is considered the classic tomato flavor; tastes great plain, mixed with salads or pasta, or cooked.

b. Pear Tomato

Extra juicy, small, similar in texture to cherry tomato but tastes milder (leaning more toward sweet than rich); ideal when eaten plain; also called yellow teardrop.

c. Plum Tomato

Less acidic than common tomato; sweeter flavor works well in pasta sauces and when dried; often used for the popular sun-dried variety at supermarkets; also called roma.

d. Grape Tomato

So called because of its small size and because it grows in a cluster like grapes; popular with kids because it's easy to snack on and very sweet.

e. Cherry Tomato

Favored in salad bars; sweet yet rich, and so tender you can cut it with a fork.

Challenge: I need a quick recipe for preparing asparagus.

Chilled Asparagus Salad

Fresh springtime asparagus has plenty of flavor on its own. But toss it with a few extra ingredients and it magically creates a filling side dish or light lunch.

Start to Finish: 25 minutes

½   cup mayonnaise or salad dressing
¼   cup plain yogurt
½   teaspoon finely shredded orange peel
⅓   cup orange juice
⅛   teaspoon lemon-pepper seasoning
1   pound fresh asparagus spears
6   cups torn butterhead (Boston or Bibb) lettuce
1   small red onion, cut into thin wedges (½ cup)
1   11-ounce can mandarin orange sections, drained

1. For dressing, stir together mayonnaise, yogurt, orange peel, orange juice, and lemon-pepper seasoning; set aside.

2. Snap off and discard woody bases from asparagus. In a saucepan, cook asparagus in a small amount of lightly salted boiling water for 3 to 5 minutes or until crisp-tender; drain. Plunge asparagus into ice water to chill; drain. Toss with lettuce, onion, orange sections, and dressing. Makes 4 to 6 servings.

Per serving: 277 cal., 23 g fat (4 g sat. fat), 11 mg chol., 180 mg sodium, 16 g carbo., 3 g fiber, 4 g pro.

Grilled Asparagus with Lemon

Long asparagus are ideal for grilling because they lay across the grill grate without falling in. Partially cooking the asparagus keeps it from burning before it's tender.

Prep: 15 minutes   **Marinate:** 30 minutes
Grill: 3 minutes

1   to 1½ pounds fresh asparagus spears
2   tablespoons olive oil
2   tablespoons lemon juice
½   teaspoon salt
¼   teaspoon ground black pepper
    Lemon wedges

1. Snap off and discard woody bases from asparagus. If desired, scrape off scales. In a large skillet, cook the asparagus in a small amount of boiling water for 3 minutes. Drain well. Meanwhile, for marinade, in a 2-quart rectangular baking dish, stir together olive oil, lemon juice, salt, and pepper. Add drained asparagus, turning to coat. Cover and marinate at room temperature for 30 minutes. Drain asparagus, discarding marinade. Place asparagus on a grill tray or in a grill basket.

2. For a charcoal grill, grill asparagus on the rack of an uncovered grill directly over medium heat for 3 to 5 minutes or until asparagus is tender and beginning to brown, turning once halfway through grilling. (For a gas grill, preheat grill. Reduce heat to medium. Place asparagus on grill rack over heat. Cover and grill as above.)

3. To serve, arrange asparagus on a serving platter. Serve with lemon wedges. Makes 4 to 6 side-dish servings.

Per serving: 87 cal., 7 g fat (1 g sat. fat), 0 mg chol., 294 mg sodium, 7 g carbo., 3 g fiber, 3 g pro.

Challenge: What is a good vegetable to toss on the grill?

Home Run Garlic Rolls

Since garlic complements many savory dishes, this homemade version of garlic bread can be eaten with almost any meal.

Prep: 20 minutes **Rise:** 1½ hours
Bake: 15 minutes

1 **16-ounce loaf frozen white or whole wheat bread dough, thawed**
1 **tablespoon butter, melted**
2 **cloves garlic, minced**
2 **tablespoons grated Parmesan cheese**

1. Lightly grease a 13×9×2-inch baking pan; set aside. Shape dough into 24 balls; place in prepared pan. Cover; let rise in a warm place until nearly double (1½ to 2 hours).

2. Preheat oven to 350°F. In a small bowl, stir together melted butter and garlic. Brush butter mixture over rolls. Sprinkle with Parmesan. Bake for 15 to 20 minutes or until golden. Remove rolls from pans and cool slightly on a wire rack. Serve warm. Makes 24 rolls (12 servings).

Per serving: 55 cal., 1 g fat (0 g sat. fat), 2 mg chol., 99 mg sodium, 9 g carbo., 0 g fiber, 1 g pro.

Challenge: I need a bread I can serve with just about anything.

how to keep garlic fresh

Garlic should be stored loosely covered, away from light and heat. Freezing destroys its texture; storing it in oil at room temperature can make it poisonous. When buying fresh garlic, make sure it's free of sprouts—a sign of age.

easy tip
That annoying little cling-on clove skin isn't easy to remove. Next time, push or pound the broad side of a knife against a clove—the skin comes right off!

Garlic Lovers Unite

Related to onions, shallots, and leeks, garlic grew in central Asia more than 6,000 years ago. Today it's a favorite around the world.

❋ **Roast it.** Roasting garlic mellows its intense raw flavor. That mellowness mixes well into homemade soups and tastes delicious when stirred in with beans and greens. Or stir it into butter or olive oil and relish with bread. Another option is to stir it into mayonnaise for a zesty sandwich spread.

❋ **Chop it.** A little chopped garlic goes a long way. Add it to stir-fries and sauteed vegetables or rub it on meat, seafood, or poultry before cooking. For a quick supper, try tossing a touch of it with chopped tomatoes, basil, hot cooked pasta, and/or cooked shrimp.

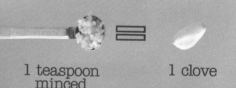

1 teaspoon minced

1 clove

Bet you didn't know: Chicago gets its name from the Native American word for a variety of wild garlic called "chicagoua."

Parmesan Twists

These twists can be made savory or sweet—depending on the topping. The main recipe, Parmesan Twists, works as a side dish while the Cinnamon-Sugar Twists variation can be relished as an after-dinner sweet.

Prep: 10 minutes **Bake:** 10 minutes

1   **11-ounce package (12) refrigerated breadsticks**
2   **tablespoons butter or margarine, melted**
2   **to 3 tablespoons grated Parmesan cheese**
    Pizza sauce or cheese dip, warmed

1. Preheat oven to 375°F. Grease a large baking sheet; set aside. Separate breadsticks. Brush each with melted butter; sprinkle with Parmesan. Twist each breadstick several times. Arrange on prepared baking sheet.

2. Bake for 10 to 13 minutes or until golden. Cool on a wire rack. Serve with pizza sauce or cheese dip for dipping. Makes 12 twists.

Cinnamon-Sugar Twists: Prepare as above except omit Parmesan and pizza sauce or cheese dip. In a small bowl, combine 2 tablespoons sugar and ¼ teaspoon ground cinnamon. Sprinkle breadsticks with sugar mixture after brushing with butter. Twist and bake as above. Serve with applesauce or fruit preserves for dipping.

Per twist (both variations): 95 cal., 3 g fat (1 g sat. fat), 5 mg chol., 199 mg sodium, 15 g carbo., 0 g fiber, 2 g pro.

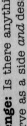

Challenge: Is there anything I can serve as a side *and* dessert?

Corn Bread Mini Muffins

Use a corn muffin mix to make short work of homemade corn bread. A luscious honey butter spread makes it a bit more special.

Prep: 15 minutes **Bake:** 10 minutes
Cool: 5 minutes

Nonstick cooking spray
¼ cup butter or margarine, softened
1 tablespoon honey
   Dash cayenne pepper or several
      dashes bottled hot pepper sauce
⅓ cup buttermilk
1 egg, slightly beaten
1 8.5-ounce package corn muffin mix
½ cup frozen whole kernel corn, thawed
½ cup shredded cheddar cheese
      (2 ounces)*

1. Preheat oven to 400°F. Lightly coat twenty-four 1¾-inch muffin cups with cooking spray; set aside.

2. For butter spread, in a small bowl, stir together butter, honey, and cayenne pepper; set aside.

3. In a medium bowl, stir together buttermilk and egg. Add muffin mix; stir just until moistened. Stir in corn and cheese. Spoon batter into prepared muffin cups, filling two-thirds full.

4. Bake for 10 to 12 minutes or until golden and a wooden toothpick inserted in centers comes out clean. Cool in muffin cups on a wire rack for 5 minutes. Remove from muffin cups; serve warm with butter spread. Makes 24 muffins.

* Note: Looking to save a few bucks? Instead of expensive packaged cheese, buy a block of cheese and shred it yourself.

Per muffin: 77 cal., 4 g fat (2 g sat. fat), 17 mg chol., 105 mg sodium, 9 g carbo., 0 g fiber, 2 g pro.

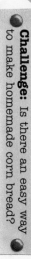

Challenge: Is there an easy way to make homemade corn bread?

make now, serve later

Make-ahead meals—whether stored for 24 hours in the fridge or 3 months in the freezer—are a guaranteed lifesaver on busy weeknights. A little forethought is required, but the reward is an easy homemade meal—just heat and eat!

Parmesan Chicken & Broccoli

Prep: 30 minutes **Bake:** 40 minutes
Freeze: up to 3 months

1	cup converted rice
½	cup sliced green onion (4)
12	ounces skinless, boneless chicken breast halves, cut into strips
¾	teaspoon dried Italian seasoning, crushed
1	clove garlic, minced
1	tablespoon cooking oil
1	16-ounce jar reduced-fat Alfredo pasta sauce
3	cups frozen cut broccoli
⅓	cup grated Parmesan cheese
¼	cup diced cooked ham
1	2-ounce jar diced pimiento, drained
	Ground black pepper

1. Cook rice according to package directions; remove from heat and stir in the green onion. Divide the rice mixture among four 12- to 16-ounce au gratin dishes or casseroles; set aside.

2. In a large skillet, cook the chicken strips, Italian seasoning, and garlic in hot oil over medium heat for 4 to 6 minutes or until chicken is no longer pink. Remove from heat. Stir in Alfredo sauce, broccoli, Parmesan, ham, and pimiento. Season to taste with pepper. Spoon chicken mixture over rice in dishes. Cover with freezer wrap, label, and freeze up to 3 months.*

3. To serve, thaw frozen dishes overnight in the refrigerator. Preheat oven to 350°F. Remove freezer wrap; cover each dish with foil. Bake for 20 minutes. Uncover and bake about 20 minutes more or until heated through. Makes 4 servings.

*Note: To serve immediately, after preparing casseroles, cover and bake in a 350°F oven for 15 minutes. Uncover and bake about 15 minutes more or until heated through.

Per serving: 660 cal., 25 g fat (12 g sat. fat), 109 mg chol., 1,277 mg sodium, 71 g carbo., 5 g fiber, 39 g pro.

Baked Penne with Meat Sauce

Prep: 30 minutes **Bake:** 75 minutes
Freeze: up to 1 month

8   ounces dried penne pasta
1   14.5-ounce can diced tomatoes, undrained
½   of a 6-ounce can (⅓ cup) Italian-style tomato paste
⅓   cup dry red wine or tomato juice
⅓   cup water
½   teaspoon sugar
½   teaspoon dried oregano, crushed, or 2 teaspoons snipped fresh oregano
¼   teaspoon salt
¼   teaspoon ground black pepper
1   pound lean ground beef
½   cup chopped onion (1 medium)
¼   cup sliced pitted ripe olives
1   cup shredded reduced-fat mozzarella cheese (4 ounces)

1. Cook pasta according to package directions; drain well.

2. In a bowl, stir together undrained tomatoes, tomato paste, wine, water, sugar, dried oregano (if using), salt, and pepper.

3. In a large skillet, brown ground beef and onion over medium heat. Drain off fat. Stir in tomato mixture. Bring to boiling; reduce heat. Cover and simmer for 10 minutes. Stir in pasta, fresh oregano (if using), and olives.

4. Divide the mixture among six 10- to 12-ounce casseroles. (Or use one 3-quart rectangular baking dish.)* Cover with freezer wrap, label, and freeze up to 1 month.

5. To serve, preheat oven to 350°F. Remove freezer wrap; cover each casserole with foil. Bake about 70 minutes or until heated through. Sprinkle with mozzarella cheese. Bake, uncovered, about 5 minutes more or until cheese melts. Makes 6 servings.

*Note: To serve in a 3-quart baking dish, after freezing, remove freezer wrap. Cover dish with foil. Bake about 1½ hours or until heated through; stir carefully once. Sprinkle with mozzarella cheese. Bake, uncovered, 5 minutes more or until cheese melts.

Per serving: 342 cal., 10 g fat (4 g sat. fat), 51 mg chol., 465 mg sodium, 37 g carbo., 2 g fiber, 22 g pro.

Bean & Beef Enchilada Casserole

Prep: 25 minutes **Bake:** 40 minutes
Chill: up to 24 hours

½ **pound lean ground beef**
½ **cup chopped onion (1 medium)**
1 **teaspoon chili powder**
½ **teaspoon ground cumin**
1 **15-ounce can pinto beans, rinsed
   and drained**
1 **4-ounce can diced green chile peppers,
   undrained**
1 **8-ounce carton dairy sour cream or
   light sour cream**
2 **tablespoons all-purpose flour**
¼ **teaspoon garlic powder**
8 **6-inch corn tortillas**
1 **10-ounce can enchilada sauce or one
   10.5-ounce can tomato puree**
1 **cup shredded cheddar cheese
   (4 ounces)**
   Chopped tomato (optional)
   Sliced green onion (optional)

1. In a large skillet, cook the ground beef, onion, chili powder, and cumin over medium heat until onion is tender and meat is no longer pink. Drain off fat. Stir in drained pinto beans and undrained chile peppers; set aside.

2. In a small bowl, stir together sour cream, flour, and garlic powder; set aside.

3. Place half of the tortillas in the bottom of a lightly greased 2-quart rectangular baking dish; cut to fit if necessary. Top with half of the meat mixture, half of the sour cream mixture, half of the enchilada sauce, and ½ cup cheese. Repeat layers, except reserve remaining ½ cup cheese. Cover dish with plastic wrap; chill in refrigerator up to 24 hours.

4. To serve, preheat oven to 350°F. Remove plastic wrap; cover dish with foil. Bake 35 to 40 minutes or until bubbly. Sprinkle with reserved ½ cup cheese. Bake, uncovered, about 5 minutes more or until cheese melts. If desired, top with chopped tomato and sliced green onion. Makes 6 servings.

Per serving: 429 cal., 24 g fat (12 g sat. fat), 64 mg chol., 632 mg sodium, 36 g carbo., 6 g fiber, 15 g pro.

Chili-Cheese Hoagies

For the bold diners at your table, serve these crowd-pleasing
hoagies with pickled jalapeño pepper slices.

Prep: 35 minutes   **Bake:** 35 minutes
Chill: up to 24 hours

- 1   pound lean ground beef
- 1   cup chopped onion (1 large)
- 1   cup chopped green and/or red sweet
      pepper (2 small)
- 2   cloves garlic, minced
- 1   14.5-ounce can diced tomatoes,
      undrained
- ½   teaspoon ground cumin
- ¼   teaspoon ground black pepper
- 8   hoagie buns or French-style rolls
- 8   thin slices Monterey Jack cheese or
      Monterey Jack cheese with jalapeño
      peppers (8 ounces)
- 8   thin slices cheddar cheese (8 ounces)
      Pickled jalapeño pepper slices
      (optional)

1. In a large skillet, cook ground beef, onion, sweet pepper, and garlic over medium heat until meat is brown. Drain off fat. Add undrained tomato, cumin, and black pepper. Bring to boiling; reduce heat. Simmer, uncovered, about 15 minutes or until thickened, stirring occasionally. Cool the meat mixture for 30 minutes or chill until ready to assemble the sandwiches.

2. Split rolls lengthwise. Hollow out roll bottoms, leaving a ¼-inch-thick shell. Place a slice of Monterey Jack cheese, cut to fit, on bottom half of hoagie. Spoon meat mixture on top of cheese. Top meat mixture with a slice of cheddar cheese. If desired, sprinkle with pickled jalapeño pepper slices. Add hoagie top. Repeat with remaining hoagies. Wrap each sandwich in parchment paper, then in foil. Chill up to 24 hours.

3. Preheat oven to 375°F. Place wrapped hoagies on a baking sheet. Bake for 35 to 40 minutes or until cheese is melted and filling is hot. Makes 8 sandwiches.

Per serving: 738 cal., 31 g fat (15 g sat. fat), 91 mg chol., 1,274 mg sodium, 79 g carbo., 5 g fiber, 36 g pro.

Pizza Supreme

Homemade frozen pizza beats purchased frozen pizza
any day. Mix and match toppings as you like.

Prep: 30 minutes   **Bake:** 25 minutes
Freeze: up to 1 month

1   15-ounce can pizza sauce
2   12-inch (10 ounces each) thin Italian
      bread shells* (such as Boboli) or
      purchased baked pizza crust
1   pound bulk Italian sausage, ground
      beef, or ground pork, cooked and
      drained; or 1½ cups diced cooked
      ham or Canadian-style bacon
      (6 ounces)
1   cup sliced fresh mushrooms or sliced
      green sweet peppers
½   cup sliced green onions (4) or sliced
      pitted ripe olives
3   cups shredded mozzarella cheese
      (12 ounces)

1. Spread pizza sauce evenly on crusts. Top pizzas with meat, mushroom, green onion, and cheese.

2. Cover pizzas with plastic wrap and freeze until firm. Wrap frozen pizzas in moistureproof and vaporproof wrap. Wrap in heavy foil or place in a large resealable freezer bag; seal. Label and freeze for up to 1 month.

3. To serve, preheat oven to 375°F. Unwrap one pizza and place on baking sheet. Bake about 25 minutes or until cheese is bubbly. Makes 3 to 4 servings per pizza.

Tip: For a crisper crust, bake pizza directly on oven rack.

*Note: If you prefer to use a thicker pizza crust, increase baking time to about 35 minutes.

Per serving: 685 cal., 37 g fat (14 g sat. fat), 100 mg chol., 1,586 mg sodium, 18 g carbo., 2 g fiber, 36 g pro.

Pork & Noodles

Prep: 30 minutes   **Chill:** up to 24 hours

8   ounces dried Chinese egg noodles
1½ pounds fresh asparagus spears,
     trimmed and cut into 2-inch-long
     pieces
4   medium carrots, cut into thin ribbons
     or bite-size strips (2 cups)
1   pound cooked lean pork, cut into
     thin strips
1   recipe Soy-Sesame Vinaigrette
     Sesame seeds (optional)
     Sliced green onion (optional)

1. Cook noodles according to package directions; drain. Rinse with cold water until cool; drain.

2. If using fresh asparagus, cook in a covered saucepan in a small amount of lightly salted boiling water for 4 to 6 minutes or until crisp-tender. Drain asparagus well.

3. In a large bowl, combine noodles, asparagus, carrot, and pork. Cover and chill in the refrigerator for 2 to 24 hours.

4. To serve, prepare Soy-Sesame Vinaigrette and gently toss with mixture. If desired, sprinkle with sesame seeds and green onion. Makes 8 (1½-cup) servings.

Soy-Sesame Vinaigrette: In a screw-top jar, combine ½ cup reduced-sodium soy sauce, ¼ cup rice vinegar or vinegar, ¼ cup honey, 2 tablespoons salad oil, and 2 teaspoons toasted sesame oil. Cover and shake well to mix. Chill for 2 to 24 hours.

Per serving: 338 cal., 12 g fat (3 g sat. fat), 71 mg chol., 654 mg sodium, 35 g carbo., 3 g fiber, 23 g pro.

Baked Rotini with Ham

*This creamy, colorful dish is a
real kid-pleaser.*

Prep: 25 minutes **Bake:** 25 minutes
Stand: 10 minutes **Chill:** up to 24 hours

8 **ounces dried tricolor rotini
   (3 cups)**
1 **16- to 17-ounce jar Alfredo
   pasta sauce**
½ **cup milk**
½ **cup shredded mozzarella cheese
   (2 ounces)**
2 **ounces cooked ham, chopped
   (½ cup)**
1 **teaspoon dried Italian
   seasoning, crushed**
⅛ **teaspoon ground black pepper**
¼ **cup grated Parmesan cheese**

1. Cook rotini according to package directions; drain and return to pan. Stir in Alfredo sauce, milk, mozzarella, ham, Italian seasoning, and pepper.

2. Transfer rotini mixture to four 7- to 8-ounce au gratin dishes or ramekins or a 1½-quart au gratin dish. Sprinkle with Parmesan cheese. Cover and chill for up to 24 hours.

3. To serve, preheat oven to 350°F. Cover with foil and bake for 25 to 30 minutes for the individual dishes or about 45 minutes for the casserole dish or until mixture is heated through. Let stand for 10 minutes. Stir before serving. Makes 4 servings.

Per serving: 503 cal., 28 g fat (13 g sat. fat), 121 mg chol., 1,084 mg sodium, 51 g carbo., 2 g fiber, 20 g pro.

Vegetable Shepherd's Pie

Prep: 25 minutes **Cook:** 30 minutes
Bake: 1 hour **Chill:** overnight

1	14-ounce can vegetable broth or chicken broth
¾	cup water
1	cup dry lentils, rinsed and drained
3	cloves garlic, minced
1½	pounds parsnips or 9 carrots, peeled and cut into ½-inch-thick slices (about 3½ cups)
6	purple boiling onions (8 ounces), quartered, or 1 medium red onion, cut into wedges
1	14.5-ounce can diced tomatoes with Italian herbs, undrained
2	tablespoons tomato paste
4	medium potatoes, peeled and cut up
3	tablespoons butter or margarine
1	tablespoon snipped fresh thyme or ½ teaspoon dried thyme, crushed
½	teaspoon salt
¼	to ⅓ cup milk
1½	cups shredded Colby and Monterey Jack or cheddar cheese (6 ounces)

1. In a large saucepan, stir together broth, water, lentils, and garlic. Bring to boiling; reduce heat. Cover and simmer for 20 minutes. Add parsnip and onion. Return to boiling; reduce heat. Cover and simmer for 10 to 15 minutes or until vegetables and lentils are just tender. Remove from heat. Stir in tomatoes and the tomato paste.

2. In a 2-quart saucepan, cook potato in lightly salted boiling water for 20 to 25 minutes or until tender; drain. Mash potato. Add butter, thyme, and salt. Gradually beat in milk until potato is light and fluffy. Stir in 1 cup of the cheese until melted.

3. Spread lentil mixture into a 2- to 2½-quart au gratin dish. Spoon potato mixture over lentil mixture. Cover dish with plastic wrap; chill in refrigerator overnight.

4. To serve, preheat oven to 350°F. Remove plastic wrap; cover dish with foil. Bake for 50 minutes. Uncover and bake for 10 to 15 minutes more or until heated through. Sprinkle with remaining ½ cup cheese. Makes 6 servings.

Per serving: 449 cal., 16 g fat (10 g sat. fat), 42 mg chol., 1,122 mg sodium, 58 g carbo., 17 g fiber, 20 g pro.

chill and store

Reheating chilled or frozen dishes is a great way to pull a meal together fast. Here are three simple tips:

❋ Store fragile items, such as cakes and cookies, on top of sturdy items, such as casseroles and meats.

❋ Thaw all foods other than baked goods in the refrigerator; baked goods can thaw at room temperature.

❋ Heat foods to a safe serving temperature before serving. Bring soups, sauces, and gravies to a full boil before serving. Heat all other leftovers to 165°F.

Quick freezer tip
Avoid UFOs—unidentified frozen objects—by labeling packages with the recipe name, number of servings, and date placed in the freezer.

More on storage
Below are some guidelines for chilling and freezing certain meals, but remember that not every dish will freeze well. Follow specific instructions outlined in individual recipes.

FOOD	STORE	REFRIGERATE 40°F up to:	FREEZE 0°F up to:
Casseroles	Line baking dish with heavy-duty foil. Place casserole contents in lined dish. Spray foil with nonstick spray. Wrap tightly and freeze. When frozen, lift foil-covered food out and place in freezer. To thaw, refrigerate overnight.	2–3 days	4 months
Chicken (cooked)	Package in resealable freezer bags.	2–3 days	4 months
Lasagna	See Casseroles above. Protect top of lasagna with plastic wrap or waxed paper before wrapping in foil.	2–3 days	4 months
Beef, lamb or pork (cooked)	Package in resealable freezer bags.	4 days	3 months
Soups, stews	Divide into convenient portions. Transfer to plastic freezer containers. Thaw in refrigerator for 24 hours before reheating.	4 days	3 months
Veggie, potato, or rice dishes	See Casseroles above.	3–4 days	3 months

Homemade sauces

Thick and meaty, creamy and rich—no matter what the style of sauce, it's guaranteed to add spunk to dinner.

TUESDAY

THURSDAY

SUNDAY

MONDAY

Spicy Tomato Sauce

*For even more kick on your pasta, choose
a spicy Italian sausage for this sauce.*
Prep: 15 minutes   **Cook:** 15 minutes

½ **pound uncooked bulk sweet or hot
    Italian sausage**
½ **pound lean ground beef**
½ **cup chopped onion (1 medium)**
1 **teaspoon minced garlic (2 cloves)**
2 **14.5-ounce cans diced tomatoes with
    garlic and onion, undrained**
2 **teaspoons dried basil, crushed**
¼ **teaspoon crushed red pepper (optional)**
    Hot cooked pasta

1. In a large skillet, cook sausage, ground beef,
onion, and garlic over medium heat until sausage
is brown, stirring to break up meat. Drain off fat.
Stir in undrained tomatoes, basil, and, if desired,
crushed red pepper. Bring to boiling; reduce heat.
Simmer, uncovered, for 15 to 18 minutes or until
desired consistency.

2. Serve immediately or divide sauce between
two airtight containers. Cover and refrigerate for
up to 3 days or freeze for up to 3 months. Thaw
overnight in the refrigerator before using. To serve,
place desired amount of sauce in a saucepan; heat
through. Serve over or toss with hot cooked pasta.
Makes 4 cups.

Per ¼ cup: 83 cal., 5 g fat (2 g sat. fat), 19 mg chol.,
332 mg sodium, 4 g carbo., 5 g pro.

Roasted Red Pepper Sauce

Prep: 15 minutes   **Cook:** 5 minutes

2   12-ounce jars roasted red sweet
     peppers, drained
1   large onion, chopped
2   teaspoons minced garlic (4 cloves)
1   tablespoon olive oil
1   tablespoon sugar
1   tablespoon balsamic vinegar
1   teaspoon dried thyme, crushed
½   teaspoon dried oregano, crushed
¼   teaspoon salt
⅛   teaspoon ground black pepper
     Hot cooked pasta
     Finely shredded Parmesan cheese
       (optional)

1. Place drained sweet peppers in a food processor. Cover and process until smooth; set aside.

2. In a medium saucepan, cook onion and garlic in hot oil over medium-high heat until tender. Add pureed peppers, sugar, vinegar, thyme, oregano, salt, and black pepper. Cook and stir until heated through.

3. Serve immediately or divide mixture among ½-cup airtight containers. Cover and refrigerate for up to 1 week or freeze for up to 3 months. Thaw overnight in the refrigerator before using. To serve, place desired amount of sauce in a saucepan; heat through. Serve over or toss with hot cooked pasta. If desired, sprinkle with Parmesan cheese. Makes 2½ cups.

Per ½ cup: 75 cal., 3 g fat (0 g sat. fat), 0 mg chol., 120 mg sodium, 12 g carbo., 2 g fiber, 1 g pro.

Homemade Pesto

When it's time to reheat and eat, stir 2 tablespoons
pesto with 1 cup hot cooked pasta.
Start to Finish: 15 minutes

  3 cups firmly packed fresh basil leaves
     (3 ounces)
⅔ cup walnuts
⅔ cup grated Parmesan or Romano cheese
½ cup olive oil
  4 cloves garlic, peeled and quartered
½ teaspoon salt
¼ teaspoon ground black pepper

1. In a food processor or blender, combine basil, nuts, cheese, olive oil, garlic, salt, and pepper. Cover and process or blend until nearly smooth, stopping and scraping sides as necessary.
2. Place pesto in a storage container. Cover the surface with plastic wrap, then cover the container. Store in the refrigerator for 1 to 2 days. Or, to freeze in a standard ice cube tray, spoon 2 tablespoons pesto into each slot; cover tightly. Freeze for up to 3 months. Thaw at room temperature before using. Makes 1¼ cups.

Per 2 tablespoons: 365 cal., 19 g fat (3 g sat. fat), 5 mg chol., 200 mg sodium, 40 g carbo., 3 g fiber, 10 g pro.

Homemade Alfredo Sauce

A little cornstarch in this sauce keeps it from curdling
after it thaws and helps it reheat to a nice,
creamy consistency—perfect for pasta!
Start to Finish: 20 minutes

1¼ cups whipping cream
  1 cup chicken broth
  1 tablespoon cornstarch
¼ teaspoon ground black pepper
⅛ teaspoon ground nutmeg
  1 tablespoon olive oil
  2 teaspoons minced garlic (4 cloves)
½ cup grated Parmesan cheese
    Hot cooked pasta

1. In a medium bowl, stir together the cream, broth, cornstarch, pepper, and nutmeg; set aside. In a medium saucepan, heat oil over medium heat. Add garlic; cook and stir for 30 seconds. Add broth mixture; cook and stir until thickened and bubbly. Cook and stir for 2 minutes more. Stir in cheese.
2. Serve immediately or divide mixture among ½-cup airtight containers. Cover and refrigerate for up to 3 days or freeze for up to 3 months. Thaw overnight in the refrigerator before using. To serve, place desired amount of sauce in a saucepan; heat just to boiling. Serve over hot cooked pasta. Makes 2½ cups.

Per ¼ cup: 139 cal., 14 g fat (8 g sat. fat), 45 mg chol., 169 mg sodium, 2 g carbo., 0 g fiber, 2 g pro.

super-saucy

Reheating chilled or frozen sauces is a great way to pull a meal together fast—simply fix your favorite pasta, pour on the sauce, and you're ready to eat. Follow these tips for a quick, safe dinner:

❋ **Heat foods to a safe temperature**. Bring sauces just to boiling before serving.

❋ **Love the sauce but tired of the pasta?** No problem! Mix pasta sauces with ground beef for a saucy spin on sloppy joes or drizzle over chicken breasts and top with mozzarella for a low-carb dish.

Veggie tip

Pasta sauce is a great way to sneak in extra veggies. To pack in even more nutrition (plus add texture), stir canned diced tomatoes or fresh zucchini or squash into the sauce.

chill-and-store sauces

Pasta sauce is the ultimate make now, serve later dish. Most sauces refrigerate and freeze well, so make a few batches at once and stockpile them for later. Just make sure you seal your storage container tightly to avoid freezer burn.

SAUCE	STORE	FRIDGE	FREEZE	THAW
Alfredo	Divide sauce among ½-cup airtight containers and cover.	3 days	3 months	Overnight in the refrigerator
Marinara	Divide sauce among ½-cup airtight containers and cover.	1 week	3 months	Overnight in the refrigerator
Meat	Divide sauce between two airtight containers and cover.	3 days	3 months	Overnight in the refrigerator
Pesto	Spoon 2 tablespoons of sauce into each slot of a standard ice cube tray; cover tightly.	1 to 2 days	3 months	Room temperature
Wine sauce	Place sauce in storage container and cover.	3 days	Do not freeze	

quick, quicker, quickest

30 minutes

25 minutes

20 minutes or less

quick

30 minutes

Oven-Fried Pork Chops

*Coating the chops with the corn bread stuffing mix gives them
a delightful, crispy crust, helping them stay juicy and moist inside.*

Prep: 10 minutes **Bake:** 20 minutes

1	**egg**
2	**tablespoons fat-free milk**
1	**cup packaged corn bread stuffing mix**
4	**pork loin chops, cut ½ inch thick (1 to 1½ pounds total)**
1	**20-ounce package frozen roasted russet potato pieces**

1. Preheat oven to 425°F. In a shallow dish, beat egg with a fork; stir in milk. Place dry stuffing mix in another shallow dish. Trim fat from chops. Dip pork chops into egg mixture. Coat both sides with stuffing mix. Arrange pork chops in a single layer on one side of 15×10×1-inch baking pan. Add potato pieces to the other side of the same pan, mounding potatoes as needed to fit.

2. Bake, uncovered, for 20 minutes or until pork is done (160°F) and potatoes are lightly browned and crisp, turning pork and stirring potatoes once. Makes 4 servings.

Per serving: 513 cal., 19 g fat (4 g sat. fat), 115 mg chol, 1,271 mg sodium, 51 g carbo., 2 g fiber, 31 g pro.

shopping list

○ 8-ounce package corn bread stuffing mix
○ 4 pork loin chops, cut ½ inch thick (1 to 1½ pounds total)
○ 20-ounce package frozen roasted russet potato pieces

pantry items

○ 1 egg
○ fat-free milk

30
minutes

Chicken-Vegetable Ratatouille

Start to Finish: 30 minutes

1   cup chopped onion
1   teaspoon bottled
     minced garlic
1   tablespoon olive oil or
     cooking oil
1   medium eggplant, cut
     into 1-inch pieces
2   cups frozen zucchini,
     carrots, cauliflower,
     lima beans, and
     Italian beans
1   14½-ounce can diced
     tomatoes, undrained

1   teaspoon dried Italian
     seasoning, crushed
¾   teaspoon seasoned salt
¼   teaspoon ground black
     pepper
2⅔   cups dried penne
     (mostaccioli), cut ziti,
     or wagon wheel
     macaroni (8 ounces)
1½   cups chopped cooked
     chicken (about
     8 ounces)

1. In a 4-quart Dutch oven, cook onion and garlic in hot oil over medium heat for 2 minutes. Stir in eggplant, frozen vegetables, undrained tomatoes, Italian seasoning, seasoned salt, and pepper. Bring to boiling; reduce heat. Simmer, uncovered, for 10 to 12 minutes or until eggplant is tender.

2. Meanwhile, in a large saucepan, cook pasta according to package directions. Drain. Cover and keep warm.

3. Add chicken to vegetable mixture; cook about 1 minute more or until heated through. Serve chicken mixture over pasta. Makes 4 or 5 servings.

Per serving: 442 cal., 9 g fat (2 g sat. fat), 50 mg chol., 578 mg sodium, 64 g carbo., 11 g fiber, 28 g pro.

shopping list

○ 2 medium onions
○ 1 medium eggplant
○ 10- or 16-ounce loose-
  pack frozen zucchini,
  carrots, cauliflower,
  lima beans, and
  Italian beans
○ 14½-ounce can diced
  tomatoes
○ seasoned salt
○ 8 ounces dried penne
  (mostaccioli)
○ 8 ounces cooked
  chicken

pantry items

○ bottled minced garlic
○ olive oil
○ dried Italian seasoning
○ ground black pepper

30
minutes

30 minutes

Stroganoff-Style Beef with Broccoli

Start to Finish: 30 minutes

½	cup light dairy sour cream
¼	teaspoon dried dillweed
1	pound boneless beef top round steak, trimmed and cut into bite-size strips
1	tablespoon cooking oil
1	small onion, cut into ½-inch-thick slices
½	teaspoon bottled minced garlic

3 cups dried wide noodles (6 ounces)
3 cups broccoli florets
3 tablespoons all-purpose flour
1 14-ounce can beef broth
3 tablespoons tomato paste
1 teaspoon Worcestershire sauce
Ground black pepper

1. In a bowl, stir together sour cream and dillweed; set aside. In a skillet, cook beef in hot oil over medium-high heat until desired doneness. Remove beef; set aside. Add onion and garlic to the skillet; cook 8 to 10 minutes or until onion is tender.

2. Meanwhile, cook noodles according to package directions, adding broccoli for the last 3 minutes of cooking; drain well. Cover noodles and broccoli and keep warm.

3. Sprinkle flour over onion mixture in skillet. Stir to coat. Add broth, tomato paste, and Worcestershire sauce. Cook and stir until thickened and bubbly. Return beef to skillet; heat through. Season to taste with pepper. Remove from heat. Stir in sour cream mixture. Serve on top of noodles and broccoli. Makes 4 servings.

Per serving: 440 cal., 12 g fat (4 g sat. fat), 96 mg chol., 513 mg sodium, 45 g carbo., 4 g fiber, 37 g pro.

shopping list

- 8-ounce carton light dairy sour cream
- dried dillweed
- 1 pound boneless beef top round steak
- 1 small onion
- 6 ounces dried wide noodles
- 1 head broccoli
- 6-ounce can tomato paste

pantry items

- cooking oil
- bottled minced garlic
- all-purpose flour
- 14-ounce can beef broth
- Worcestershire sauce
- ground black pepper

30 minutes

shopping list

- two 3-ounce packages ramen noodles
- chili oil
- 12 ounces beef flank steak
- 1 piece fresh ginger
- 6- to 7-ounce bag fresh baby spinach leaves
- 6-ounce package shredded carrots
- 1 bunch fresh cilantro

pantry items

- bottled minced garlic
- 14-ounce can beef broth
- soy sauce

Asian Beef & Noodle Bowl

Start to Finish: 30 minutes

4	cups water
2	3-ounce packages ramen noodles (any flavor)
2	teaspoons chili oil or 2 teaspoons cooking oil plus 1/8 teaspoon cayenne pepper
12	ounces beef flank steak or top round steak, cut into thin, bite-size strips
1	teaspoon grated fresh ginger

1	teaspoon bottled minced garlic (2 cloves)
1	cup beef broth
2	tablespoons soy sauce
2	cups baby spinach leaves or torn fresh spinach
1	cup packaged coarsely shredded fresh carrot
1/4	cup snipped fresh cilantro

1. In a large saucepan, bring the water to boiling. If desired, break up noodles; drop noodles into the boiling water. (Reserve the flavor packets for another use.) Return to boiling; boil for 2 to 3 minutes or just until noodles are tender but still firm, stirring occasionally. Drain noodles; set aside.

2. Meanwhile, in an extra-large skillet, heat oil over medium-high heat. Add beef, ginger, and garlic; cook and stir for 2 to 3 minutes or until beef is desired doneness. Carefully stir broth and soy sauce into skillet. Bring to boiling; reduce heat. Add spinach, carrot, and noodles to skillet; stir to combine. Heat through. Stir in cilantro. Makes 4 servings.

Per serving: 381 cal., 17 g fat (3 g sat. fat), 34 mg chol., 1,503 mg sodium, 30 g carbo., 2 g fiber, 26 g pro.

Beef & Veggies

Start to Finish: 30 minutes

12	ounces lean ground beef	1	medium zucchini, halved lengthwise and sliced $\frac{1}{4}$ inch thick
1	medium (1$\frac{1}{4}$ pounds) butternut squash, peeled, seeded, and cubed (about 3 cups)	$\frac{1}{4}$	cup water
2	cloves garlic, minced	$\frac{1}{4}$	cup chopped fresh cilantro
1	teaspoon ground cumin	2	to 3 cups hot cooked white or brown rice
$\frac{1}{2}$	teaspoon salt		Bottled hot pepper sauce (optional)
$\frac{1}{8}$	teaspoon ground cinnamon		
1	14$\frac{1}{2}$-ounce can diced tomatoes, undrained		

1. In a large skillet, cook ground beef, squash, garlic, cumin, salt, and cinnamon over medium heat until beef is no longer pink. Drain off fat.

2. Stir in undrained tomatoes; bring to boiling; reduce heat. Cover and simmer about 8 minutes or until squash is just tender. Stir in zucchini and the water. Cover and simmer about 4 minutes more or until zucchini is tender. Stir in cilantro. Serve over hot cooked rice. If desired, season to taste with bottled hot pepper sauce. Makes 4 to 6 servings.

Per serving: 313 cal., 9 g fat (3 g sat. fat), 54 mg chol., 504 mg sodium, 39 g carbo., 3 g fiber, 20 g pro.

30
minutes

shopping list

○ 12 ounces lean ground beef
○ 1 medium butternut squash
○ ground cumin
○ 14.5-ounce can diced tomatoes
○ 1 medium zucchini
○ 1 bunch fresh cilantro
○ white or brown rice
○ bottled hot pepper sauce (optional)

pantry items

○ garlic
○ salt
○ ground cinnamon

Chicken Dinner Burgers

Prep: 15 minutes **Cook:** 12 minutes

1   egg, slightly beaten
½   teaspoon salt
¼   teaspoon ground black
      pepper
1   pound uncooked lean
      ground chicken or
      lean ground turkey
¼   cup fine dry bread
      crumbs

1   tablespoon olive oil
¼   cup barbecue sauce
4   slices Texas toast or
      other thick-sliced
      bread
      Prepared deli coleslaw
      (optional)
      Pickle slices (optional)

shopping list

○ 1 pound uncooked
   lean ground chicken
○ 8-ounce package fine
   dry bread crumbs
○ 1 loaf Texas toast
○ 1 pound prepared deli
   coleslaw (optional)
○ 12-ounce jar sliced
   pickles (optional)

pantry items

○ egg
○ salt
○ ground black pepper
○ olive oil
○ barbecue sauce

1. In a medium bowl, combine egg, salt, and pepper. Add chicken and bread crumbs; mix well. Shape the chicken mixture into four ¾-inch-thick patties.

2. In a large nonstick skillet, cook patties over medium heat in hot oil about 10 minutes or until an instant-read thermometer inserted into the thickest part of the burger registers 165°F, turning once halfway through cooking time. Brush patties on each side with barbecue sauce. Cook for 1 minute more on each side to glaze.

3. Place burgers on slices of Texas toast. If desired, top with a spoonful of coleslaw and a few pickle slices. Makes 4 servings.

Per serving: 371 cal., 17 g fat (1 g sat. fat), 103 mg chol., 912 mg sodium, 27 g carbo., 0 g fiber, 26 g pro.

30 minutes

30 minutes

Rice 'n' Bean Tostadas

Quick-cooking brown rice, canned chili beans, shredded cheese,
and purchased tostada shells make easy work of these tostadas.

Prep: 25 minutes **Bake:** 5 minutes

1½	cups water	1	8-ounce can whole kernel corn, drained
1½	cups quick-cooking brown rice	8	purchased tostada shells
1	medium onion, chopped	3	cups shredded lettuce
1	15-ounce can chili beans with chili gravy, undrained	½	cup shredded cheddar cheese (2 ounces)
		1	cup quartered cherry tomatoes

1. Preheat oven to 350°F. In a saucepan, bring water to boiling. Stir in rice and onion. Return to boiling; reduce heat. Cover; simmer for 5 minutes. Remove from heat; stir. Cover; let stand for 5 minutes. Stir undrained chili beans and drained corn into rice mixture. Heat through.

2. Place tostada shells on a baking sheet. Bake for 5 minutes or until heated through.

3. To assemble, place 2 tostada shells on each dinner plate. Top tostadas with shredded lettuce and the rice-bean mixture. Sprinkle with cheddar cheese and top with tomato. Makes 4 servings.

Per serving: 438 cal., 12 g fat (4 g sat. fat), 15 mg chol., 621 mg sodium, 70 g carbo., 11 g fiber, 15 g pro.

shopping list

- ◯ 6.2-ounce package quick-cooking brown rice
- ◯ 1 medium onion
- ◯ 15-ounce can chili beans with chili gravy
- ◯ 8-ounce can whole kernel corn
- ◯ tostada shells
- ◯ 8- to 10-ounce package shredded lettuce
- ◯ 8-ounce package shredded cheddar cheese
- ◯ 1 pint cherry tomatoes

shopping list

- ○ 1 package quick-cooking polenta mix
- ○ 14-ounce can vegetable broth
- ○ 1 large onion
- ○ 1 head broccoli
- ○ 7-ounce jar roasted red sweet peppers
- ○ slivered or sliced almonds

pantry items

- ○ cornstarch
- ○ olive oil
- ○ bottled minced garlic

30 minutes

Polenta with Broccoli

Start to Finish: 30 minutes

1	cup quick-cooking polenta mix
1	cup vegetable broth or chicken broth
1	tablespoon cornstarch
1	cup chopped onion (1 large)
4	teaspoons olive oil
3	teaspoons bottled minced garlic

3	cups coarsely chopped broccoli florets
½	of a 7-ounce jar (½ cup) roasted red sweet peppers, drained and chopped
¼	cup slivered or sliced almonds or chopped walnuts, toasted

1. Prepare polenta according to package directions. Cover and keep warm. Stir together broth and cornstarch; set aside.

2. In a large skillet, cook and stir onion in hot oil over medium heat about 4 minutes or until just tender. Add garlic; cook and stir for 30 seconds more. Add broccoli; cook and stir for 3 to 4 minutes or until crisp-tender. Stir in roasted sweet pepper.

3. Stir cornstarch mixture; add to vegetables. Cook and stir until thickened and bubbly. Cook and stir for 2 minutes more.

4. To serve, divide polenta among 4 plates. Spoon the vegetable mixture over polenta. Sprinkle with nuts. Makes 4 servings.

Per serving: 317 cal., 13 g fat (2 g sat. fat), 3 mg chol., 623 mg sodium, 45 g carbo., 6 g fiber, 10 g pro.

Grilled Steak, Mango & Pear Salad

Prep: 15 minutes **Grill:** 14 minutes

12 ounces boneless beef
    top loin steak
    (1 inch thick)
½ teaspoon salt
¼ teaspoon ground black
    pepper
1 10-ounce package torn
    mixed salad greens
    (about 8 cups)

1 24-ounce jar
    refrigerated sliced
    mango, drained
1 medium pear, peeled,
    cored, and chopped
¾ cup refrigerated low-fat
    or fat-free blue
    cheese salad
    dressing

1. Sprinkle both sides of steak with salt and the ¼ teaspoon ground black pepper.
2. Place steak on the rack of an uncovered grill directly over medium heat. Grill until desired doneness, turning once halfway through grilling. Allow 14 to 18 minutes for medium-rare doneness (145°F) or 18 to 22 minutes for medium doneness (160°F).

3. To serve, thinly slice steak across the grain. Arrange greens on a serving platter; top with meat, mango, and pear. Top with blue cheese salad dressing. Makes 4 servings.

Per serving: 307 cal., 5 g fat (2 g sat. fat), 50 mg chol., 900 mg sodium, 49 g carbo., 4 g fiber, 19 g pro.

30
minutes

shopping list

○ 12 ounces boneless beef top loin steak (1 inch thick)
○ 10-ounce package torn mixed salad greens
○ 24-ounce jar refrigerated sliced mango
○ 1 medium pear
○ refrigerated blue cheese salad dressing

pantry items

○ salt
○ ground black pepper

quicker

25 minutes

25 minutes

Rosemary Chicken with Vegetables

Start to Finish: 25 minutes

4   medium skinless, boneless chicken breast halves
½   teaspoon lemon-pepper seasoning
2   tablespoons olive oil
4   ounces refrigerated plain linguine
1   teaspoon bottled minced garlic
2   medium zucchini and/or yellow summer squash, sliced ¼ inch thick (2½ cups)
½   cup apple juice
2   teaspoons snipped fresh rosemary or ½ teaspoon dried rosemary, crushed
2   tablespoons dry white wine or chicken broth
2   teaspoons cornstarch
1   cup halved cherry or grape tomatoes
Fresh rosemary sprigs (optional)

1. Sprinkle chicken with lemon-pepper seasoning. In a skillet, cook chicken in oil over medium heat for 8 to 10 minutes or until no longer pink; turn once. Remove chicken. Cover; keep warm. Cook pasta according to package directions.

2. Add garlic to skillet; cook for 15 seconds. Add zucchini, apple juice, and rosemary. Bring to boiling; reduce heat. Cover and simmer for 2 minutes.

3. In a bowl, stir together wine and cornstarch; add to skillet. Cook and stir until thickened and bubbly; cook for 2 minutes more. Stir in tomatoes. Serve vegetables and pasta with chicken. If desired, garnish with rosemary sprigs. Makes 4 servings.

Per serving: 326 cal., 10 g fat (2 g sat. fat), 95 mg chol., 247 mg sodium, 25 g carbo., 2 g fiber, 33 g pro.

25 minutes

shopping list

- ◯ 9-ounce package refrigerated cheese-filled ravioli
- ◯ 1 medium yellow summer squash
- ◯ 4 plum tomatoes
- ◯ 15-ounce can garbanzo beans
- ◯ fresh thyme
- ◯ 9- to 10-ounce package fresh spinach
- ◯ grated Parmesan cheese (optional)

pantry items

- ◯ bottled minced garlic
- ◯ olive oil
- ◯ ground black pepper

Ravioli with Fresh Vegetables

Start to Finish: 25 minutes

1   9-ounce package refrigerated cheese-filled ravioli or tortellini

2   teaspoons bottled minced garlic

2   teaspoons olive oil

1¼   cups thinly sliced yellow summer squash (1 medium)

4   plum tomatoes, quartered

1   15-ounce can garbanzo beans, rinsed and drained

2   teaspoons snipped fresh thyme or ½ teaspoon dried thyme, crushed

¼   teaspoon ground black pepper

4   cups shredded fresh spinach
    Olive oil or cooking oil (optional)
    Grated Parmesan cheese (optional)

1. Cook ravioli according to package directions; drain well.

2. Meanwhile, in a skillet, cook and stir garlic in 2 teaspoons hot oil over medium heat for 30 seconds. Add squash, tomato, garbanzo beans, thyme, and pepper. Cook and stir over medium-high heat 4 to 5 minutes or until squash is crisp-tender and mixture is heated through.

3. Add hot ravioli to vegetable mixture. Toss lightly. Arrange spinach on 4 serving plates; top with ravioli mixture. If desired, drizzle with additional olive oil and sprinkle with Parmesan cheese. Makes 4 servings.

Per serving: 304 cal., 7 g fat (2 g sat. fat), 25 mg chol., 688 mg sodium, 48 g carbo., 7 g fiber, 15 g pro.

Shrimp with Basil on Fettuccine

Start to Finish: 25 minutes

1   pound frozen peeled
    and deveined
    medium shrimp
    (1½ pounds medium
    shrimp in shell)
6   ounces refrigerated
    spinach or plain
    fettuccine

2   teaspoons snipped
    fresh basil or
    tarragon or
    1 teaspoon dried
    basil or tarragon,
    crushed
2   tablespoons butter or
    margarine

1. Thaw shrimp, if frozen. Prepare the fettuccine according to package directions. In a large skillet, cook shrimp and basil in hot butter over medium-high heat for 2 to 3 minutes or until shrimp turn pink, stirring frequently. Serve warm over fettuccine. Makes 4 servings.

Per serving: 301 cal., 9 g fat (5 g sat. fat), 225 mg chol., 264 mg sodium, 24 g carbo., 1 g fiber, 29 g pro.

25 minutes

shopping list
○ 1 pound frozen peeled, deveined medium shrimp
○ 9-ounce package refrigerated spinach fettuccine
○ fresh basil

pantry items
○ butter

Skillet Tuna & Biscuits

Prep: 10 minutes **Bake:** 12 minutes **Cook:** 5 minutes

1¼ cups Homemade Alfredo Sauce (page 117) or one 10-ounce container reduced-fat Alfredo pasta sauce
1 10-ounce package frozen peas and carrots
1 4-ounce can sliced mushrooms, drained
1 teaspoon lemon juice
¼ teaspoon dried dillweed
1 12-ounce can tuna, drained and flaked
1 cup packaged biscuit mix
⅓ cup fat-free milk
¼ cup shredded cheddar cheese (1 ounce)

1. Preheat oven to 400°F. In a large oven-going skillet, combine pasta sauce, peas and carrots, drained mushrooms, lemon juice, and dillweed. Cook and stir over medium heat until bubbly and heated through. Stir in drained tuna. Cover to keep warm.

2. In a medium bowl, stir together biscuit mix, milk, and half of the cheese. Drop mixture into 4 mounds on top of tuna mixture. Sprinkle with the remaining cheese.

3. Bake for 12 to 15 minutes or until biscuits are golden. Makes 4 servings.

Per serving: 434 cal., 22 g fat (10 g sat. fat), 85 mg chol., 1,032 mg sodium, 32 g carbo., 3 g fiber, 29 g pro.

25 minutes

Smashed Veggie-Cheese Sandwiches

Prep: 20 minutes **Cook:** 3 minutes

8	½-inch-thick slices country French white or wheat bread	½	cup fresh spinach leaves or broccoli slaw mix
4	teaspoons olive oil or cooking oil	¼	cup thinly sliced red onion or red sweet pepper strips
2	tablespoons honey mustard or bottled ranch salad dressing	1	32-ounce can or bottle (4 cups) ready-to-serve tomato soup
4	ounces thinly sliced cheddar or farmer cheese	1	cup chopped roma tomato (3 medium)
½	cup thinly sliced cucumber or roma tomato	1	tablespoon balsamic vinegar

1. Brush one side of bread slices lightly with oil. Brush other side of bread slices with honey mustard. Top the mustard side of four of the slices with cheese. Top cheese with cucumber, spinach, and red onion. Top with remaining bread slices, mustard sides down.

2. Preheat an indoor electric grill or a large skillet over medium heat. Place the sandwiches on the grill rack. If using a covered grill, close lid. Grill sandwiches until bread is golden and cheese is melted. (For a covered grill, allow 3 to 5 minutes. For an uncovered grill or skillet, allow 6 to 8 minutes, turning once halfway through grilling.) With a long serrated knife, cut sandwiches in half.

3. Meanwhile, in a medium saucepan stir together soup, tomato, and balsamic vinegar. Heat through. Serve soup with sandwiches. Makes 4 servings.

Per serving: 413 cal., 13 g fat (3 g sat. fat), 9 mg chol., 1,380 mg sodium, 60 g carbo., 4 g fiber, 11 g pro.

shopping list

- 1 loaf country French white bread
- honey mustard
- 4-ounce block cheddar cheese
- 1 small cucumber
- fresh spinach leaves
- 1 small red onion
- 32-ounce can ready-to-serve tomato soup
- 3 medium roma tomatoes

pantry items

- olive oil
- balsamic vinegar

shopping list

- 12-ounce jar pickled peppers
- 8-ounce jar pickle relish
- 1 small onion
- poppy seeds
- 1-pound package jumbo hot dogs
- 1 package hot dog buns

pantry items

- ketchup

25 minutes

Saucy Dogs

Pickled peppers make these saucy hot dogs a little sassy.
Prep: 10 minutes **Grill:** 14 minutes

⅓ cup ketchup	¼ teaspoon poppy seeds
¼ cup chopped pickled pepper	4 jumbo hot dogs (about 1 pound total)
2 tablespoons pickle relish	4 hot dog buns, split and toasted
2 tablespoons chopped onion	

1. For sauce, in a small bowl, stir together ketchup, pickled pepper, relish, onion, and poppy seeds. Set aside.

2. For a charcoal grill, grill hot dogs on the rack of an uncovered grill directly over medium heat for 12 to 14 minutes or until heated through, turning and brushing with sauce halfway through grilling. (For a gas grill, preheat grill. Reduce heat to medium. Place hot dogs on grill rack over heat. Cover and grill as above.) Remove from grill.

3. Serve hot dogs in toasted buns; top with additional sauce. Makes 4 servings.

Per serving: 247 cal., 8 g fat (3 g sat. fat), 30 mg chol., 1,130 mg sodium, 34 g carbo., 2 g fiber, 10 g pro.

Pulled Chicken Peanut Salad

Roasted chicken from the supermarket deli and packaged washed salad greens keep the prep time for this sumptuous salad to a minimum.

Start to Finish: 25 minutes

2 tablespoons frozen orange juice concentrate, thawed
1 tablespoon water
2 teaspoons toasted sesame oil
¼ teaspoon salt
⅛ teaspoon coarsely ground black pepper

6 cups torn mixed salad greens
2 cups coarsely shredded cooked chicken
1 11-ounce can mandarin orange sections, drained
¼ cup cocktail peanuts

1. For dressing, in a small bowl, stir together juice concentrate, water, sesame oil, salt, and pepper. Set aside.

2. Arrange greens on salad plates. Top with chicken, oranges, and peanuts. Drizzle with dressing. Makes 4 servings.

Per serving: 263 cal., 12 g fat (3 g sat. fat), 62 mg chol., 247 mg sodium, 15 g carbo., 2 g fiber, 24 g pro.

shopping list

○ 12-ounce can frozen orange juice concentrate
○ toasted sesame oil
○ 10-ounce package mixed salad greens
○ 1 deli chicken
○ 11-ounce can mandarin orange sections
○ cocktail peanuts

pantry items

○ salt
○ coarsely ground black pepper

25
minutes

quickest

20 minutes or less

shopping list

○ 4 boneless pork loin chops
○ 1 medium red apple
○ 1 package chopped pecans

pantry items

○ salt
○ ground black pepper
○ butter
○ brown sugar

20 minutes

Apple-Pecan Pork Chops

Brown sugar and butter create a sweet sauce that marries well with pork chops and apples. Choose a tart apple for more flavor and contrast.

Start to Finish: 20 minutes

4   boneless pork loin chops (¾ to 1 inch thick)
    Salt and ground black pepper
2   tablespoons butter

1   medium red apple, cored and thinly sliced
¼   cup chopped pecans
2   tablespoons packed brown sugar

1. Trim fat from pork. Sprinkle with salt and pepper. Set aside.

2. In a large skillet, melt butter over medium heat until it sizzles. Add apple; cook and stir for 2 minutes. Push apple to side of skillet. Add pork chops; cook for 4 minutes. Turn chops, moving apple aside as needed. Spoon apple over chops. Sprinkle with pecans and brown sugar.

3. Cover and cook 4 to 8 minutes more, or until an instant-read thermometer inserted in center of chops registers 160°F. Serve apple and cooking juices over chops. Makes 4 servings.

Per serving: 250 cal., 13 g fat (5 g sat. fat), 66 mg chol., 360 mg sodium, 12 g carbo., 1 g fiber, 22 g pro.

shopping list

- ○ two 15-ounce cans Great Northern beans
- ○ 12 ounces cooked smoked ham
- ○ 9- to 10-ounce package fresh spinach

pantry items

- ○ olive oil
- ○ garlic

20 minutes

Greens, Beans & Ham

Start to Finish: 20 minutes

2	15-ounce cans Great Northern beans
1	tablespoon olive oil
6	cloves garlic, minced
2	cups cooked smoked ham, cut into bite-size strips

3	cups chopped fresh spinach or one 10-ounce package frozen spinach, thawed and well drained

1. Drain beans, reserving liquid. In a large nonstick skillet, heat oil over medium heat. Add garlic; cook and stir for 1 minute. Add beans and ham to the skillet. Cook about 5 minutes or until heated through, stirring occasionally. Stir in spinach; cover and cook for 2 to 5 minutes more or until fresh greens are wilted or frozen spinach is heated through. If desired, thin mixture with some of the reserved liquid. Makes 4 servings.

Per serving: 353 cal., 6 g fat (1 g sat. fat), 12 mg chol., 537 mg sodium, 51 g carbo., 11 g fiber, 27 g pro.

No-Bake Tuna-Noodle Casserole
Start to Finish: 20 minutes

8 ounces dried cavatappi, elbow, bow-tie, or penne pasta
1½ cups desired frozen vegetables (optional)
¼ to ½ cup milk
1 6.5-ounce container light semisoft cheese with garlic and herb
1 12-ounce can solid white tuna, drained and broken into chunks
Salt
Ground black pepper

1. Cook pasta in lightly salted water according to package directions. If desired, add frozen vegetables during the last 4 minutes of cooking. Drain and return to pan.
2. Add ¼ cup of the milk and the cheese to pasta in pan. Cook and stir over medium heat until cheese is melted and pasta is coated, adding additional milk as needed to create a creamy consistency. Gently fold in tuna; heat through. Season to taste with salt and pepper. Makes 4 servings.

Per serving: 419 cal., 11 g fat (6 g sat. fat), 68 mg chol., 693 mg sodium, 46 g carbo., 1 g fiber, 33 g pro.

shopping list
- 8 ounces dried cavatappi
- 9- to 10-ounce package frozen vegetables
- 6.5-ounce container semisoft cheese with garlic and herb
- 12-ounce can white tuna

pantry items
- milk
- salt
- ground black pepper

20 minutes

20 minutes

shopping list

- ○ 1 head iceberg lettuce
- ○ 1 medium cucumber
- ○ 1 small sweet pepper
- ○ 1 small red onion
- ○ 4 ounces fresh whole mushrooms
- ○ 2 medium carrots
- ○ 2 ounces sharp cheddar cheese
- ○ bottled salad dressing
- ○ bacon (optional)

{ Add a little fun (and take away a little stress) with a food processor. }

Row Salad

Start to Finish: 20 minutes

½	head iceberg lettuce
1	medium cucumber
1	small orange, red, or green sweet pepper, halved and seeded
½	small red onion
4	ounces fresh whole mushrooms

2	medium carrots
2	ounces sharp cheddar cheese
1¼	cups bottled salad dressing
	Crumbled crisp-cooked bacon (optional)

1. Use a food processor to slice and shred vegetables and cheese (or slice and shred ingredients by hand). If desired, cover and refrigerate salad ingredients until ready to serve.

2. To serve, arrange the vegetables and cheese in rows on a serving platter. Serve with dressing and, if desired, bacon. Makes 6 servings.

Per serving: 314 cal., 27 g fat (5 g sat. fat), 10 mg chol., 513 mg sodium, 16 g carbo., 2 g fiber, 4 g pro.

shopping list

○ 1 pound boneless,
   skinless chicken
   breast tenders
○ 10-ounce package
   torn mixed salad
   greens
○ 1 pint fresh
   blueberries and/or
   raspberres
○ fresh basil
○ bottled balsamic
   vinaigrette salad
   dressing

pantry items

○ cooking oil

Quick Chicken Salad with Berries

*If you make this with fresh raspberries, use a bottled
raspberry vinaigrette salad dressing.*

Start to Finish: 20 minutes

20 minutes

1 pound boneless,
   skinless chicken
   breast tenders
1 tablespoon cooking oil
6 cups purchased torn
   mixed salad greens
1½ cups fresh blueberries
   and/or raspberries

2 tablespoons shredded
   fresh basil leaves
½ cup bottled balsamic
   vinaigrette salad
   dressing or your
   favorite salad
   dressing

1. In a 12-inch heavy skillet, cook chicken in hot oil over medium-high heat for 6 to 8 minutes or until no longer pink, turning once. Cool slightly. Use two forks to shred chicken.

2. In a large bowl, toss together the greens, blueberries, and basil. Drizzle vinaigrette over salad mixture; toss gently to coat. To serve, divide greens mixture among serving plates. Top with shredded chicken. Makes 6 main-dish servings.

Per serving: 194 cal., 10 g fat (1 g sat. fat), 44 mg chol., 280 mg sodium, 9 g carbo., 2 g fiber, 18 g pro.

20 minutes

Mu Shu Style Pork Roll-Ups

Start to Finish: 20 minutes

4 10-inch flour tortillas	2 cups loose-pack frozen stir-fry vegetables (any combination)
1 teaspoon toasted sesame oil	
12 ounces lean boneless pork, cut into strips	¼ cup bottled plum or hoisin sauce

1. Preheat oven to 350°F. Wrap tortillas tightly in foil. Heat in oven for 10 minutes to soften. (Or wrap tortillas in microwave-safe paper towels; microwave on 100-percent power 15 to 30 seconds or until tortillas are softened.)

2. Meanwhile, in a large skillet, heat oil over medium-high heat. Add pork strips; cook and turn for 2 to 3 minutes or until done. Add stir-fry vegetables. Cook and stir for 3 to 4 minutes or until vegetables are crisp-tender.

3. Spread each tortilla with 1 tablespoon of the plum sauce; place a quarter of the meat mixture just below the center of each tortilla. Fold the bottom edge of each tortilla up and over the filling. Fold in the sides until they meet; roll up over the filling. Makes 4 servings.

Per serving: 296 cal., 8 g fat (2 g sat. fat), 53 mg chol., 325 mg sodium, 32 g carbo., 1 g fiber, 22 g pro.

Deli-Style Submarines

Use a single type of meat or pile on an assortment in this meal-size sandwich.
Ranch-flavor sour cream dip adds a little extra zip.

Start to Finish: 20 minutes

1   16-ounce loaf French bread
½   of an 8-ounce carton light dairy sour cream ranch dip
1   cup shredded lettuce
¾   cup shredded fresh carrot

8   ounces thinly sliced cooked roast beef, ham, or turkey
½   of a medium cucumber, seeded and shredded
4   ounces thinly sliced mozzarella or provolone cheese

1. Cut French bread in half horizontally. Spread ranch dip on cut sides of bread. On the bottom half of the bread, layer lettuce, carrot, roast beef, cucumber, and cheese. Replace top half of bread. Cut sandwich into 8 portions. Secure portions with decorative toothpicks. Makes 8 servings.

Make-Ahead Directions: Prepare as directed, except do not cut sandwich into pieces. Wrap sandwich in plastic wrap and chill for up to 4 hours. Cut and serve as directed.

Per serving: 250 cal., 6 g fat (3 g sat. fat), 24 mg chol., 743 mg sodium, 34 g carbo., 2 g fiber, 14 g pro.

shopping list

- ◯ 16-ounce loaf French bread
- ◯ 8-ounce carton light dairy sour cream ranch dip
- ◯ 10-ounce bag shredded lettuce
- ◯ 10-ounce bag shredded fresh carrot
- ◯ 8 ounces thinly sliced roast beef
- ◯ 1 medium cucumber
- ◯ 4 ounces thinly sliced mozzarella cheese

20 minutes

Honey Chicken Sandwiches

Start to Finish: 20 minutes

3	tablespoons honey
2	teaspoons snipped fresh thyme or ½ teaspoon dried thyme, crushed
1	small red onion, halved and thinly sliced
12	ounces cut-up cooked chicken
4	baked biscuits, split

1. In a medium skillet, combine honey and thyme; stir in red onion. Cook and stir over medium-low heat just until hot (do not boil). Stir in chicken; heat through. Arrange chicken mixture on biscuit bottoms. Add tops. Makes 4 servings.

Per serving: 342 cal., 12 g fat (3 g sat. fat), 76 mg chol., 443 mg sodium, 31 g carbo., 1 g fiber, 27 g pro.

20 minutes

shopping list

○ fresh thyme
○ 1 small red onion
○ 12 ounces cut-up cooked chicken
○ 4 baked biscuits

pantry items

○ honey

shopping list

○ 1 package 8- or 9-inch
  plain flour tortillas
○ 10-ounce jar low-fat
  mayonnaise
○ fresh basil
○ 12 ounces thinly
  sliced cooked chicken
○ 7-ounce jar roasted
  red sweet peppers

pantry items

○ garlic
○ cayenne pepper
  (optional)

15 minutes

Basil Chicken Wraps

Start to Finish: 15 minutes

4   8- or 9-inch plain flour
    tortillas or tomato-
    or spinach-flavor
    flour tortillas
½   cup Basil Mayonnaise
    Fresh basil leaves

12   ounces thinly sliced
     cooked chicken cut
     into thin strips
½   cup roasted red sweet
     pepper, cut into
     thin strips

1. Place the stack of flat tortillas on foil; wrap tightly. Heat in a 350°F oven until warm.

2. Prepare Basil Mayonnaise; spread onto warm tortillas. Arrange basil leaves, chicken, and sweet pepper on tortillas. Fold up bottoms; roll up. Makes 4 servings.

Basil Mayonnaise: Stir together ½ cup low-fat mayonnaise or salad dressing, 1 tablespoon snipped fresh basil, and 1 small clove garlic, minced. If desired, stir in ⅛ teaspoon cayenne pepper. Makes about ½ cup.

Per wrap: 366 cal., 15 g fat (3 g sat. fat), 44 mg chol., 1,330 mg sodium, 37 g carbo., 2 g fiber, 21 g pro.

shopping list
- ○ 1 pound creamy deli coleslaw
- ○ 1 small tomato
- ○ curry powder
- ○ 6-ounce can tuna
- ○ peanuts
- ○ 4 ciabatta rolls
- ○ 1 head butterhead lettuce (Bibb or Boston)
- ○ 8-ounce container dairy sour cream dip with chives (optional)

15 minutes

Curried Tuna Sandwiches
Start to Finish: 15 minutes

1½ cups creamy deli coleslaw	4 ciabatta rolls, sliced horizontally
1 small tomato, seeded and chopped	4 large butterhead (Bibb or Boston) lettuce leaves
1 teaspoon curry powder	Dairy sour cream dip with chives (optional)
1 6-ounce can tuna, drained and flaked	
¼ cup chopped peanuts	

1. In a small bowl, stir together coleslaw, tomato, and curry powder. Fold in drained tuna and chopped peanuts.

2. To serve, spoon the tuna mixture into sliced ciabatta rolls and top with lettuce leaves. If desired, top with dip. Makes 4 servings.

Tip: If you don't love curry, this sandwich fix-up works well with other combinations too. Substitute ranch seasoning for the curry powder and chopped cucumber for the chopped peanuts for a rich and creamy sandwich with a little crunch.

Per serving: 254 cal., 9 g fat (2 g sat. fat), 21 mg chol., 434 mg sodium, 28 g carbo., 3 g fiber, 17 g pro.

Twisted Tuna Salad

Start to Finish: 15 minutes

1   12-ounce can chunk
    white tuna (water-
    pack), drained
⅓   cup bottled creamy
    Italian salad dressing
⅓   cup finely chopped
    fresh or canned
    pineapple, drained

¼   cup finely chopped red
    sweet pepper
4   to 8 Boston lettuce
    leaves
2   pita bread rounds,
    halved

1. In a medium bowl, combine drained tuna, salad dressing, drained pineapple, and sweet pepper. Place the lettuce leaves in the pita halves. Fill each pita half with tuna mixture. Makes 4 servings.

Per serving: 275 cal., 11 g fat (2 g sat. fat), 36 mg chol., 819 mg sodium, 21 g carbo., 1 g fiber, 23 g pro.

shopping list

○ 12-ounce can chunk
   white tuna
   (water-pack)
○ bottled creamy Italian
   salad dressing
○ 1 fresh pineapple
○ 1 red sweet pepper
○ 1 head Boston lettuce
○ 1 package pita bread
   rounds

15
minutes

Parmesan Chicken Salad Sandwiches

Start to Finish: 10 minutes

½ cup low-fat mayonnaise
1 tablespoon lemon juice
2 teaspoons snipped fresh basil
2½ cups chopped cooked chicken or turkey
¼ cup grated Parmesan cheese

¼ cup thinly sliced green onion
3 tablespoons finely chopped celery
Salt
Ground black pepper
12 slices wheat bread, toasted

1. For dressing, in a small bowl, stir together mayonnaise, lemon juice, and basil. Set aside.

2. For salad, in a medium bowl, combine chicken, cheese, green onion, and celery. Pour dressing over chicken mixture; toss to coat. Season to taste with salt and pepper. Serve immediately or cover and chill in the refrigerator for 1 to 4 hours. Serve on toasted wheat bread. Makes 6 main-dish servings.

Per serving: 194 cal., 12 g fat (3 g sat. fat), 61 mg chol., 366 mg sodium, 2 g carbo., 0 g fiber, 18 g pro.

shopping list

○ 10-ounce jar low-fat mayonnaise
○ fresh basil
○ 16 ounces chopped cooked chicken
○ grated Parmesan cheese
○ 3 green onions
○ 1 celery stalk
○ 1 loaf sliced wheat bread

pantry items

○ lemon juice
○ salt
○ ground black pepper

10
minutes

Fast Chicken & Rice

High heat and thin pieces of chicken make for a short cooking time.
Use your favorite stir-fry sauce to tie it all together.

Start to Finish: 10 minutes

10 minutes

½ cup frozen peas
1 8.8-ounce package cooked brown or white rice (microwave pack)
1 pound chicken breast tenders, halved crosswise

1 tablespoon cooking oil
¼ cup bottled stir-fry sauce
Packaged oven-roasted sliced almonds

1. Stir peas into rice pouch. Heat rice pouch according to package directions.
2. Meanwhile, in a large skillet, cook and stir chicken in hot oil over medium-high heat for 2 to 3 minutes or until no longer pink. Stir rice mixture into skillet. Stir in stir-fry sauce; heat through. Sprinkle each serving with sliced almonds. Makes 4 servings.

Per serving: 311 cal., 9 g fat (1 g sat. fat), 66 mg chol., 453 mg sodium, 25 g carbo., 2 g fiber, 31 g pro.

shopping list

- ○ 16-ounce package coleslaw mix
- ○ 6 ounces sliced cooked turkey breast
- ○ 3-ounce package ramen noodles
- ○ bottled vinaigrette salad dressing
- ○ 11- or 15-ounce can mandarin orange sections
- ○ toasted sliced almonds (optional)

10
minutes

Quick & Crunchy Turkey Salad
Start to Finish: 10 minutes

1   16-ounce package coleslaw mix

6   ounces sliced cooked turkey breast, diced

1   3-ounce package ramen noodles

⅔   cup bottled vinaigrette salad dressing

1   11- or 15-ounce can mandarin orange sections, drained
Toasted sliced almonds (optional)

1. In a large salad bowl, combine the slaw mixture and turkey. Remove seasoning packet from noodles; reserve for another use. Crumble noodles and add to slaw mixture. Pour the dressing over the salad; toss to coat. Gently fold in orange sections. If desired, top with almonds. Makes 4 main-dish servings.

Per serving: 326 cal., 14 g fat (1 g sat. fat), 15 mg chol., 895 mg sodium, 31 g carbo., 3 g fiber, 12 g pro.

express lane recipes

Deli-roasted chicken has been your go-to plan for a quick dinner many a night, but here are some great ways to amp up the already succulent flavor.

roast chicken

Pulled Chicken Sandwiches

Prep: 25 minutes   **Cook:** 7 minutes

1   2½-pound deli-roasted chicken
1   medium onion, cut into ¼-inch-thick
      slices
1   tablespoon olive oil
⅓   cup cider vinegar or white
      wine vinegar
½   cup tomato sauce
3   to 4 tablespoons seeded and finely
      chopped fresh red and/or green hot
      chile pepper
2   tablespoons snipped fresh thyme
2   tablespoons molasses
2   tablespoons water
½   teaspoon salt
4   sandwich buns, split

1. Remove meat from chicken (discard skin and bones). Use two forks to shred meat (2½ to 3 cups).

2. In a large skillet, cook onion in hot oil over medium heat 5 minutes or until tender; stir to separate rings. Add vinegar; cook 1 minute more. Stir in tomato sauce, chile, thyme, molasses, 2 tablespoons water, and ½ teaspoon salt. Bring to boiling. Add chicken; stir to coat. Heat through. Serve on buns. Makes 4 sandwiches.

Per sandwich: 445 cal., 12 g fat (3 g sat. fat), 84 mg chol., 990 mg sodium, 51 g carbo., 2 g fiber, 33 g pro.

Mexican Chicken Casserole

Prep: 15 minutes **Bake:** 15 minutes

1   15-ounce can black beans, rinsed
    and drained
½   cup chunky salsa
½   teaspoon ground cumin
1   2½-pound deli-roasted chicken
¼   cup shredded Monterey Jack cheese
    with jalapeño peppers
    Dairy sour cream (optional)

1. Preheat oven to 350°F. In a small bowl, stir together drained beans, ¼ cup of the salsa, and the cumin. Divide bean mixture among 4 au gratin dishes or casseroles. Set aside.

2. Cut chicken into quarters. Place one piece on bean mixture in each dish. Spoon remaining ¼ cup salsa evenly over chicken pieces. Sprinkle evenly with cheese. Bake for 15 to 20 minutes or until heated through. If desired, top with sour cream. Makes 4 servings.

Per serving: 468 cal., 23 g fat (7 g sat. fat), 140 mg chol., 596 mg sodium, 16 g carbo., 5 g fiber, 50 g pro.

Chicken Linguine with Pesto Sauce

Start to Finish: 20 minutes

- 8 ounces dried linguine
- 1 10-ounce package frozen vegetables
- 1 10-ounce container refrigerated Alfredo pasta sauce or 1 cup jarred Alfredo sauce
- ⅓ cup purchased basil pesto
- ¼ cup milk
- ½ of a 2½-pound deli-roasted chicken
  Grated Parmesan cheese

1. In a 4-quart Dutch oven, cook pasta according to package directions; add vegetables during last 5 minutes of cooking. Drain; return to Dutch oven.
2. Meanwhile, combine Alfredo sauce, pesto, and ¼ cup milk; set aside. Remove meat from chicken (discard skin and bones). Shred meat (2½ cups).
3. Add chicken to pasta and vegetables in Dutch oven. Add sauce mixture; toss gently to coat. Heat through over medium-low heat. If desired, stir in additional milk to reach desired consistency. Sprinkle each serving with cheese. Makes 4 servings.

Per serving: 801 cal., 48 g fat (4 g sat. fat), 109 mg chol., 546 mg sodium, 54 g carbo., 3 g fiber, 37 g pro.

Chicken Quesadillas

Start to Finish: 25 minutes

- 1 2½-pound deli-roasted chicken
- 4 8- to 10-inch flour tortillas
  Fresh spinach leaves
- 1 8-ounce can sliced mushrooms, drained
- 2 cups shredded Monterey Jack cheese
  Salsa (optional)
  Guacamole (optional)

1. Remove meat from chicken (discard skin and bones). Chop meat, reserving 2 cups. Cover and chill or freeze remaining meat for another use.
2. Spoon the 2 cups chicken evenly on bottom halves of tortillas. Top with spinach and drained mushrooms. Sprinkle cheese evenly over mushrooms. Fold tortillas in half. Heat on a griddle over medium heat until browned on both sides and cheese is melted. If desired, serve with salsa and guacamole. Makes 4 servings.

Per serving: 472 cal., 28 g fat (15 g sat. fat), 120 mg chol., 513 mg sodium, 18 g carbo., 2 g fiber, 37 g pro.

Kids love 'em for their taste, moms love 'em for their ease. These five recipes bring both attributes of breaded chicken pieces to the table in new ways.

breaded chicken

Southwest Chicken Wraps
Start to Finish: 20 minutes

½ of a 28-ounce package frozen cooked,
  breaded chicken strips (about 24 strips)
½ of an 8-ounce tub light cream cheese
1 green onion, thinly sliced
1 tablespoon snipped fresh cilantro
6 7- to 8-inch flour tortillas
1 red sweet pepper, seeded and cut into
  bite-size strips
½ cup shredded reduced-fat or regular
  Monterey Jack cheese (2 ounces)
  Bottled salsa (optional)

1. Bake chicken strips according to directions.
2. Meanwhile, in a small bowl, stir together the cream cheese, green onion, and cilantro. Spread over tortillas. Top with pepper strips and shredded cheese. Top with hot chicken strips. Roll up tortillas; secure tortillas with toothpicks. Cut in half to serve. Serve with salsa, if desired. Makes 6 servings.
  Per serving: 356 cal., 20 g fat (6 g sat. fat), 54 mg chol., 610 mg sodium, 27 g carbo., 1 g fiber, 18 g pro.

Chicken Salad with Strawberries
Any shape of frozen cooked chicken would work in this salad. Change the fruit according to what's in season, such as apples, pears, oranges, or grapes.
Start to Finish: 20 minutes

1 11-ounce package frozen cooked, breaded
  chicken nuggets or strips
1 10-ounce package mixed salad greens
2 cups sliced fresh strawberries
¼ cup fresh basil leaves, cut into strips
½ cup bottled balsamic vinaigrette
  salad dressing

1. Bake chicken nuggets according to package directions.
2. Meanwhile, in a very large bowl, toss together the greens, strawberries, and basil. Divide among serving plates and top with chicken. Drizzle salad dressing over the top. Makes 6 main-dish servings.
  Per serving: 244 cal., 15 g fat (3 g sat. fat), 29 mg chol., 487 mg sodium, 19 g carbo., 2 g fiber, 8 g pro.

Easy Chicken Marinara

Start to Finish: 25 minutes

4   frozen cooked, breaded chicken breast
     patties
2   cups purchased marinara sauce
½   to 1 cup shredded mozzarella cheese
     (2 to 4 ounces)
     Hot cooked spaghetti

1. Place chicken patties on a baking sheet. Bake according to package directions. Meanwhile, pour sauce into a saucepan and heat through over medium heat.

2. Remove baking sheet from oven; turn chicken patties over. Spoon about ¼ cup sauce over each chicken patty. Top each with cheese. Return to oven and bake for 4 to 5 minutes more or until cheese melts.

3. Serve chicken patties over spaghetti with remaining sauce. Makes 4 servings.

Per serving: 283 cal., 15 g fat (4 g sat. fat), 36 mg chol., 919 mg sodium, 24 g carbo., 3 g fiber, 14 g pro.

Chicken with Buttermilk Gravy

Lemon peel adds flavor and character to this comfort-food recipe. Another time, try it with orange peel.

Start to Finish: 15 minutes

6   frozen cooked, breaded chicken breast
     patties
1   24-ounce package refrigerated mashed
     potatoes
1   1-ounce envelope chicken gravy mix
1   cup buttermilk
¼   to ½ teaspoon finely shredded lemon peel
¼   teaspoon dried sage, crushed

1. Bake chicken patties according to package directions. Heat potatoes according to package directions.

2. Meanwhile, in a small saucepan, prepare chicken gravy mix according to package directions, except use the 1 cup buttermilk in place of the water called for and add lemon peel and sage. Place chicken patties on serving plates. Mound potatoes on top of patties. Spoon some of the gravy over the top. Pass remaining gravy. Makes 6 servings.

Per serving: 301 cal., 13 g fat (3 g sat. fat), 26 mg chol., 776 mg sodium, 33 g carbo., 2 g fiber, 14 g pro.

Sweet & Sour Chicken

Either breaded or grilled chicken breast strips or
nuggets would work well in this recipe.

Prep: 15 minutes   **Cook:** 5 minutes

1   11-ounce package frozen cooked,
      breaded chicken strips or nuggets
1   tablespoon cooking oil
1   medium red sweet pepper, cut into
      bite-size strips
½   cup thinly sliced carrot (1 medium)
1   cup fresh pea pods, tips and stems removed
1   8-ounce can pineapple chunks, undrained
      (juice pack)
½   cup bottled sweet-and-sour sauce
2   to 3 cups hot cooked rice

1. Bake chicken strips according to package directions.
2. Meanwhile, in a large nonstick skillet, heat oil over medium-high
heat. Add sweet pepper and carrot; cook and stir for 3 minutes. Add pea
pods; cook and stir about 1 minute more or until vegetables are crisp-tender.
3. Add undrained pineapple chunks and sweet-and-sour sauce to skillet; heat through.
Spoon vegetable mixture over hot cooked rice and top with chicken. Makes 4 to 6 servings.

Per serving: 371 cal., 10 g fat (2 g sat. fat), 19 mg chol., 460 mg sodium, 56 g carbo., 2 g fiber, 13 g pro.

Soups, stir-fries, sandwiches, and more—
power up five creative meals with these
irresistible little bites of protein.

meatballs

Meatballs Stroganoff

Start to Finish: 30 minutes

1 12- to 16-ounce package frozen cooked
    meatballs
1 cup lower-sodium beef broth
1 4-ounce can sliced mushrooms, drained
1 8-ounce carton dairy sour cream
2 tablespoons all-purpose flour
½ cup milk
1 tablespoon Dijon-style mustard
4 cups hot cooked wide egg noodles

1. In a large skillet, combine meatballs, broth, and drained mushrooms. Bring to boiling; reduce heat. Cover; simmer 15 minutes or until heated through.
2. In a bowl, stir together sour cream and flour. Whisk in milk and mustard. Stir sour cream mixture into skillet. Cook and stir until thickened and bubbly; simmer 1 minute more. Serve over hot cooked noodles. If desired, stir in snipped *fresh parsley.* Makes 6 to 8 servings.

    Per serving: 424 cal., 25 g fat (12 g sat. fat), 73 mg chol., 696 mg sodium, 36 g carbo., 3 g fiber, 16 g pro.

Meatball & Red Pepper Pasta

Start to Finish: 30 minutes

1 cup thinly sliced carrot (2 medium)
½ cup chopped onion (1 medium)
2 cloves garlic, minced
1 tablespoon olive oil or cooking oil
2 12-ounce packages frozen cooked
    Italian-style meatballs (24 meatballs)
1 26-ounce jar spicy red pepper
    pasta sauce
8 ounces dried spaghetti or
    bow-tie pasta
    Finely shredded Parmesan cheese

1. In a large skillet, cook carrot, onion, and garlic in hot oil over medium heat for 5 minutes or until tender. Stir in meatballs and pasta sauce. Bring to boiling; reduce heat. Simmer, covered, 15 minutes or until meatballs are heated through.
2. Cook pasta according to package directions until just tender; drain. Serve meatballs and sauce over hot cooked pasta. Sprinkle with Parmesan cheese. Makes 6 servings.

    Per serving: 591 cal., 31 g fat (13 g sat. fat), 77 mg chol., 1,225 mg sodium, 46 g carbo., 8 g fiber, 26 g pro.

Quick Meatball Minestrone
Start to Finish: 25 minutes

1   12- to 16-ounce package frozen cooked
     Italian-style meatballs
3   14-ounce cans lower-sodium beef broth
1   15- to 16-ounce can Great Northern or
     cannellini beans, rinsed and drained
1   14.5-ounce can diced tomatoes with basil,
     garlic, and oregano, undrained
1   10-ounce package frozen mixed vegetables
1   cup dried small pasta (such as macaroni)
1   teaspoon sugar

1. In a 4-quart Dutch oven, stir together meatballs, broth, drained beans, undrained tomatoes, and vegetables. Bring to boiling. Stir in pasta. Return to boiling; reduce heat. Simmer, uncovered, about 10 minutes or until pasta is tender and meatballs are heated through. Stir in sugar. Makes 6 to 8 servings.

Per serving: 413 cal., 15 g fat (7 g sat. fat), 40 mg chol., 1,242 mg sodium, 47 g carbo., 8 g fiber, 24 g pro.

Sweet & Sour Meatballs
Start to Finish: 30 minutes

1   20-ounce can pineapple chunks
¾   cup maple syrup or maple-flavor syrup
½   cup cider vinegar
1   12- to 16-ounce package frozen
     cooked meatballs
2   medium red sweet peppers
¼   cup cold water
2   tablespoons cornstarch
½   teaspoon salt
2   cups hot cooked Asian noodles or rice

1. Drain pineapple; reserve liquid. In a large saucepan, stir together pineapple liquid, syrup, and vinegar. Add meatballs. Bring to boiling; reduce heat. Simmer, covered, for 15 minutes.

2. Remove seeds from sweet peppers and cut into ¾-inch pieces. Add to meatballs. Simmer, covered, for 5 minutes.

3. In a bowl, stir together water, cornstarch, and salt until smooth. Stir into meatball mixture. Cook and stir 1 to 2 minutes or until thickened and bubbly. Stir in pineapple chunks; heat through. Serve over hot cooked noodles. Makes 4 servings.

Per serving: 667 cal., 23 g fat (9 g sat. fat), 30 mg chol., 972 mg sodium, 107 g carbo., 5 g fiber, 14 g pro.

Meatball Hoagies

For easier eating, choose smaller ¹/₂-ounce meatballs when making these sandwiches.
Start to Finish: 30 minutes

1   **medium onion, thinly sliced**
1   **medium red or green sweet pepper, seeded and cut into thin strips**
1   **tablespoon olive oil**
1   **16-ounce package frozen cooked Italian meatballs**
2   **cups refrigerated marinara sauce**
¼   **teaspoon crushed red pepper**
6   **slices provolone cheese (6 ounces)**
6   **hoagie buns or ciabatta rolls, split**

1. In a saucepan, cook onion and sweet pepper in hot oil over medium heat for 4 to 5 minutes or until crisp-tender. Add meatballs, marinara sauce, and crushed red pepper. Bring to boiling; reduce heat. Simmer, covered, about 15 minutes or until meatballs are heated through.

2. To serve, place provolone cheese on bottom halves of rolls. Spoon meatball mixture onto each roll. If desired, broil sandwiches 4 to 5 inches from heat for 1 to 2 minutes or until cheese melts. Makes 6 sandwiches.

Per serving: 696 cal., 29 g fat (11 g sat. fat), 44 mg chol., 1,642 mg sodium, 84 g carbo., 7 g fiber, 26 g pro.

Hamburgers are great—but every night?
Keep ground beef from becoming a
bummer with these six fresh choices.

ground beef

French Onion Burgers

Prep: 20 minutes   Broil: 14 minutes

1	tablespoon olive oil
3	cups sliced onion (3 large)
$^1/_4$	teaspoon salt
$^3/_4$	teaspoon coarsely ground black pepper
$1^1/_2$	pounds lean ground beef
2	tablespoons Worcestershire sauce
2	cloves garlic, minced
$^3/_4$	cup shredded Swiss cheese or reduced-fat Swiss cheese (3 ounces)
4	$^3/_4$-inch-thick slices French bread

1. In a skillet, heat oil over medium heat. Add onion; cook 10 minutes or until golden, stirring occasionally. Stir in salt and $^1/_4$ teaspoon of the pepper. Cover and keep warm.

2. Meanwhile, in a large bowl, combine beef, Worcestershire sauce, the remaining $^1/_2$ teaspoon pepper, and the garlic. Divide beef mixture into 8 equal portions. Shape each portion into a 4-inch-diameter patty. Place one-fourth of the cheese on each of four of the patties. Top with remaining patties, pressing down lightly and sealing edges to enclose cheese.

3. Place burgers on the unheated rack of a broiler pan. Broil 4 inches from the heat for 14 to 18 minutes or until done (160°F), turning once halfway through broiling.

4. Add bread slices to pan for the last 1 to 2 minutes of broiling or until toasted, turning once. Serve patties on toasted bread slices topped with onions. Makes 4 servings.

Per serving: 535 cal., 27 g fat (11 g sat. fat), 127 mg chol., 576 mg sodium, 32 g carbo., 2 g fiber, 40 g pro.

Easy Goulash

Prep: 20 minutes   Cook: 6 hours (low) or 3 hours (high)   Stand: 5 minutes

1	pound lean ground beef
$^1/_2$	of a 24-ounce package frozen loose-pack diced hash brown potatoes with onions and peppers (about $3^1/_2$ cups)
1	15-ounce can tomato sauce
1	14.5-ounce can diced tomatoes with basil, garlic, and oregano, undrained
$^1/_2$	cup shredded cheddar cheese (2 ounces)
	Hot cooked noodles

1. In a large skillet, cook ground beef over medium heat until brown. Drain off fat.

2. In a $3^1/_2$- or 4-quart slow cooker, stir together meat, frozen potatoes, tomato sauce, and undrained tomatoes.

3. Cover and cook on low-heat setting for 6 to 8 hours or on high-heat setting for 3 to 4 hours. Turn off cooker. Sprinkle cheese over meat mixture. Let stand about 5 minutes or until cheese melts. Serve with noodles. Makes 4 servings.

Per serving: 535 cal., 33 g fat (14 g sat. fat), 109 mg chol., 1,371 mg sodium, 34 g carbo., 4 g fiber, 27 g pro.

Polenta with Italian Beef Stew

Prep: 25 minutes **Cook:** 15 minutes

1	pound lean ground beef
1	14.5-ounce can diced tomatoes with basil, garlic, and oregano, undrained
3	medium carrots, cut into $^{1}/_{2}$-inch slices
2	medium onions, cut into thin wedges
1	large red sweet pepper, cut into 1-inch pieces
$^{1}/_{2}$	cup beef broth
3	tablespoons tomato paste
$^{1}/_{4}$	teaspoon salt
$^{1}/_{4}$	teaspoon ground black pepper
1	teaspoon bottled minced garlic
1	medium zucchini, halved lengthwise and cut into $^{1}/_{4}$-inch slices
$^{1}/_{3}$	cup purchased basil pesto or Homemade Pesto (page 117)
1	16-ounce tube refrigerated cooked polenta

1. In a large skillet, cook ground beef over medium heat until brown. Drain off fat. Stir in undrained tomatoes, carrot, onion, sweet pepper, beef broth, tomato paste, salt, black pepper, and garlic. Bring to boiling; reduce heat. Cover and simmer for 10 to 15 minutes or until carrot is tender. Stir in zucchini and pesto. Cover and simmer 5 minutes more.

2. Meanwhile, prepare polenta according to package directions. Serve meat mixture with polenta. Makes 6 servings.

Per serving: 362 cal., 16 g fat (3 g sat. fat), 50 mg chol., 978 mg sodium, 34 g carbo., 5 g fiber, 20 g pro.

Chili Macaroni

Start to Finish: 30 minutes

12 ounces lean ground beef or uncooked
    ground turkey
$^1/_2$ cup chopped onion (1 medium)
1 14.5-ounce can diced tomatoes
    and green chiles, undrained
$1^1/_4$ cups tomato juice
2 teaspoons chili powder
$^1/_2$ teaspoon garlic salt
1 cup dried wagon wheel macaroni
1 cup frozen cut green beans
1 cup shredded cheddar cheese
    (4 ounces)
    Tortilla chips

1. In a very large skillet, cook ground beef and onion over medium heat until meat is brown. Drain off fat. Stir undrained tomatoes, tomato juice, chili powder, and garlic salt into meat mixture. Bring to boiling. Stir in pasta and green beans. Return to boiling; reduce heat. Cover and simmer about 15 minutes or until pasta and beans are tender.

2. Top with shredded cheddar cheese and serve with tortilla chips. Makes 4 servings.

Per serving: 443 cal., 20 g fat (9 g sat. fat), 83 mg chol., 881 mg sodium, 37 g carbo., 5 g fiber, 29 g pro.

Upside-Down Pizza Casserole

*Put the crust on top of this "pizza" by topping
the ground beef mixture with biscuits.*

Prep: 20 minutes   **Bake:** 15 minutes

$1^1/_2$ pounds lean ground beef
1 15-ounce can Italian-style tomato sauce
$1^1/_2$ cups shredded mozzarella cheese
    (6 ounces)
1 10-ounce package refrigerated biscuits
    (10 biscuits)

1. Preheat oven to 400°F. In a large skillet, cook ground beef over medium heat until brown. Drain off fat. Stir in tomato sauce; heat through. Transfer beef mixture to a 2-quart rectangular baking dish or 10-inch deep-dish pie plate. Sprinkle with cheese. Flatten each biscuit with your hands; arrange the biscuits on top of cheese.

2. Bake, uncovered, about 15 minutes or until biscuits are golden. Makes 10 small or 5 large servings.

Per small serving: 321 cal., 20 g fat (8 g sat. fat), 58 mg chol., 551 mg sodium, 15 g carbo., 1 g fiber, 17 g pro.

Greek-Style Lasagna

Prep: 45 minutes   **Bake:** 35 minutes
Stand: 10 minutes

9	dried lasagna noodles
1	pound lean ground beef or lamb
1	medium onion, chopped (½ cup)
2	cloves garlic, minced
1	8-ounce can tomato sauce
¼	cup dry red wine or beef broth
1	teaspoon dried oregano, crushed
¼	teaspoon ground cinnamon
3	tablespoons butter
3	tablespoons all-purpose flour
¼	teaspoon ground black pepper
1¾	cups milk
½	cup grated Parmesan cheese
1	2¼-ounce can sliced pitted ripe olives, drained
8	ounces crumbled feta cheese
1	cup shredded white cheddar cheese (4 ounces)

1. Preheat oven to 350°F. Cook noodles according to package directions; drain. Rinse with cold water; drain well and set aside.

2. In a large skillet, brown meat, onion, and garlic. Drain off fat. Stir in tomato sauce, wine, oregano, and cinnamon. Bring to boiling; reduce heat. Simmer, uncovered, 10 minutes.

3. In a saucepan, melt butter; stir in flour, pepper, and milk. Cook and stir until thickened and bubbly; cook and stir 1 minute more. Stir in Parmesan; set aside.

4. To assemble, layer noodles, meat sauce, cheese sauce, olives, and cheeses. Bake, uncovered, about 35 to 40 minutes or until heated through. Let stand 10 minutes before serving. Makes 12 servings.

Per serving: 330 cal., 20 g fat (11 g sat. fat), 67 mg chol., 516 mg sodium, 19 g carbo., 1 g fiber, 17 g pro.

food safety 101
how to handle ground beef

As the list of health concerns grows and prevention measures seem more daunting, it's comforting to know one ailment is relatively easy to stop: foodborne illness.

Simply wash your hands, wash food prep surfaces, cook food to at least 160°F, and store food smartly. That's it. No pricey prescriptions or 12-step programs.

Concerns about *E. coli* bacteria are common (perhaps rivaled only by worries about salmonella). But you don't have to give up the delicious, hearty flavor of ground beef out of fear of contamination. Follow these four easy steps to dine on hamburgers, goulash, chili, and meatballs without a care:

✳ Wash your hands for at least 20 seconds in warm, soapy water before and after working with any raw beef product.

✳ Make sure any surface—cutting board, countertop, etc.—is clean before food prep begins. Wash surfaces immediately after working with any raw beef product. If possible, use two cutting boards—one for cutting meat, the other for chopping vegetables.

✳ Cook ground beef to at least 160°F. Check the temperature with a clean meat thermometer. Immediately refrigerate or freeze any leftovers in a sealed container. Reheat leftover ground beef to at least 165°F.

✳ Don't cross-contaminate. Trays or tubes of ground beef can leak juices into the shopping cart or refrigerator. Separate raw meat from fresh produce in the cart and the fridge, and place containers in plastic bags to keep juices contained. At home, store raw meat on the bottom shelf in the refrigerator to keep juices from dripping onto other items.

Good news! According to studies conducted by the CDC and the FDA, the incidence of *E. coli* found in beef products has decreased by 42 percent since 1996.

Quick-frozen shrimp is one of the fastest (and best tasting) ways to get dinner on the table. Here are five choices to make your workweek "shrimp-ilicious."

Shrimp Gumbo

Start to Finish: 40 minutes

8   ounces bulk hot Italian sausage
1   large onion, chopped
1   large green sweet pepper, chopped
2   stalks celery, thinly sliced
3   cloves garlic, chopped
2   14½-ounce cans reduced-sodium stewed
      tomatoes, undrained
1   14-ounce can reduced-sodium chicken broth
1   teaspoon paprika
¼   teaspoon ground black pepper
⅛   to ¼ teaspoon cayenne pepper
1   pound frozen uncooked medium shrimp,
      thawed, peeled, and deveined
1   cup instant white rice

1. Cook sausage, onion, sweet pepper, and celery until sausage is browned. Drain. Add garlic, undrained tomatoes, broth, paprika, black pepper, and cayenne. Bring to boiling; reduce heat. Simmer, covered, for 10 minutes.

2. Add shrimp; cook, covered, 4 minutes more, until shrimp are opaque. Remove from heat. Stir in rice. Cover; let stand 5 minutes. Serve hot. Makes 6 servings.

Per serving: 338 cal., 14 g fat (5 g sat. fat), 144 mg chol., 971 mg sodium, 28 g carbo., 4 g fiber, 24 g pro.

Mexican Shrimp Tostadas

Start to Finish: 20 minutes

4   purchased tostada shells
2   cups shredded lettuce
1   15-ounce can black beans, drained
20 frozen cooked large shrimp, thawed,
      peeled, and deveined
1   tablespoon lime juice
1   medium tomato, cut into 16 thin
      wedges
¼   cup dairy sour cream
    Sliced green onion
    Salsa

1. Place one tostada shell on each of 4 serving plates. Top with some lettuce and one-fourth of the beans. Arrange 5 shrimp in a circle over the drained beans; sprinkle shrimp with lime juice.

2. Arrange 4 tomato wedges on each tortilla and top with a tablespoon of the dairy sour cream and some green onion. Serve with salsa. Makes 4 servings.

Per serving: 273 cal., 6 g fat (2 g sat. fat), 227 mg chol., 670 mg sodium, 25 g carbo., 6 g fiber, 32 g pro.

Shrimply Divine Pasta

Start to Finish: 20 minutes

1	6-ounce package rotini
1½	teaspoons bottled minced garlic
1	tablespoon olive oil
12	ounces frozen uncooked medium shrimp, thawed, peeled, and deveined
1	cup chicken broth
1	tablespoon cornstarch
1	teaspoon Italian herb seasoning
4	cups packaged baby spinach
	Finely shredded Parmesan cheese

1. Cook pasta according to package directions. Drain; keep warm. Rinse shrimp; pat dry.
2. In a skillet, cook garlic in oil over medium-high heat for 15 seconds. Add shrimp. Cook for 2 to 3 minutes or until shrimp are opaque. Remove shrimp. Add broth, cornstarch, and Italian seasoning to skillet. Cook and stir until thickened and bubbly. Add spinach. Cook until wilted. Return shrimp to skillet; stir. Toss with pasta and Parmesan cheese. Makes 4 servings.

Per serving: 333 cal., 7 g fat (1 g sat. fat), 136 mg chol., 422 mg sodium, 39 g carbo., 3 g fiber, 25 g pro.

Jerk-Spiced Shrimp with Wilted Spinach

Start to Finish: 25 minutes

12	ounces frozen uncooked medium shrimp, thawed, peeled, and deveined
1½	teaspoons Jamaican jerk seasoning
3	cloves garlic, minced
2	tablespoons olive oil
8	cups torn fresh spinach

1. Rinse shrimp; pat dry with paper towels. In a small bowl, toss together shrimp and jerk seasoning; set aside.
2. In a large skillet, cook garlic in 1 tablespoon of hot oil for 15 to 30 seconds. Add half of the spinach. Cook and stir about 1 minute or until spinach is just wilted. Transfer to a serving platter. Repeat with remaining spinach. Cover; keep warm.
3. Carefully add remaining oil to skillet. Add shrimp. Cook and stir for 2 to 3 minutes or until shrimp are opaque. Spoon shrimp over wilted spinach. Makes 4 servings.

Per serving: 159 cal., 8 g fat (1 g sat. fat), 129 mg chol., 315 mg sodium, 2 g carbo., 6 g fiber, 19 g pro.

Grilled Shrimp Kabobs

For fiery flavor, slather the kabobs with a hot and spicy variety of barbecue sauce.

Prep: 20 minutes
Grill: 6 minutes

1 pound frozen large shrimp in shells
1 medium green and/or red sweet pepper, cut into 16 pieces
¼ of a medium fresh pineapple, cut into chunks
4 green onions, cut into 2- to 3-inch pieces
¼ cup bottled low-carb barbecue sauce

1. Thaw shrimp. Peel and devein shrimp, keeping tails intact. Rinse shrimp; pat dry with paper towels. Alternately thread shrimp, sweet pepper pieces, pineapple chunks, and green onions onto 8 long metal or wood skewers.

2. For a charcoal grill, grill kabobs on the greased grill rack of an uncovered grill directly over medium coals for 6 to 10 minutes or until shrimp are opaque, turning once and brushing with barbecue sauce halfway through grilling. (For a gas grill, preheat grill. Reduce heat to medium. Place kabobs on greased grill rack over heat. Cover and grill as above.) Makes 4 servings.

Per serving: 127 cal., 2 g fat (0 g sat. fat), 129 mg chol., 257 mg sodium, 9 g carbo., 1 g fiber, 18 g pro.

They're not just for snacking anymore!
Introduce easy-to-prepare fish sticks to the
dinner table with five kickin' meal ideas.

frozen fish

Fish Tacos

Start to Finish: 20 minutes

1	11-ounce package (18) frozen baked, breaded fish sticks
3	tablespoons low-fat mayonnaise or salad dressing
1	teaspoon lime juice
1½	cups packaged shredded cabbage with carrot (coleslaw mix)
8	corn tortillas
	Mango Salsa

1. Bake fish according to package directions. Cut each fish stick in half crosswise.

2. Meanwhile, in a bowl, stir together mayonnaise and lime juice. Add cabbage; toss to coat. Divide coleslaw mixture among tortillas. Add fish and top with mango salsa. Makes 4 servings.

Mango Salsa: In a bowl, stir together 1 cup seeded, peeled, and chopped mango; ¾ cup finely chopped red sweet pepper; ¼ cup sliced green onion; ½ teaspoon finely shredded lime peel; 1 tablespoon lime juice; ¼ teaspoon salt; and ¼ teaspoon ground black pepper. Makes 1½ cups.

Per serving: 334 cal., 12 g total fat (2 g sat. fat), 22 mg chol., 655 mg sodium, 47 g carbo., 4 g fiber, 10 g pro.

Pizza-Style Fish Sticks

Don't knock 'em before you try 'em! These wacky-sounding sticks are delicious!

Prep: 15 minutes   **Bake:** 20 minutes

1	11-ounce package (18) frozen baked, breaded fish sticks
1	8-ounce can pizza sauce
1	cup shredded provolone or mozzarella cheese (4 ounces)
2	tablespoons shredded fresh basil (optional)

1. Preheat oven to 425°F. Arrange fish sticks in a 2-quart square or rectangular baking dish. Spoon sauce over sticks. Sprinkle with cheese. Bake, uncovered, about 20 minutes or until heated through. Sprinkle with basil, if desired. Makes 4 servings.

Per serving: 336 cal., 20 g fat (7 g sat. fat), 36 mg chol., 839 mg sodium, 22 g carbo., 1 g fiber, 17 g pro.

Something's Fishy Sandwiches

Prep: 10 minutes   **Bake:** per package directions

1   11-ounce package (18) frozen baked,
       breaded fish sticks
4   thin slices tomato
½   teaspoon dried basil, crushed
⅛   teaspoon ground black pepper
1   cup shredded mozzarella, cheddar, Swiss,
       or American cheese (4 ounces)
2   tablespoons desired creamy salad
       dressing
4   kaiser rolls, split and toasted

1. Arrange fish sticks close together on a baking sheet. Bake according to package directions.
2. Top fish with tomato slices. Sprinkle with basil and pepper; top with cheese. Bake for 2 to 3 minutes more or until cheese is melted.

3. Spread salad dressing on bottoms of rolls. Add fish and top halves of rolls. Makes 4 servings.

Per serving: 414 cal., 14 g fat (5 g sat. fat), 35 mg chol., 875 mg sodium, 50 g carbo., 1 g fiber, 20 g pro.

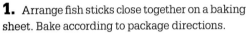

Spinach & Fish Salad

Start to Finish: 25 minutes

1   11-ounce package (18) frozen baked,
       breaded fish sticks
4   cups baby spinach leaves
1   medium onion, cut into thin wedges
1   tablespoon olive oil or cooking oil
1   medium red or yellow sweet pepper,
       cut into thin strips
3   tablespoons balsamic vinegar
1   tablespoon honey

1. Bake fish according to package directions. Place spinach in a bowl. Top with fish; cover to keep warm.
2. Meanwhile, in a skillet, cook onion in hot oil over medium heat 5 to 6 minutes or until tender and slightly golden. Add sweet pepper; cook and stir 1 minute more. Remove from heat. Add onion mixture to spinach and fish; toss to combine. Transfer to a serving platter.

3. In a bowl, stir together the balsamic vinegar and honey. Add to skillet. Cook and stir until heated through, about 1 minute. Spoon vinegar mixture over fish and spinach. Makes 4 servings.

Per serving: 279 cal., 14 g fat (2 g sat. fat), 25 mg chol., 356 mg sodium, 29 g carbo., 3 g fiber, 10 g pro.

Sweet & Sour Fish Sticks

Start to Finish: 25 minutes

¾ **cup bottled sweet-and-sour sauce**
1 **11-ounce package (18) frozen baked, breaded fish sticks**
1 **red sweet pepper, cut into strips**
1 **tablespoon cooking oil**
1 **cup snow pea pods, trimmed**
1 **8.8-ounce pouch cooked brown or white rice**

1. Set aside ¼ cup of the sweet-and-sour sauce in a small microwave-safe bowl or measuring cup. Bake fish sticks according to package directions.
2. Meanwhile, in a large skillet, cook pepper strips in hot oil over medium-high heat for 3 minutes. Add pea pods and cook for 1 to 2 minutes more or until vegetables are crisp-tender. Stir in the remaining ½ cup sauce to coat; heat through. Prepare rice according to package directions.
3. Heat reserved sauce in microwave on 100-percent power (high) for 30 to 40 seconds or until heated through. Serve vegetable mixture over rice. Top with fish sticks. Drizzle with warm sauce. Makes 4 servings.

Per serving: 406 cal., 17 g fat (3 g sat. fat), 16 mg chol., 643 mg sodium, 52 g carbo., 2 g fiber, 11 g pro.

Hash brown potatoes—they're not just for breakfast anymore! Add some extra ingredients for flavor and heartiness, and this potato favorite can be transformed into four satisfying meals.

Pork & Potato Skillet

This one-pan dinner is perfect for a busy weeknight.

Start to Finish: 30 minutes

- 4   4-ounce boneless pork loin chops
- ¾   teaspoon seasoned salt
- 2   tablespoons cooking oil
- ⅓   cup chopped onion (1 small)
- 1   medium red sweet pepper, cut into
  ¾-inch pieces
- 3   cups frozen diced hash brown potatoes
- 2   cups frozen peas and carrots
- 1   teaspoon dried thyme, crushed

1. Sprinkle both sides of pork chops evenly with ½ teaspoon of the seasoned salt. In a very large skillet, heat 1 tablespoon of the oil over medium-high heat.

Cook chops in hot oil for 3 minutes. Turn chops. Cook for 3 minutes more or until brown. Remove chops from skillet.

2. Carefully add remaining 1 tablespoon oil to skillet. Add onion and sweet pepper; cook and stir for 1 minute. Add potatoes, peas and carrots, thyme, and remaining ¼ teaspoon seasoned salt; mix well. Cook for 6 minutes, stirring frequently.

3. Place chops on top of potato mixture in skillet; cover. Reduce heat to medium. Cook for 7 to 9 minutes more or until chops are no longer pink and potatoes are brown. Makes 4 servings.

Per serving: 406 cal., 15 g fat (3 g sat. fat), 72 mg chol., 422 mg sodium, 39 g carbo., 5 g fiber, 29 g pro.

Grilled Potato & Onion Packets

Start to Finish: 30 minutes

- 1 teaspoon dried thyme, crushed
- ½ teaspoon garlic salt
- ½ teaspoon paprika
- ⅛ teaspoon ground black pepper
  Nonstick cooking spray
- 4 cups frozen diced hash brown potatoes
- 1 sweet onion, halved and thinly sliced
- 2 tablespoons olive oil
- ¼ cup dairy sour cream and chive dip (optional)

1. For seasoning mixture, stir together thyme, garlic salt, paprika, and pepper; set aside. Fold a 48×18-inch piece of heavy foil in half to make a double thickness of foil that measures 24×18 inches. Lightly coat the foil with cooking spray.

2. Place potatoes and onion in center of foil. Drizzle potatoes and onions with oil. Sprinkle with seasoning mixture.

3. Bring up opposite edges of foil; seal with a double fold. Fold remaining edges to enclose the vegetables, leaving space for steam.

4. For a charcoal grill, grill the foil packet on the rack of an uncovered grill directly over medium heat for 20 to 25 minutes or until the potatoes are tender. (For a gas grill, preheat grill. Reduce heat to medium. Place packet on grill rack over heat. Cover and grill as above.) If desired, serve with dip. Makes 4 to 6 servings.

Per serving: 329 cal., 20 g fat (6 g sat. fat), 0 mg chol., 161 mg sodium, 36 g carbo., 3 g fiber, 4 g pro.

Shredded Potatoes with Sausage & Apples

Start to Finish: 30 minutes

- 2 tablespoons olive oil
- 2 tablespoons butter
- 5 cups frozen shredded hash brown potatoes
- 1 tablespoon snipped fresh thyme or 1 teaspoon dried thyme, crushed
- ¼ teaspoon ground black pepper
- 6 ounces cooked smoked sausage, coarsely chopped
- 1 medium apple, such as Golden Delicious, cut into thin wedges
  Salt to taste

1. In a 10-inch cast-iron or nonstick skillet, heat the oil and 1 tablespoon of the butter over medium heat. Add potatoes in an even layer. Cook for 8 minutes, stirring occasionally, until lightly browned. Stir in half of the thyme and the pepper. With a wide metal spatula, press potatoes down firmly. Cook about 8 minutes more or until potatoes are tender.

2. Meanwhile, in a medium skillet, melt the remaining 1 tablespoon butter over medium heat. Add sausage and apple. Cook about 10 minutes or until apple is tender, stirring occasionally. Stir in remaining thyme.

3. Cut potato mixture into 4 wedges and place on serving plates; top wedges with apple mixture. Add salt to taste. Makes 4 servings.

Per serving: 365 cal., 28 g fat (10 g sat. fat), 47 mg chol., 381 mg sodium, 21 g carbo., 2 g fiber, 8 g pro.

Hash Brown Casserole
Prep: 20 minutes **Bake:** 50 minutes

1 10.75-ounce can reduced-fat and
   reduced-sodium condensed cream
   of chicken soup or condensed cream
   of chicken soup
1 8-ounce carton light dairy sour cream
   or dairy sour cream
4 cups frozen shredded hash brown
   potatoes
1 cup diced cooked ham (4 ounces)
1 cup cubed American cheese (4 ounces)
¼ cup chopped onion
⅛ teaspoon ground black pepper
1 cup cornflakes
3 tablespoons butter, melted

1. Preheat oven to 350°F. In a large bowl, stir together soup and sour cream. Stir in frozen potatoes, ham, cheese, onion, and pepper. Spread the mixture evenly into a 2-quart square baking dish. In a small bowl, combine cornflakes and butter. Sprinkle over potato mixture.
2. Bake, uncovered, for 50 to 55 minutes or until hot and bubbly. Let stand for 10 minutes before serving. Makes 6 servings.

Per serving: 351 cal., 19 g fat (11 g sat. fat), 63 mg chol., 953 mg sodium, 35 g carbo., 2 g fiber, 13 g pro.

How do you get five servings of vegetables a day? Keep it easy and delicious, and you'll have no problem getting your fill.

frozen veggies

Crumb-Topped Vegetables

Get the kids involved in making this side dish by letting them crush the crackers in the bag.

Start to Finish: 10 minutes

1   12-ounce package frozen cut green beans in microwavable steaming bag (such as Birds Eye Steamfresh)
1   cup cheese-flavor crackers, crushed
½   teaspoon dried thyme, crushed
2   tablespoons butter, melted
¼   cup finely shredded Parmesan cheese

1. Cook beans according to package directions.

2. Meanwhile, place the crackers and thyme in a small resealable plastic bag. Release the air from the bag and seal bag. With your hands, crush the crackers until they resemble fine crumbs. Add melted butter to the bag. Seal bag and shake to combine.

3. Place beans in a serving dish. Top with cracker mixture. Sprinkle Parmesan cheese over top. Makes 4 to 6 servings.

Per serving: 168 cal., 10 g fat (6 g sat. fat), 20 mg chol., 249 mg sodium, 13 g carbo., 2 g fiber, 4 g pro.

Quick & Cheesy Veggies

*Walnuts add a nice crunch to this side dish. If some
members of the family don't care for the crunchy nut
topping, sprinkle it on individual servings.*

Start to Finish: 10 minutes

1   12-ounce package frozen broccoli and
    cauliflower in microwavable
    steaming bag
1   cup shredded American cheese
    (4 ounces)
2   tablespoons chopped walnuts, toasted

1. Cook vegetables according to package
directions. Transfer vegetables to a serving bowl.
Stir in cheese; let stand for 1 minute. Toss until
cheese is melted and vegetables are coated.
Sprinkle with nuts. Makes 4 servings.

Per serving: 158 cal., 11 g fat (6 g sat. fat), 27 mg chol.,
445 mg sodium, 5 g carbo., 2 g fiber, 8 g pro.

outside the box

Sure, mac 'n' cheese is great on its own, but turn it into something that will make the family flip! Add a little love (and flavor) to your favorite packaged foods with these clever fix-ups.

Italian-Style Macaroni Salad
Prep: 20 minutes **Chill:** 10 minutes

1. Prepare one 7.25-ounce package macaroni and cheese dinner mix according to package directions, adding 1 cup frozen stir-fry pepper and onion strips during the last 2 minutes of cooking the pasta. Transfer pasta mixture to a large bowl. Cover; chill in freezer for 10 minutes, stirring once. Stir in one large seeded, chopped tomato (¾ cup) and ⅓ cup bottled Italian salad dressing. Makes 4 servings.

Per serving: 394 cal., 17 g fat (8 g sat. fat), 34 mg chol., 902 mg sodium, 49 g carbo., 2 g fiber, 11 g pro.

Here, your lunchtime go-to gets a makeover. Add zip, zing, and pizzazz to this family pantry favorite, all with the stir of a spoon. Stepping outside the box has never been easier!

Pizza-Style Mac & Cheese

Start to Finish: 25 minutes

1. Prepare one 7.25-ounce package macaroni and cheese dinner mix according to package directions. Stir in ½ cup pizza sauce. Stir in one drained 6-ounce can or jar sliced or chopped mushrooms, ¼ cup chopped pitted ripe olives, and ¼ cup chopped pepperoni; heat through, stirring occasionally. Sprinkle with grated Parmesan cheese. Makes 4 servings.

Per serving: 404 cal., 17 g fat (8 g sat. fat), 45 mg chol., 1,174 mg sodium, 49 g carbo., 2 g fiber, 14 g pro.

Mac & Cheese with Smoked Sausage

Start to Finish: 25 minutes

1. Prepare one 7.25-ounce package macaroni and cheese dinner mix according to package directions. Stir in 6 ounces cooked smoked sausage, halved lengthwise and sliced, and ¾ cup canned roasted red sweet peppers, drained and coarsely chopped. Heat through. If desired, sprinkle with snipped Italian (flat-leaf) parsley. Makes 4 servings.

Per serving: 466 cal., 24 g fat (11 g sat. fat), 58 mg chol., 965 mg sodium, 46 g carbo., 2 g fiber, 16 g pro.

Turn a plain box of rice pilaf mix into an irresistible side dish or main dish with these three sumptuous ideas. You'll have everyone in the family raving!

Autumn Vegetable Pilaf
Start to Finish: 35 minutes

1. Preheat oven to 400°F. Prepare one 6- to 7.2-ounce box rice pilaf mix according to package directions, except omit butter or oil. Stir together 2 tablespoons olive oil; 2 tablespoons cider vinegar; 2 cloves garlic, minced; and 1 teaspoon dried thyme. Add 1 sweet potato, peeled and cubed; 1 zucchini, cubed; and 1 small red onion, cut into wedges; stir to coat. Spread vegetables in a 15×10×1-inch baking pan. Roast, uncovered, 20 to 25 minutes or until vegetables are lightly browned and tender. Remove and stir into hot rice pilaf; top with ⅓ cup chopped toasted walnuts. Makes 6 servings.

Per serving: 233 cal., 9 g fat (1 g sat. fat), 0 mg chol., 328 mg sodium, 34 g carbo., 3 g fiber, 4 g pro.

Asian Chicken & Rice Salad

Start to Finish: 25 minutes

1. Prepare one 6- to 7.2-ounce box rice pilaf mix according to package directions. In a large bowl, stir together rice mix, 2 cups shredded or chopped cooked chicken, one 14-ounce can whole baby corn (drained), ½ cup chopped sweet pepper, ½ cup halved snow peas (or 1 stalk thinly sliced celery), and ¼ cup sliced green onion. Add ½ cup bottled Asian salad dressing, stirring gently to combine. Serve immediately or cover and chill for up to 24 hours. If desired, sprinkle with toasted sesame seeds before serving. Makes 4 to 6 servings.

Per serving: 429 cal., 14 g fat (3 g sat. fat), 62 mg chol., 1,057 mg sodium, 46 g carbo., 5 g fiber, 26 g pro.

Bayou Shrimp & Rice

Prep: 20 minutes **Cook:** 20 minutes

1. In a 4-quart Dutch oven, stir together one 14.5-ounce can undrained Cajun- or Mexican-style stewed tomatoes (chopped), one 14-ounce can chicken broth, 1 cup chopped onion, 1 cup chopped green sweet pepper, one 6- to 7.2-ounce box rice pilaf mix, 2 cloves garlic (minced), and 1 teaspoon Cajun seasoning. Bring to boiling; reduce heat. Cover and simmer for 20 to 25 minutes or until rice is tender and liquid is nearly absorbed. Stir occasionally. Stir in 8 ounces cooked, peeled, and deveined shrimp and 8 ounces cooked, sliced kielbasa; heat through. Makes 4 to 5 servings.

Per serving: 461 cal., 18 g fat (8 g sat. fat), 137 mg chol., 1,864 mg sodium, 49 g carbo., 3 g fiber, 25 g pro.

Skip the full-fat gravy. A bowl of mashed potatoes has tastier accompaniments with these mix-and-serve ideas.

Boursin Mashed Potatoes

Boursin is a soft triple-cream cheese seasoned with herbs and garlic. It melts to a supercreamy texture with the mashed potatoes.
Start to Finish: 10 minutes

1. Heat a 1.5-pound package refrigerated mashed potatoes according to package directions. Transfer warm potatoes to a serving bowl. Stir in one 5.2-ounce container semisoft cheese with garlic and herbs (Boursin) and 3 tablespoons snipped fresh parsley. If desired, top with canned french-fried onions. Makes 4 to 6 servings.

Per serving: 301 cal., 17 g fat (8 g sat. fat), 34 mg chol., 287 mg sodium, 27 g carbo., 1 g fiber, 7 g pro.

Bacon & Spinach Mashed Potatoes

This colorful side dish has flavors to please the whole family, and it's a good way to introduce spinach to your kids.

Start to Finish: 15 minutes

1. Heat a 1.5-pound package refrigerated mashed potatoes according to package directions. Transfer warm potatoes to a serving bowl. Stir in ¾ cup shredded cheddar cheese, 3 slices of crisp-cooked and crumbled bacon, and 2 cups of baby spinach leaves, shredded. If desired, top with additional bacon and spinach leaves. Makes 4 to 6 servings.

Per serving: 255 cal., 12 g fat (5 g sat. fat), 29 mg chol., 538 mg sodium, 24 g carbo., 2 g fiber, 12 g pro.

Pesto & Red Pepper Potatoes

Try the Homemade Pesto on page 117 in this recipe. Two frozen cubes are enough to do the trick.

Start to Finish: 10 minutes

1. Heat a 1.5-pound package refrigerated mashed potatoes according to package directions. Transfer warm potatoes to a serving bowl. Stir in ¼ cup of roasted red sweet peppers, drained and cut into strips. Gently swirl in ¼ cup purchased basil pesto or Homemade Pesto (page 117). If desired, top with ¼ cup of roasted red sweet peppers, drained and cut into strips, and shredded Parmesan cheese. Makes 4 to 6 servings.

Per serving: 268 cal., 14 g fat (1 g sat. fat), 6 mg chol., 456 mg sodium, 27 g carbo., 2 g fiber, 8 g pro.

Biscuit mix + flavor = a rockin' good addition to mealtime.

Pesto Biscuits
Prep: 15 minutes   **Bake:** 10 minutes

1. Preheat oven to 450°F. In a medium bowl, stir together 2¼ cups biscuit mix, ½ cup milk, and ¼ cup purchased basil pesto until a soft dough forms. Turn dough out onto a lightly floured surface. Lightly knead 10 times or until nearly smooth. Pat dough to ½ inch thick. Using a 2½-inch round cookie cutter, cut dough into rounds. Place rounds on an ungreased baking sheet. Brush lightly with 2 teaspoons olive oil and sprinkle with 2 tablespoons finely shredded Parmesan cheese. Bake about 10 minutes or until golden. Serve warm. Makes 10 to 12 biscuits.

Per serving: 165 cal., 8 g fat (2 g sat. fat), 4 mg chol., 426 mg sodium, 19 g carbo., 1 g fiber, 4 g pro.

Blueberry-Orange Scones
Prep: 20 minutes   **Bake:** 12 minutes

1. Preheat oven to 400°F. In a large bowl, stir together 2¼ cups biscuit mix, ⅓ cup milk, 1 egg, and 1 teaspoon finely shredded orange peel until a soft dough forms. Carefully fold in ½ cup fresh blueberries. Turn dough out onto a lightly floured surface. Lightly knead 10 times or until nearly smooth. Pat dough into a 6-inch circle. Cut into 6 wedges. Arrange wedges on an ungreased baking sheet. Brush with additional milk and sprinkle lightly with sugar. Bake for 12 to 14 minutes or until golden. Serve warm. Makes 6 servings.

Per serving: 230 cal., 8 g fat (2 g sat. fat), 37 mg chol., 598 mg sodium, 33 g carbo., 1 g fiber, 5 g pro.

the one-pan plan

Dinner
in a flash,
all in one pan—it's
a busy cook's dream
come true! Whether it's
in a skillet, saucepan,
or baking dish, all you
need to do is turn on
the heat. Best part?
Cleanup's
a breeze!

Skillet-Style Lasagna
Start to Finish: 30 minutes

8   ounces uncooked lean ground
      chicken or turkey
½   cup chopped onion (1 medium)
2   cups purchased spaghetti sauce
1   cup water
2   cups dried extra-wide noodles
1½ cups coarsely chopped zucchini
      (1 medium)
½   cup fat-free ricotta cheese
2   tablespoons grated Parmesan or
      Romano cheese
1   tablespoon snipped fresh parsley
½   cup shredded part-skim mozzarella
      cheese (2 ounces)
      Snipped fresh parsley (optional)

1. In a skillet, brown chicken and onion over medium heat; drain fat. Stir in spaghetti sauce and water. Bring to boiling; stir in uncooked noodles and zucchini. Reduce heat. Cover and simmer 10 minutes or until pasta is tender.

2. Meanwhile, in a bowl, combine ricotta cheese, Parmesan cheese, and 1 tablespoon parsley. Spoon cheese mixture onto pasta in 4 mounds. Sprinkle each with mozzarella cheese. Cover and cook over low heat 4 to 5 minutes or until mozzarella is melted. Remove from heat; let stand, uncovered, 10 minutes before serving. If desired, sprinkle with parsley. Makes 6 servings.

Per serving: 186 cal., 3 g total fat (2 g sat. fat), 45 mg chol., 519 mg sodium, 21 g carbo., 2 g fiber, 17 g pro.

One-Pot Spaghetti

Start to Finish: 40 minutes

8   ounces ground beef or bulk
      pork sausage
1   cup sliced fresh mushrooms
      or one 6-ounce jar sliced
      mushrooms, drained
½   cup chopped onion
      (1 medium)
1   clove garlic, minced, or
      ⅛ teaspoon garlic powder
1   14-ounce can chicken broth
      or beef broth
1¾   cups water
1   6-ounce can tomato paste
1   teaspoon dried oregano,
      crushed
½   teaspoon dried basil or
      marjoram, crushed
¼   teaspoon ground
      black pepper
6   ounces dried spaghetti,
      broken
¼   cup grated Parmesan
      cheese

1. In a large saucepan, cook the ground beef, fresh mushrooms (if using), onion, and garlic over medium heat until meat is brown and onion is tender. Drain off fat.

2. Stir in the jarred mushrooms (if using), broth, water, tomato paste, oregano, basil, and pepper. Bring to boiling. Add the broken spaghetti, a little at a time, stirring constantly. Return to boiling; reduce heat. Boil gently, uncovered, for 17 to 20 minutes or until spaghetti is tender and sauce is of the desired consistency, stirring frequently. Serve with Parmesan cheese. Makes 4 servings.

Per serving: 362 cal., 12 g fat (5 g sat. fat), 39 mg chol., 857 mg sodium, 44 g carbo., 4 g fiber, 21 g pro.

Popover Pizza Casserole

Prep: 30 minutes **Bake:** 25 minutes

12 ounces ground turkey or
ground beef
¾ cup chopped onion (1 large)
¾ cup chopped green sweet pepper
(1 medium)
½ of a 3.5-ounce package sliced pepperoni
1 14- to 15.5-ounce jar or can pizza sauce
1 4-ounce can mushroom stems and
pieces, drained
1 teaspoon dried Italian seasoning,
crushed
½ teaspoon fennel seeds, crushed
2 eggs
1 cup milk
1 tablespoon cooking oil
1 cup all-purpose flour
1½ cups broccoli florets
1 cup shredded mozzarella cheese
(4 ounces)
2 tablespoons grated Parmesan cheese

1. In an oven-safe large skillet, cook turkey, onion, and sweet pepper over medium heat until meat is brown and vegetables are tender. Drain off fat. Halve pepperoni slices. Stir pepperoni, pizza sauce, drained mushrooms, Italian seasoning, and fennel into meat mixture. Bring to boiling; reduce heat. Simmer, uncovered, for 10 minutes; stir occasionally.

2. Preheat oven to 400°F. In a bowl, combine eggs, milk, and oil. Whisk for 1 minute. Add flour; whisk 1 minute more or until smooth. Top meat mixture in skillet with broccoli; sprinkle with mozzarella cheese. Pour milk mixture over meat mixture in skillet; cover completely. Sprinkle with Parmesan cheese. Bake, uncovered, 25 to 30 minutes or until topping is puffed and golden brown. Serve immediately. Makes 6 servings.

Per serving: 379 cal., 18 g fat (7 g sat. fat), 145 mg chol., 818 mg sodium, 29 g carbo., 3 g fiber, 24 g pro.

Hamburger-Mash Surprise

Prep: 25 minutes **Bake:** 30 minutes
Stand: 5 minutes

¾   **cup shredded cheddar cheese
(3 ounces)**
2   **cups refrigerated mashed potatoes**
12   **ounces lean ground beef**
½   **cup chopped onion**
2   **cups sliced zucchini or yellow
summer squash**
1   **14½-ounce can diced tomatoes with
basil, oregano, and garlic, undrained**
½   **of a 6-ounce can (⅓ cup) no-sodium
tomato paste**
¼   **teaspoon ground black pepper
Paprika (optional)**

1. Preheat oven to 375°F. Stir ½ cup of the cheese into the potatoes; set aside. In a large oven-safe skillet,* cook ground beef and onion until meat is no longer pink and onion is tender. Drain off fat. Stir in squash, undrained tomatoes, tomato paste, and pepper. Bring to boiling. Remove from heat.

2. Spoon mashed potato mixture into a large reasealable plastic bag. Seal bag; snip off a corner of the plastic bag. Starting at one end of the skillet, pipe the potato mixture in rows across the top of meat mixture until meat mixture is covered. (Or spoon mashed potato mixture in mounds on top of hot mixture.) Sprinkle with remaining ¼ cup cheese. If desired, sprinkle potato mixture with paprika.

3. Bake, uncovered, for 30 minutes or until mashed potato top is golden brown. Let stand 5 minutes before serving. Makes 6 servings

*Tip: If you don't own an oven-safe skillet, transfer beef-vegetable mixture to a 2-quart casserole dish at the end of step 1. Continue as directed.

Per serving: 284 cal., 14 g fat (6 g sat. fat), 53 mg chol., 602 mg sodium, 21 g carbo., 2 g fiber, 18 g pro.

Crunchy Beef Wraps

Beef, cabbage, and corn come together in a savory
saucy mixture that is wrapped up in hot tortillas
and ready to go! Perfect for lunch, dinner,
or a little something in between.

Start to Finish: 20 minutes

8	8-inch flour tortillas
¾	pound lean ground beef
½	cup chopped red or green onion
2	cups packaged shredded cabbage with carrot (coleslaw mix)
1	cup frozen whole kernel corn
¼	cup bottled barbecue sauce
1	teaspoon toasted sesame oil
	Barbecue sauce (optional)

1. Preheat oven to 350°F. Stack tortillas and wrap in foil. Heat in the oven for 10 minutes. Meanwhile, in a large skillet, cook ground beef and onion over medium heat until meat is brown. Drain well. Stir in cabbage mix and corn. Cover; cook about 4 minutes or until vegetables are tender, stirring once. Stir in barbecue sauce and sesame oil. Cook and stir until heated through.

2. Spoon ½ cup filling onto each tortilla below center. Fold bottom edge up and over filling. Fold opposite sides in, just until they meet. Roll up from bottom. If desired, serve with additional barbecue sauce. Makes 4 servings (2 wraps each).

Per serving: 388 cal., 14 g total fat (5 g sat. fat), 54 mg chol., 409 mg sodium, 44 g carbo., 4 g fiber, 21 g pro.

Steak & Mushrooms

Start to Finish: 30 minutes

4 beef tenderloin steaks, cut 1 inch thick
(about 1 pound)
Salt and ground black pepper
1 tablespoon olive oil
1 tablespoon bottled minced garlic
½ cup chopped red onion
1 medium green sweet pepper, cut into
thin strips
1 8-ounce package presliced button
mushrooms (3 cups)
¼ cup onion-flavor beef broth or
beef broth
¼ cup whipping cream

1. Season meat lightly with salt and black pepper. In a large skillet, heat oil over medium-high heat until very hot. Add meat. Reduce heat to medium and cook for 10 to 13 minutes or to desired doneness, turning once. Transfer steaks to a serving platter; keep warm.

2. In the same skillet, cook and stir garlic, onion, sweet pepper, and mushrooms over medium-high heat about 6 minutes or until tender and most of the liquid has evaporated. Stir in broth and cream. Bring to boiling. Boil gently, uncovered, over medium heat about 4 minutes or until slightly thickened, stirring occasionally. Spoon mushroom mixture over steaks. Makes 4 servings.

Per serving: 298 cal., 18 g fat (7 g sat. fat), 90 mg chol., 191 mg sodium, 7 g carbo., 1 g fiber, 26 g pro.

Garlic-Mustard Steak Sandwiches

Prep: 15 minutes **Broil:** 13 minutes

4 to 6 hoagie rolls, split
2 tablespoons honey mustard
½ teaspoon dried thyme, crushed
1 clove garlic, minced
¼ teaspoon coarsely ground black pepper
1 to 1½ pounds beef flank steak
1 large red onion, sliced ½ inch thick
4 to 6 slices Swiss cheese
   Honey mustard (optional)

1. Preheat broiler. Place rolls, cut sides up, on a broiler pan. Broil 4 to 5 inches from heat for 1 to 2 minutes or until toasted. Set aside. In a bowl, mix mustard, thyme, garlic, and pepper.

2. Trim fat from steak. Score steak on both sides by making shallow diagonal cuts at 1-inch intervals in a diamond pattern. Brush both sides of steak with mustard mixture.

3. Place steak on broiler pan. Place onion slices beside steak. Broil 4 to 5 inches from heat for 12 to 17 minutes or until steak is desired doneness and onion is tender, turning steak and onion slices once.

4. Thinly slice steak at an angle across the grain. Separate onion slices into rings. Arrange steak strips, onion rings, and cheese on roll bottoms. Broil 1 minute or until cheese starts to melt. Add roll tops. If desired, pass additional mustard at the table. Makes 4 to 6 servings.

Per serving: 685 cal., 22 g fat (9 g sat. fat), 65 mg chol., 844 mg sodium, 78 g carbo., 4 g fiber, 43 g pro.

Microwave Meat Loaf with Tomato Sauce

Start to Finish: 40 minutes

1 8-ounce can pizza sauce
½ cup shredded zucchini
¼ cup rolled oats
¼ cup finely chopped onion
3 tablespoons snipped fresh parsley
1 teaspoon bottled minced garlic
1 teaspoon dried thyme, crushed
¼ teaspoon salt
¼ teaspoon ground black pepper
1 pound lean ground beef
½ pound uncooked ground turkey breast

1. In a bowl, combine 2 tablespoons of the pizza sauce, the zucchini, oats, onion, 2 tablespoons of the parsley, ½ teaspoon of the garlic, the thyme, salt, and pepper. Add beef and turkey; mix well. Shape meat mixture into a 7×4×2-inch loaf. Place loaf in a greased 9-inch microwave-safe pie plate or greased 2-quart square baking dish.

2. Cover meat loaf with waxed paper. Microwave on 100-percent power (high) for 5 minutes, turning plate once (if your microwave has a turntable, there is no need to turn the dish). Tilt dish slightly and spoon off drippings. In a small bowl, stir together the remaining pizza sauce, remaining 1 tablespoon parsley, and remaining ½ teaspoon garlic. Pour evenly over meat loaf. Cover with waxed paper; microwave on 50-percent power (medium) for 21 to 24 minutes or until cooked through (165°F), turning plate twice. Makes 6 servings.

Per serving: 243 cal., 12 g fat (5 g sat. fat), 66 mg chol., 380 mg sodium, 7 g carbo., 1 g fiber, 24 g pro.

Spiced Meatball Stew

Start to Finish: 30 minutes

1	16-ounce package frozen prepared Italian-style meatballs
3	cups green beans, cut into 1-inch pieces, or frozen cut green beans
2	cups peeled baby carrots
1	14½-ounce can beef broth
2	teaspoons Worcestershire sauce
½	to ¾ teaspoon ground allspice
1	piece (1-inch) stick cinnamon
2	14.5-ounce cans stewed tomatoes, undrained

1. In a Dutch oven, combine meatballs, green beans, carrots, beef broth, Worcestershire sauce, allspice, and cinnamon. Bring to boiling; reduce heat. Cover and simmer for 10 minutes. Stir in undrained tomatoes. Return to boiling; reduce heat. Cover; simmer 5 minutes more or until vegetables are tender. Remove cinnamon stick.

To Make Ahead: Prepare as directed. Freeze stew in an airtight freezer container. To reheat, place frozen stew in a large saucepan. Heat, covered, over medium heat about 30 minutes, stirring occasionally to break apart. Makes 10 cups.

Per serving: 233 cal., 13 g fat (6 g sat. fat), 37 mg chol., 938 mg sodium, 18 g carbo., 4 g fiber, 12 g pro.

Peppered Pork Chops & Pilaf

For a speedier supper, pick up assorted cut-up vegetables from the salad bar at your local supermarket.

Start to Finish: 25 minutes

4   3-ounce boneless pork loin chops, cut ¾ inch thick
2   teaspoons seasoned pepper blend
1   tablespoon olive oil
3   cups vegetables, such as broccoli, carrots, onions, and/or sweet peppers, cut into bite-size pieces
1   14-ounce can chicken broth
2   cups uncooked instant brown rice
¼   cup roasted red sweet pepper strips

1. Sprinkle both sides of chops with the seasoned pepper blend. In a large skillet, cook chops in hot oil over medium heat for 5 minutes. Turn chops. Cook for 3 to 7 minutes more or until slightly pink in the center and juices run clear (160°F). Remove chops from skillet; cover and keep warm.
2. Add vegetables, broth, and rice to skillet. Bring to boiling; reduce heat. Cover and simmer for 5 to 7 minutes or until rice is tender and vegetables are crisp-tender. Return pork chops to skillet; cover and heat through. Garnish with roasted red pepper strips. Makes 4 servings.

Per serving: 305 cal., 9 g fat (2 g sat. fat), 47 mg chol., 606 mg sodium, 32 g carbo., 4 g fiber, 24 g pro.

Glazed Teriyaki Pork Chops with Potatoes

Prep: 20 minutes   **Broil:** 9 minutes

4   boneless pork loin chops,
        cut ¾ inch thick
¼   cup bottled teriyaki glaze
12   ounces tiny new potatoes,
        quartered
1   tablespoon olive oil
1   tablespoon toasted sesame oil
¼   teaspoon salt
⅛   teaspoon ground black pepper
1   cup pea pods, halved lengthwise
        Bottled teriyaki glaze (optional)

1. Preheat broiler. Brush both sides of chops with the ¼ cup teriyaki glaze. Arrange chops on half of the broiler pan; set aside.

2. In a large bowl, toss potatoes with olive oil, sesame oil, salt, and pepper until coated. Arrange potatoes in a single layer next to chops.

3. Broil 4 inches from heat for 9 to 11 minutes or until pork is done (160°F) and potatoes are tender, turning pork and potatoes once.

4. Place pea pods in a large bowl. Add potatoes and toss to combine. Serve pork with potatoes and pea pods. If desired, pass additional teriyaki glaze. Makes 4 servings.

Per serving: 394 cal., 15 g fat (4 g sat. fat), 86 mg chol., 626 mg sodium, 23 g carbo., 2 g fiber, 38 g pro.

Oriental Pork & Vegetables

Prep: 10 minutes **Cook:** 8 minutes

6 ounces wide rice noodles or rice stick
   noodles, broken if desired
2 teaspoons sesame oil or olive oil
1 16-ounce package frozen stir-fry
   vegetables
1 12-ounce pork tenderloin, cut into
   ¼-inch-thick slices
¼ cup bottled teriyaki sauce
2 tablespoons plum sauce

1. Discard spice packet from ramen noodles, if using, or save for another use. Prepare noodles as directed on package. Set aside and keep warm.

2. Heat 12-inch nonstick skillet over medium-high heat. Add 1 teaspoon of the sesame oil. Cook and stir vegetables for 4 to 6 minutes or until crisp-tender. Remove vegetables from skillet. Set aside and keep warm.

3. Add remaining 1 teaspoon oil to skillet. Add pork and cook over medium-high heat for 4 to 6 minutes or until no longer pink, turning slices once. Stir in vegetables (drained if necessary), teriyaki sauce, and plum sauce; heat through. Toss pork mixture with noodles. Makes 4 servings.

Note: Find bottled teriyaki and plum sauces in the Asian aisle of your supermarket.

Per serving: 341 cal., 5 g fat (1 g sat. fat), 55 mg chol., 820 mg sodium, 48 g carbo., 3 g fiber, 22 g pro.

Vermicelli with Sausage & Spinach

Start to Finish: 25 minutes

1 pound cooked smoked sausage, halved lengthwise and cut into ½-inch-thick slices

¾ cup chopped onion (1 large)

2 large cloves garlic, chopped

2 teaspoons olive oil

2 14-ounce cans reduced-sodium chicken broth

¼ cup water

8 ounces dried vermicelli or angel hair pasta, broken in half

1 9-ounce package fresh prewashed baby spinach

¼ teaspoon freshly ground black pepper

⅓ cup whipping cream

1. In a 4-quart Dutch oven, cook sausage, onion, and garlic in hot oil over medium-high heat until onion is tender and sausage is lightly browned.

2. Add broth and the water; bring to boiling. Add pasta; cook for 3 minutes, stirring frequently. Add spinach and pepper; cook about 1 minute more or until spinach is wilted. Stir in cream. Serve immediately. Makes 4 to 6 servings.

Per serving: 782 cal., 47 g fat (18 g sat. fat), 104 mg chol., 2,556 mg sodium, 52 g carbo., 4 g fiber, 38 g pro.

Rotini-Kielbasa Skillet

Start to Finish: 35 minutes

2 cups dried rotini pasta (about 6 ounces)
1 tablespoon olive oil
1 medium onion, cut into wedges
2 cloves garlic, minced
1 pound cooked turkey kielbasa, halved lengthwise
    and sliced diagonally
1 small zucchini, coarsely chopped
1 yellow or orange sweet pepper, cut into small strips
1 teaspoon dried Italian seasoning, crushed
⅛ teaspoon cayenne pepper
8 roma tomatoes, cored and chopped (about 1 pound)

1. Cook pasta according to package directions; drain. Meanwhile, in a large skillet, heat oil over medium-high heat. Add onion and garlic; cook for 1 minute. Add kielbasa; cook and stir until onion is tender.

2. Add zucchini, sweet pepper, Italian seasoning, and cayenne pepper; cook and stir for 5 minutes. Stir in tomatoes and pasta. Heat through. Makes 6 servings.

Per serving: 267 cal., 10 g fat (2 g sat. fat), 47 mg chol., 677 mg sodium, 29 g carbo., 2 g fiber, 15 g pro.

Greek Skillet Supper

Prep: 20 minutes   **Cook:** 15 minutes

8 ounces lean ground lamb or
    ground beef
¾ cup chopped onion (1 large)
2 cloves garlic, minced
1 14½-ounce can beef broth
1½ cups dried medium shell macaroni
2 cups frozen mixed vegetables
1 14.5-ounce can tomatoes, undrained
    and cut up
2 tablespoons tomato paste
⅛ teaspoon ground cinnamon
⅛ teaspoon ground nutmeg
2 teaspoons snipped fresh
    marjoram
½ cup crumbled
    feta cheese
    (2 ounces)

1. In a large skillet, cook meat, onion, and garlic over medium heat until meat is brown and onion is tender. Drain off fat. Stir in broth and macaroni. Bring to boiling; reduce heat. Cover; simmer for 10 minutes.

2. Stir in vegetables, undrained tomatoes, tomato paste, cinnamon, and nutmeg. Return to boiling; reduce heat. Simmer, uncovered, 5 to 10 minutes or until vegetables are tender. Stir in marjoram. Sprinkle with feta and, if desired, additional marjoram. Makes 4 servings.

Per serving: 400 cal., 12 g fat (6 g sat. fat), 50 mg chol., 783 mg sodium, 51 g carbo., 3 g fiber, 22 g pro.

Pesto Chicken Breasts with Veggies

Prep: 15 minutes   **Broil:** 11 minutes

4   medium skinless, boneless chicken breast halves (about 1½ pounds)
¼   cup purchased basil pesto or Homemade Pesto (page 117)
1   medium zucchini or yellow summer squash
3   tablespoons olive oil
¼   teaspoon salt
⅛   teaspoon ground black pepper
1   8-ounce loaf or half of a 16-ounce loaf Italian bread, halved lengthwise
2   tablespoons grated Parmesan cheese

1. Preheat broiler. Brush both sides of chicken with pesto; arrange chicken on one end of a broiler pan. Broil 4 inches from heat for 5 minutes. Remove pan and turn chicken.

2. Meanwhile, cut zucchini lengthwise into ¼-inch-thick slices. Brush slices with 1½ tablespoons of the olive oil and sprinkle with salt and pepper. Arrange zucchini on pan next to chicken.

3. Broil for 5 to 8 minutes more or until chicken is done (170°F) and zucchini is tender, turning zucchini once. Transfer chicken and zucchini to a serving platter; cover to keep warm.

4. Brush cut sides of bread with the remaining 1½ tablespoons olive oil. Sprinkle with Parmesan. Place bread, cut sides up, on broiler pan. Broil 4 inches from heat for 1 to 2 minutes or until toasted. Cut bread crosswise into slices and serve with chicken and zucchini. Makes 4 servings.

Per serving: 531 cal., 25 g fat (3 g sat. fat), 86 mg chol., 713 mg sodium, 33 g carbo., 2 g fiber, 41 g pro.

Greek-Style Chicken Skillet

To add even more interest to this dish, choose a
flavored couscous mix in place of the plain couscous.

Start to Finish: 40 minutes

4   skinless, boneless chicken breast
    halves (about 1¼ pounds total)
    Salt and ground black pepper
1   tablespoon olive oil or cooking oil
1½ cups sliced zucchini (1 medium)
¾   cup chopped green sweet pepper
    (1 medium)
1   medium onion, sliced and separated
    into rings
2   cloves garlic, minced
⅛   teaspoon ground black pepper
¼   cup water
1   10.75-ounce can condensed
    tomato soup
2   cups hot cooked couscous or
    small pasta (orzo)
½   cup crumbled feta cheese (2 ounces)
    Lemon wedges

1. Season chicken with salt and black pepper to taste. In a large skillet, cook chicken in hot oil over medium heat for 12 to 15 minutes or until no longer pink (170°F), turning once. Remove chicken from skillet; keep warm.

2. Add zucchini, sweet pepper, onion, garlic, and black pepper to skillet. Add the water; reduce heat. Cover and cook for 5 minutes, stirring once or twice. Stir in soup. Bring to boiling; reduce heat. Cover and simmer for 5 minutes more, stirring once.

3. Return chicken to skillet, turning to coat. Serve with couscous, feta, and lemon wedges. Makes 4 servings.

Per serving: 401 cal., 10 g fat (4 g sat. fat), 99 mg chol., 827 mg sodium, 36 g carbo., 4 g fiber, 41 g pro.

Zesty Chicken with Black Beans & Rice

Start to Finish: 30 minutes

1	pound skinless, boneless chicken breast halves, cut into 2-inch pieces
2	tablespoons cooking oil
1	6- to 7.4-ounce package Spanish rice pilaf mix
1¾	cups water
1	15-ounce can black beans, rinsed and drained
1	14½-ounce can diced tomatoes, undrained
	Sour cream, sliced green onion, and lime wedges (optional)

1. In a large skillet, brown the chicken pieces in 1 tablespoon of the oil over medium heat. Remove from skillet; keep warm.

2. Add rice mix and remaining 1 tablespoon oil to skillet; cook and stir for 2 minutes. Stir in seasoning packet from rice mix, the water, drained beans, and undrained tomatoes; add chicken. Bring to boiling; reduce heat. Cover; simmer about 20 minutes or until rice is tender. If desired, serve with sour cream, green onion, and lime wedges. Makes 4 servings.

Per serving: 424 cal., 9 g fat (2 g sat. fat), 66 mg chol., 1,080 mg sodium, 52 g carbo., 6 g fiber, 37 g pro.

Shrimp and Couscous Jambalaya

Start to Finish: 25 minutes

12	ounces fresh medium shrimp, peeled and deveined
1	cup sliced celery (2 stalks)
¾	cup chopped green sweet pepper (1 medium)
½	cup chopped onion (1 medium)
½	teaspoon Cajun seasoning
¼	teaspoon dried oregano, crushed
2	tablespoons cooking oil
1	14-ounce can reduced-sodium chicken broth
1	cup quick-cooking couscous
½	cup chopped tomato (1 medium)
	Bottled hot pepper sauce and lemon wedges (optional)

1. Rinse shrimp and pat dry; set aside. In a large skillet, cook celery, sweet pepper, onion, Cajun seasoning, and oregano in oil over medium heat until tender. Add broth; bring to boiling. Stir in shrimp; remove from heat. Stir in couscous and tomato. Cover; let stand 5 minutes. If desired, serve with hot pepper sauce and lemon. Makes 4 servings.

Per serving: 317 cal., 8 g fat (1 g sat. fat), 98 mg chol., 462 mg sodium, 42 g carbo., 9 g fiber, 18 g pro.

Dilled Shrimp with Rice

Start to Finish: 25 minutes

1   **tablespoon butter**
1½ **cups shredded carrot (3 medium)**
1   **cup sugar snap peas**
⅓   **cup sliced green onion (3)**
1   **pound cooked, peeled, and**
     deveined shrimp
2   **cups cooked rice**
1   **teaspoon finely shredded lemon peel**
¾   **cup chicken or vegetable broth**
1   **tablespoon snipped fresh dill**
     or ½ teaspoon dried dillweed

1. In a large skillet, melt butter over medium heat. Add carrot, peas, and onion; cook and stir 2 to 3 minutes or until vegetables are crisp-tender.

2. Stir shrimp, rice, lemon peel, and broth into skillet; heat through. Stir in dill. Makes 4 servings.

Per serving: 291 cal., 5 g fat (2 g sat. fat), 230 mg chol., 495 mg sodium, 32 g carbo., 3 g fiber, 26 g pro.

Salmon with Tropical Rice

Prep: 15 minutes   **Bake:** 15 minutes

1   1½-pound fresh or frozen skinless
     salmon fillet, 1 inch thick
2   teaspoons olive oil
1   teaspoon lemon-pepper seasoning
1   8.8-ounce pouch cooked brown or
     white rice
1   medium mango, peeled, seeded,
     and chopped
1   tablespoon snipped fresh cilantro
1   teaspoon finely shredded lemon peel
     Lemon wedges (optional)
     Fresh cilantro sprigs (optional)

1. Preheat oven to 450°F. Thaw salmon, if frozen. Rinse fish and pat dry with paper towels. Place fish in a greased 3-quart rectangular baking dish. Drizzle olive oil over fish. Sprinkle with lemon-pepper seasoning.

2. In a medium bowl, stir together rice, mango, snipped cilantro, and lemon peel, breaking up rice with a spoon. Spoon rice mixture around fish. Bake, uncovered, for 15 minutes or until fish flakes easily when tested with a fork.

3. To serve, cut fish into 4 serving-size pieces. Serve fish on top of rice mixture. If desired, garnish each serving with lemon wedges and cilantro sprigs. Makes 4 servings.

Per serving: 462 cal., 22 g fat (4 g sat. fat), 99 mg chol., 104 mg sodium, 27 g carbo., 2 g fiber, 36 g pro.

Lemony Cod with Asparagus

Cod is a mild-flavored lean white fish. It is versatile in cooking and can be found either fresh or frozen in most supermarkets.

Prep: 10 minutes   **Broil:** 5 minutes

4	purchased soft breadsticks
2	tablespoons butter, melted
¼	teaspoon garlic salt
1	pound fresh or frozen cod fillets (½ inch thick)
12	ounces asparagus spears, trimmed
1	tablespoon lemon juice
½	teaspoon dried thyme, crushed
⅛	teaspoon ground black pepper
	Lemon wedges (optional)

1. Preheat broiler. Place breadsticks on broiler pan. Brush with 1 tablespoon of the melted butter and sprinkle with garlic salt. Broil 4 inches from heat for 1 to 2 minutes or until golden, turning once. Remove from pan and keep warm.

2. Arrange fish and asparagus in a single layer on the broiler pan. In a small bowl, stir together the remaining 1 tablespoon butter and lemon juice. Drizzle butter mixture over fish and brush over asparagus. Sprinkle fish and asparagus with thyme and pepper.

3. Broil 4 inches from heat for 4 to 6 minutes or until fish flakes easily when tested with a fork and asparagus is crisp-tender; turn asparagus once. Serve with breadsticks and, if desired, lemon wedges. Makes 4 servings.

Per serving: 293 cal., 8 g fat (4 g sat. fat), 64 mg chol., 454 mg sodium, 29 g carbo., 3 g fiber, 27 g pro.

Broiled Rice & Tuna Patties

Start to Finish: 30 minutes

1   6-ounce can tuna, drained and flaked
½   of an 8.8-ounce package cooked whole
      grain brown rice (1 cup)
½   cup finely shredded carrot (1 medium)
⅓   cup finely chopped onion (1 small)
⅓   cup chopped dry-roasted peanuts
¼   cup fine dry bread crumbs
1   tablespoon snipped fresh parsley
1   tablespoon milk
½   teaspoon dried dillweed
⅛   teaspoon ground black pepper
1   egg, lightly beaten
      Nonstick cooking spray
2   English muffins, split
4   ounces American cheese, sliced
      Pickle slices

1. Preheat broiler. In a large bowl, stir together tuna, rice, carrot, onion, peanuts, bread crumbs, parsley, milk, dillweed, and pepper. Add egg and mix well.

2. Shape mixture into four ¾-inch-thick patties. Lightly coat broiler pan with cooking spray and place patties on pan.

3. Broil 4 inches from the heat for 7 minutes. Turn patties over; add English muffin halves to rack. Broil about 2 minutes more or until patties are cooked through (160°F) and muffins are toasted.

4. Place a tuna patty on each muffin half. Top evenly with cheese. Broil for 1 to 2 minutes more or until cheese melts. Serve with pickle slices. Makes 4 servings.

Per serving: 147 cal., 5 g fat (2 g sat. fat), 22 mg chol., 265 mg sodium, 18 g carbo., 1 g fiber, 7 g pro.

A-to-Z Vegetable Soup
Start to Finish: 45 minutes

2 cups cut-up mixed fresh vegetables, such as zucchini, carrot, broccoli, and/or red sweet pepper
1 tablespoon cooking oil or olive oil
2 14-ounce cans reduced-sodium chicken broth
2 cloves garlic, minced
1 15-ounce can cannellini or Great Northern beans, rinsed and drained
½ cup dried alphabet-shape pasta or tiny shells
2 tablespoons fresh oregano leaves or 1 teaspoon dried oregano, crushed

1. In a large saucepan, cook vegetables in hot oil over medium-high heat about 5 minutes or until crisp-tender.

2. Add broth and garlic to vegetables in saucepan. Bring to boiling. Stir in drained beans, pasta, and dried oregano, if using. Return to boiling; reduce heat. Cover and simmer about 10 minutes or until pasta is just tender. Stir in fresh oregano leaves, if using. Makes 4 servings.

Per serving: 188 cal., 4 g fat (1 g sat. fat), 0 mg chol., 717 mg sodium, 33 g carbo., 6 g fiber, 12 g pro.

forget about it!

Your very own personal chef is ready and waiting inside the cupboard: your slow cooker. Simply toss in a few ingredients and turn the dial on your way out the door. When you return ... dinner's done!

Finger Lickin' BBQ Chicken

Prep: 10 minutes
Cook: 7 hours (low) or 3½ hours (high)
Slow cooker size: 3½- or 4-quart

2½ to 3 pounds chicken drumsticks, skinned, if desired
1 cup bottled barbecue sauce
⅓ cup apricot or peach preserves
2 teaspoons yellow mustard

1. Place chicken in a 3½- or 4-quart slow cooker. In a bowl, combine barbecue sauce, preserves, and mustard. Pour over chicken.
2. Cover; cook on low-heat setting for 7 to 8 hours or on high-heat setting for 3½ to 4 hours. Remove chicken to platter; cover. Transfer sauce mixture in cooker to a medium saucepan. Bring to boiling; reduce heat. Simmer, uncovered, for 10 minutes or until desired consistency. Serve sauce with chicken. Makes 4 to 6 servings.

Per serving: 456 cal., 17 g fat (4 g sat. fat), 154 mg chol., 963 mg sodium, 37 g carbo., 2 g fiber, 38 g pro.

Ginger Chicken

Prep: 20 minutes
Cook: 5 hours (low) or 2½ hours (high)
Slow cooker size: 4- or 5-quart

½ cup mango chutney
¼ cup bottled chili sauce
2 tablespoons quick-cooking tapioca
1½ teaspoons grated fresh ginger or ½ teaspoon ground ginger
12 chicken thighs, skinned (about 4 pounds)
    Hot cooked brown rice (optional)
    Sliced green onion (optional)

1. Using kitchen scissors, snip any large pieces of fruit in the chutney. In a 4- or 5-quart slow cooker, combine chutney, chili sauce, tapioca, and ginger. Add chicken, turning to coat.
2. Cover and cook on low-heat setting for 5 to 6 hours or on high-heat setting for 2½ to 3 hours. If desired, serve chicken over rice and sprinkle with green onion. Makes 6 servings.

Per serving: 264 cal., 7 g fat (2 g sat. fat), 143 mg chol., 494 mg sodium, 16 g carbo., 1 g fiber, 34 g pro.

Chicken & Noodles with Vegetables

Prep: 25 minutes

Cook: 8 hours (low) or 4 hours (high)

Slow cooker size: 3½ or 4-quart

2	cups sliced carrot (4 medium)
1½	cups chopped onion (3 medium)
1	cup sliced celery (2 stalks)
2	tablespoons snipped fresh parsley
1	bay leaf
3	medium chicken legs (drumstick-thigh portion) (about 2 pounds total), skinned
2	10.75-ounce cans reduced-fat and reduced-sodium condensed cream of chicken soup
1	teaspoon dried thyme, crushed
10	ounces dried wide noodles (about 5 cups)
1	cup frozen peas

1. In a 3½- or 4-quart slow cooker, stir together carrot, onion, celery, parsley, and bay leaf. Place chicken on top of vegetables. In a bowl, stir together soup, ½ cup *water*, thyme, and ¼ teaspoon *ground black pepper*. Pour over chicken in the slow cooker.

2. Cover and cook on low-heat setting for 8 to 9 hours or on high-heat setting for 4 to 4½ hours. Remove chicken from slow cooker; cool slightly. Discard bay leaf.

3. Cook noodles according to package directions; drain. Remove chicken from bones and shred or chop; discard bones. Stir chicken and peas into mixture in slow cooker. To serve, spoon over noodles. Makes 6 servings.

Per serving: 406 cal., 7 g fat (2 g sat. fat), 122 mg chol., 532 mg sodium, 56 g carbo., 5 g fiber, 26 g pro.

Chicken Curry Soup

Prep: 15 minutes **Cook:** 4 hours (low) or
2 hours (high) + 15 minutes (low)
Slow cooker size: 3½- or 4-quart

1	10¾-ounce can condensed cream of chicken soup
1	cup water
2	teaspoons curry powder
1¼	pounds skinless, boneless chicken thighs or breast halves, cut into ¾-inch pieces
2	cups sliced carrot (4 medium)
1	13½-ounce can unsweetened coconut milk
1	red sweet pepper, cut into thin, bite-size strips
½	cup sliced green onion (4)
	Chopped peanuts and/or toasted coconut (optional)

1. In a 3½- or 4-quart slow cooker, combine soup and water. Stir in curry powder. Add the chicken and carrot to cooker. Stir to mix.

2. Cover and cook on low-heat setting for 4 to 5 hours or on high-heat setting for 2 to 2½ hours. If using high-heat setting, turn to low. Stir in coconut milk, sweet pepper, and green onion. Cover and cook for 15 minutes more. If desired, garnish with peanuts and/or toasted coconut. Makes about 8 cups.

Per 1½ cups: 309 cal., 19 g fat (12 g sat. fat), 80 mg chol., 479 mg sodium, 13 g carbo., 2 g fiber, 22 g pro.

Southwestern White Chili

Prep: 20 minutes
Cook: 8 hours (low) or 4 hours (high)
Slow cooker size: 3½- to 5-quart

3   15½-ounce cans Great Northern beans,
    drained and rinsed
4   cups reduced-sodium chicken broth
3   cups chopped cooked chicken
2   4-ounce cans diced green chile pepper
1   cup chopped onion (2 medium)
4   cloves garlic, minced
2   teaspoons ground cumin
1   teaspoon dried oregano, crushed
¼   teaspoon cayenne pepper
2   cups shredded Monterey Jack cheese
    (8 ounces)
    Sour cream (optional)
    Fresh cilantro leaves (optional)

1. In a 3½- to 5-quart slow cooker, place beans, broth, chicken, chile pepper, onion, garlic, cumin, oregano, and cayenne. Stir to combine.

2. Cover and cook on low-heat setting for 8 to 10 hours or on high-heat setting for 4 to 5 hours. Stir in the cheese until melted. If desired, top servings with sour cream and cilantro. Makes 8 servings.

Per serving: 429 cal., 14 g total fat (7 g sat. fat), 72 mg chol., 570 mg sodium, 41 g carbo., 9 g fiber, 37 g pro.

Sausage-Corn Chowder

Prep: 15 minutes
Cook: 8 hours (low) or 4 hours (high)
Slow cooker size: 3½- to 5-quart

12 ounces cooked smoked turkey sausage, halved lengthwise and cut into ½-inch slices
3 cups frozen loose-pack diced hash brown potatoes with onions and peppers
2 medium carrots, coarsely chopped
2½ cups water
1 15- to 16½-ounce can no-salt cream-style corn
1 10¾-ounce can condensed golden mushroom soup
½ cup roasted red sweet pepper strips
1 teaspoon dried thyme, crushed

1. In a 3½- to 5-quart slow cooker, place sausage, frozen potatoes, and carrot. In a large bowl, stir together water, corn, soup, red pepper strips, and thyme. Add to cooker; stir to combine.

2. Cover and cook on low-heat setting for 8 to 10 hours or on high-heat setting for 4 to 5 hours. Makes 6 servings.

Per serving: 258 cal., 7 g total fat (2 g sat. fat), 40 mg chol., 893 mg sodium, 37 g carbo., 4 g fiber, 13 g pro.

Turkey & Wild Rice Amandine

Prep: 15 minutes

Cook: 6 hours (low) or 3 hours (high)

Slow cooker size: 4- or 5-quart

1   6-ounce jar whole mushrooms, drained

1   10.75-ounce can condensed cream of mushroom with roasted garlic soup

1   8-ounce can sliced water chestnuts, drained

1   cup wild rice, rinsed and drained

1   cup brown rice

½   cup chopped onion (1 medium)

¼   teaspoon ground black pepper

3   14-ounce cans reduced-sodium chicken broth

3   cups shredded cooked turkey or chicken (about 1 pound)

1   cup dairy sour cream

½   cup sliced almonds, toasted

1. In a 4- or 5-quart slow cooker, stir together drained mushrooms, soup, water chestnuts, uncooked wild rice, uncooked brown rice, onion, and ground black pepper. Stir in broth and ½ cup *water*.

2. Cover and cook on low-heat setting for 6 to 7 hours or on high-heat setting for 3 to 3½ hours. Stir in turkey. Top servings with sour cream and toasted almonds. Makes 10 servings.

Per serving: 340 cal., 12 g fat (4 g sat. fat), 42 mg chol., 604 mg sodium, 40 g carbo., 3 g fiber, 21 g pro.

Salsa Swiss Steak

Prep: 20 minutes

Cook: 9 hours (low) or 4½ hours (high)

Slow cooker size: 3½- or 4-quart

2   pounds boneless beef round steak, cut 1 inch thick

1   to 2 large red or green sweet peppers, cut into bite-size strips

1   medium onion, sliced

1   10.75-ounce can condensed cream of mushroom soup

1   cup bottled salsa

2   tablespoons all-purpose flour

1   teaspoon dry mustard

1. Trim fat from meat. Cut meat into 6 serving-size pieces. In a 3½- or 4-quart slow cooker, place meat, sweet pepper, and onion. In a medium bowl, stir together soup, salsa, flour, and mustard. Pour into slow cooker.

2. Cover and cook on low-heat setting for 9 to 10 hours or on high-heat setting for 4½ to 5 hours. Makes 6 servings.

Per serving: 251 cal., 6 g fat (2 g sat. fat), 65 mg chol., 574 mg sodium, 10 g carbo., 1 g fiber, 37 g pro.

Greek-Style Beef & Vegetables

Prep: 15 minutes   **Cook:** 6 hours (low) +
30 minutes (high) or 3 hours (high)
Slow cooker size: 3½- or 4-quart

1	**pound ground beef**
1	**cup chopped onion (1 large)**
3	**cloves garlic, minced**
1	**14-ounce can beef broth**
3	**cups frozen mixed vegetables**
1	**14.5-ounce can diced tomatoes, undrained**
3	**tablespoons tomato paste**
1	**teaspoon dried oregano, crushed**
⅛	**teaspoon ground cinnamon**
⅛	**teaspoon ground nutmeg**
2	**cups dried medium shell macaroni**
1	**cup shredded Monterey Jack or crumbled feta cheese (4 ounces)**

1. In a large skillet, cook ground beef, onion, and garlic over medium heat until meat is brown and onion is tender. Drain off fat. Place in a 3½- or 4-quart slow cooker. Stir in broth, mixed vegetables, undrained tomatoes, tomato paste, oregano, cinnamon, and nutmeg.

2. Cover and cook on low-heat setting for 6 to 8 hours or on high-heat setting for 3 to 4 hours. If using low-heat setting, turn to high-heat setting. Add pasta. Cover and cook about 30 minutes more or until pasta is tender. Top each serving with cheese. Makes 6 servings.

Per serving: 446 cal., 16 g fat (7 g sat. fat), 64 mg chol., 539 mg sodium, 46 g carbo., 5 g fiber, 28 g pro.

Saucy Cheeseburger Sandwiches

Prep: 20 minutes
Cook: 6 hours (low) or 3 hours (high)
Slow cooker size: 3½- to 4-quart

2½ pounds lean ground beef
1 10.75-ounce can condensed
    tomato soup
1 cup finely chopped onion (2 medium)
2 tablespoons tomato paste
1 tablespoon Worcestershire sauce
1 tablespoon yellow mustard
2 teaspoons dried Italian seasoning,
    crushed
2 cloves garlic, minced
12 to 15 hamburger buns, split and toasted
12 to 15 slices American cheese
    (9 to 12 ounces)

1. In a large skillet, brown ground beef over medium heat. Drain off fat. Transfer meat to a 3½- or 4-quart slow cooker. Stir in soup, onion, ¼ cup *water*, the tomato paste, Worcestershire sauce, mustard, Italian seasoning, ¼ teaspoon *ground black pepper*, and the garlic.

2. Cover and cook on low-heat setting for 6 to 8 hours or on high-heat setting for 3 to 4 hours. Serve on hamburger buns topped with sliced cheese. Makes 12 to 15 servings.

Per serving: 382 cal., 17 g fat (8 g sat. fat), 80 mg chol., 734 mg sodium, 28 g carbo., 1 g fiber, 26 g pro.

French Dip with Mushrooms

Prep: 25 minutes **Cook:** 8 hours (low)
or 4 hours (high) **Stand:** 10 minutes
Slow cooker size: 3½- to 6-quart

1 **3- to 3½-pound beef bottom round or rump roast**
  Nonstick cooking spray
4 **portobello mushrooms (3 to 4 inches in diameter)**
1 **14-ounce can beef broth seasoned with onion**
1 **large red onion, cut into ½-inch slices (optional)**
8 **hoagie buns, split and toasted**

1. Trim fat from meat. If necessary, cut roast to fit into a 3½- to 6-quart slow cooker. Lightly coat a large skillet with cooking spray; heat over medium heat. Brown meat on all sides in hot skillet. Place meat in the prepared cooker.

2. Clean mushrooms; remove and discard stems. Cut mushrooms into ¼-inch slices. Add to cooker. Pour broth over meat and mushrooms.

3. Cover and cook on low-heat setting for 8 to 9 hours or on high-heat setting for 4 to 4½ hours. Remove meat from cooker; cover and let stand for 10 minutes.

4. Meanwhile, using a slotted spoon, remove mushrooms; set aside. Thinly slice meat. Arrange meat, mushrooms, and, if desired, onion on toasted buns. Pour cooking juice into a measuring cup; skim off fat. Drizzle a little of the juice onto sandwiches; pour remaining juice into bowls for dipping. Makes 8 sandwiches.

Per sandwich: 646 cal., 17 g fat (4 g sat. fat), 98 mg chol., 970 mg sodium, 74 g carbo., 4 g fiber, 50 g pro.

Easy Cheesy Sloppy Joes

Prep: 25 minutes
Cook: 4½ hours (low) or 2 hours (high)
Slow cooker size: 3½- or 4-quart

3   pounds lean ground beef
1   cup chopped onion (1 large)
2   10¾-ounce cans condensed fiesta
     nacho cheese soup
¾   cup ketchup
18 hamburger or cocktail buns,
     split and toasted
     Pickles (optional)

1. In a 12-inch skillet or Dutch oven, cook ground beef and onion over medium heat until meat is browned and onion is tender. Drain off fat. In a 3½- or 4-quart slow cooker, combine meat mixture, soup, and ketchup.

2. Cover and cook on low-heat setting for 4½ hours or on high-heat setting for 2 hours. Serve meat mixture on toasted buns. If desired, garnish with pickles. Makes 18 servings.

Per serving: 288 cal., 11 g fat (4 g sat. fat), 50 mg chol., 563 mg sodium, 27 g carbo., 1 g fiber, 19 g pro.

Pesto Meatball Stew

Prep: 10 minutes
Cook: 5 hours (low) or 2½ hours (high)
Slow cooker size: 3½- or 4-quart

1   16-ounce package frozen cooked
    Italian-style meatballs (32),
    thawed
2   14½-ounce cans Italian-style stewed
    tomatoes, undrained
1   15- to 19-ounce can white kidney
    (cannellini) beans, rinsed
    and drained
¼   cup purchased basil pesto
½   cup finely shredded Parmesan cheese
    (2 ounces)

1. In a 3½- or 4-quart slow cooker, combine
the meatballs, undrained tomatoes, drained
beans, ½ cup *water*, and the pesto.
2. Cover and cook on low-heat setting for 5 to
7 hours or on high-heat setting for 2½ to
3½ hours. Ladle soup into bowls. Sprinkle with
Parmesan cheese. Makes about 7 cups.

Per 1 cup: 408 cal., 27 g fat (10 g sat. fat), 34 mg chol.,
1,201 mg sodium, 24 g carbo., 6 g fiber, 17 g pro.

Beefy Minestrone

Prep: 20 minutes
Cook: 8 hours (low) or 4 hours (high)
Slow cooker size: 3½- to 5-quart

1   pound lean ground beef
1   14-ounce can reduced-sodium
      beef broth
1¼   cups water
1   10-ounce package frozen mixed
      vegetables
1   14.5-ounce can whole peeled
      tomatoes, undrained, cut up
1   10.75-ounce can reduced-sodium and
      reduced-fat condensed tomato soup
1   tablespoon dried minced onion
1   teaspoon dried Italian seasoning,
      crushed
¼   teaspoon garlic powder

1. In a large skillet, cook beef until brown.
Drain off fat. Transfer meat to a 3½- to 5-quart
slow cooker. Stir in broth, water, vegetables,
tomatoes, tomato soup, dried onion, Italian seasoning, and garlic powder.
2. Cover and cook on low-heat setting for 8 to
10 hours or on high-heat setting for 4 to 5 hours.
If desired, top each serving with *crackers*.
Makes 4 to 6 servings.

Per serving: 346 cal., 15 g total fat (6 g sat. fat),
71 mg chol., 684 mg sodium, 26 g carbo., 4.5 g fiber,
27 g pro.

Slow Cooker Chili

This easy chili gets its zesty flavor from salsa.

Prep: 25 minutes
Cook: 10 hours (low) or 5 hours (high)
Slow cooker size: 4- or 5-quart

1½	pounds ground beef
2	15-ounce cans red kidney beans or small red beans, rinsed and drained
2	14.5-ounce cans Mexican-style stewed tomatoes, undrained
1	16-ounce jar salsa
¾	cup chopped onion (1 large)
¾	cup chopped green sweet pepper (1 medium)
1	clove garlic, minced
	Desired toppers, such as sliced green onion, corn chips, chopped tomato, and/or shredded cheddar cheese

1. In a large skillet, brown ground beef over medium heat. Drain off fat. Transfer meat to a 4- or 5-quart slow cooker. Add drained beans, undrained tomatoes, salsa, onion, sweet pepper, and garlic to beef in cooker; stir to combine.

2. Cover and cook on low-heat setting for 10 to 12 hours or on high-heat setting for 5 to 6 hours. Serve chili with desired toppers. Makes 6 servings.

Per serving: 496 cal., 26 g fat (10 g sat. fat), 74 mg chol., 1,270 mg sodium, 40 g carbo., 10 g fiber, 32 g pro.

Taco Chili

Prep: 20 minutes
Cook: 4 hours (low) or 2 hours (high)
Slow cooker size: $3\frac{1}{2}$- or 4-quart

1 **pound lean ground beef**
2 **15-ounce cans seasoned tomato sauce with diced tomatoes**
1 **15-ounce can chili beans with chili gravy**
1 **15-ounce can hominy or whole kernel corn, undrained**
1 **1.25-ounce envelope taco seasoning mix**
   Dairy sour cream (optional)
   Shredded cheddar cheese (optional)

1. In a large skillet, brown ground beef over medium heat. Drain off fat.

2. In a $3\frac{1}{2}$- or 4-quart slow cooker, combine the meat, tomato sauce, beans with chili gravy, undrained hominy, and taco seasoning mix.

3. Cover and cook on low-heat setting for 4 to 6 hours or on high-heat setting for 2 to 3 hours. If desired, top each serving with sour cream and cheddar cheese. Makes 8 cups.

Per $1\frac{1}{2}$ cups: 477 cal., 18 g fat (6 g sat. fat), 71 mg chol., 1,998 mg sodium, 49 g carbo., 12 g fiber, 35 g pro.

Spaghetti Sauce with Italian Sausage

Prep: 15 minutes
Cook: 8 hours (low) or 4 hours (high)
Slow cooker size: 3½- or 4-quart

½   pound bulk Italian sausage
¼   pound lean ground beef
½   cup chopped onion
1   clove garlic, minced
1   14.5-ounce can diced tomatoes, undrained
1   8-ounce can reduced-sodium tomato sauce
1   4-ounce can sliced mushrooms, drained
½   cup chopped green sweet pepper (1 small)
2   tablespoons quick-cooking tapioca
1   bay leaf
1   teaspoon dried Italian seasoning, crushed
⅛   teaspoon ground black pepper
    Dash salt
    Hot cooked spaghetti

1. In a large skillet, brown sausage, ground beef, onion, and garlic over medium heat until onion is tender. Drain off fat.

2. In a 3½- or 4-quart slow cooker, stir together undrained tomatoes, tomato sauce, drained mushrooms, sweet pepper, tapioca, bay leaf, Italian seasoning, black pepper, and a dash salt. Stir in meat mixture. Cover and cook on low heat setting for 8 to 10 hours or on high heat setting for 4 to 5 hours. Discard bay leaf. Serve sauce over hot cooked spaghetti. If desired, sprinkle with *fresh oregano*. Makes 4 or 5 servings.

Per serving: 481 cal., 24 g total fat (9 g sat. fat), 79 mg chol., 788 mg sodium, 40 g carbo., 5 g fiber, 25 g pro.

Cuban Pork Sandwich

Prep: 30 minutes
Cook: 10 hours (low) or 5 hours (high)
Stand: 15 minutes
Slow cooker size: 3½- or 4-quart

1	3- to 3½-pound boneless pork shoulder roast
¾	cup reduced-sodium chicken broth
1	medium onion, cut into wedges
1	cup packed cilantro leaves (1 bunch)
2	tablespoons vinegar
4	cloves garlic, minced
1	teaspoon salt
1	teaspoon ground cumin
1	teaspoon dried oregano, crushed
¼	teaspoon ground black pepper
2	red onions, thinly sliced
1	tablespoon cooking oil
¼	cup lime juice
8	ciabatta or French rolls, split

1. Trim fat from roast; set aside. In a 3½- or 4-quart slow cooker, stir together broth, onion wedges, cilantro, ¼ cup *water*, vinegar, garlic, salt, cumin, oregano, and pepper. Add meat to slow cooker; spoon mixture over meat. Cover and cook on low-heat setting for 10 to 12 hours or on high-heat setting for 5 to 6 hours.

2. Just before serving, in a skillet, cook red onion in hot oil over medium-high heat until tender but not brown. Carefully add lime juice. Cook and stir until lime juice is evaporated.

3. Transfer meat to a cutting board; cool meat slightly. Using two forks, shred meat; discard fat. Serve meat and red onions on rolls. Makes 8 servings.

Per serving: 381 cal., 13 g fat (4 g sat. fat), 110 mg chol., 721 mg sodium, 25 g carbo., 2 g fiber, 38 g pro.

Pork Chops O'Brien

Prep: 20 minutes
Cook: 7 hours (low) or 3 ½ hours (high)
Slow cooker size: 3½- or 4-quart

5   cups loose-pack frozen diced hash brown potatoes with onion and peppers, thawed
1   10.75-ounce can reduced-fat and reduced-sodium condensed cream of mushroom soup
½   cup bottled roasted red sweet peppers, drained and chopped
½   cup dairy sour cream
½   cup shredded Colby and Monterey Jack cheese (2 ounces)
¼   teaspoon ground black pepper
4   pork loin chops, cut ¾ inch thick
1   tablespoon cooking oil
1   2.8-ounce can french-fried onions

1. Stir together thawed hash brown potatoes, soup, roasted sweet pepper, sour cream, cheese, and ground black pepper. Transfer mixture to 3½- or 4-quart slow cooker.
2. Trim fat from chops. In a skillet, brown chops in hot oil over medium heat; drain fat. Place chops on hash brown mixture in cooker.
3. Cover and cook on low-heat setting for 7 to 9 hours or on high-heat setting for 3½ to 4½ hours. Sprinkle each serving with french-fried onions. Makes 4 servings.

Per serving: 670 cal., 29 g fat (9 g sat. fat), 92 mg chol., 639 mg sodium, 64 g carbo., 4 g fiber, 37 g pro.

Cajun Pork

Prep: 20 minutes   **Cook:** 7 hours (low) + 30 minutes (high) or 4 hours (high)
Slow cooker size: 3½- or 4-quart

    Nonstick cooking spray
2½   to 3 pounds boneless pork shoulder, trimmed and cut into 1-inch cubes
2   medium yellow sweet peppers, cut into 1-inch pieces
1   tablespoon Cajun seasoning
1   14½-ounce can diced tomatoes with green pepper and onion, undrained
1   16-ounce package frozen cut okra
1   6-ounce package quick-cooking brown rice, cooked according to package directions
    Bottled hot pepper sauce (optional)

1. Lightly coat a large skillet with nonstick cooking spray. Heat over medium heat. In hot skillet, cook meat, half at a time, until browned; drain off fat.
2. In a 3½- or 4-quart slow cooker, place meat and sweet pepper. Sprinkle with Cajun seasoning. Top with undrained tomatoes. Cover; cook on low-heat setting for 7 to 8 hours or on high-heat setting for 3½ to 4 hours.
3. If using low-heat setting, turn to high-heat setting. Stir in frozen okra. Cover and cook 30 minutes more. Serve over rice. If desired, pass hot pepper sauce. Makes 6 to 8 servings.

Per serving: 233 cal., 8 g fat (3 g sat. fat), 77 mg chol., 444 mg sodium, 15 g carbo., 4 g fiber, 25 g pro.

Shredded Pork Tacos

Prep: 30 minutes
Cook: 8 hours (low) or 4 hours (high)
Slow cooker size: 3½- or 4-quart

1   2½- to 3-pound boneless pork
    shoulder roast
1   cup chicken broth
½   cup enchilada sauce or bottled salsa
4   8-inch soft flour tortillas or taco shells
    Assorted toppers, such as shredded
    lettuce, finely shredded Mexican-
    blend cheese, chopped tomato, sliced
    pitted ripe olives, and/or chopped
    avocado
    Dairy sour cream (optional)

1. Trim fat from pork. If necessary, cut pork to fit
in a 3½- or 4-quart slow cooker. Place pork in
cooker. Add broth. Cover; cook on low-heat setting
for 8 to 10 hours or on high-heat setting for 4 to
5 hours. Remove meat from cooker; discard broth.
Using two forks, shred meat, discarding any fat.
Reserve 2 cups of the meat. (Place remaining meat
in an airtight container for another use; refrigerate
up to 3 days or freeze up to 3 months.)

2. In a medium saucepan, combine reserved
2 cups meat and the enchilada sauce. Cover and
cook over medium-low heat about 10 minutes or
until heated through, stirring occasionally.
Meanwhile, warm flour tortillas according to
package directions.

3. To assemble tacos, place pork mixture in
center of warm tortillas or in taco shells. Top as
desired with lettuce, cheese, tomato, olives,
and/or avocado. If desired, serve with sour cream.
Makes 4 servings.

Per serving: 616 cal., 31 g fat (10 g sat. fat), 202 mg
chol., 846 mg sodium, 20 g carbo., 3 g fiber, 61 g pro.

White & Green Chili

Prep: 20 minutes
Cook: 7 hours (low) or 3½ hours (high)
Slow cooker size: 3½- or 4-quart

1½   **pounds lean ground pork**
1   **cup chopped onion**
2   **15-ounce cans Great Northern beans, rinsed and drained**
1   **16-ounce jar green salsa**
1   **14-ounce can chicken broth**
1½   **teaspoons ground cumin**
2   **tablespoons snipped fresh cilantro**
⅓   **cup dairy sour cream (optional)**
  Fresh cilantro sprigs (optional)

1. In a large skillet, cook ground pork and onion over medium heat until meat is brown and onion is tender. Drain off fat. Transfer meat mixture to a 3½- or 4-quart slow cooker. Stir in drained beans, salsa, broth, and cumin.

2. Cover and cook on low-heat setting for 7 to 8 hours or on high-heat setting for 3½ to 4 hours.

3. Stir in the snipped cilantro. If desired, top each serving with sour cream and garnish with a cilantro sprig. Makes 6 servings.

Per serving: 348 cal., 9 g fat (4 g sat. fat), 53 mg chol., 613 mg sodium, 39 g carbo., 9 g fiber, 26 g pro.

Ribs & Kraut

Prep: 20 minutes
Cook: 7 hours (low) or 3½ hours (high)
Slow cooker size: 4- or 4½-quart

1   14-ounce can sauerkraut, drained
1   large sweet onion, sliced (2 cups)
2   medium tart cooking apples, peeled,
    cored, and sliced (about 2 cups)
2   pounds boneless pork country-
    style ribs
1   cup apple juice
    Snipped fresh chives

1. In a 4- or 4½-quart slow cooker, place sauerkraut, onion, and apple. Top with pork. Pour apple juice over all.

2. Cover and cook on low-heat setting for 7 to 8 hours or on high-heat setting for 3½ to 4 hours. Serve with a slotted spoon. Sprinkle with chives. Makes 6 to 8 servings.

Per serving: 312 cal., 12 g fat (4 g sat. fat), 96 mg chol., 541 mg sodium, 19 g carbo., 4 g fiber, 30 g pro.

Orange Sesame Ribs

Prep: 15 minutes
Cook: 8 hours (low) or 4 hours (high)
Slow cooker size: 3$\frac{1}{2}$- or 4-quart

2$\frac{1}{2}$ to 3 pounds boneless country-style
    pork ribs
    Nonstick cooking spray
1 10-ounce jar orange marmalade
1 7$\frac{1}{4}$-ounce jar hoisin sauce
3 cloves garlic, minced
1 teaspoon toasted sesame oil

1. Trim fat from ribs. Lightly coat a large skillet with cooking spray; heat over medium heat. In hot skillet, brown ribs on all sides. Drain off fat. Place ribs in a 3$\frac{1}{2}$- or 4-quart slow cooker.

2. In a medium bowl, stir together marmalade, hoisin sauce, garlic, and sesame oil. Pour over ribs in cooker; stir to coat meat with sauce.

3. Cover and cook on low-heat setting for 8 to 10 hours or on high-heat setting for 4 to 5 hours. Transfer meat to a serving platter. Skim fat from sauce. Spoon some sauce over the meat. Pass remaining sauce. Makes 4 servings.

Per serving: 532 cal., 16 g fat (5 g sat. fat), 101 mg chol., 696 mg sodium, 66 g carbo., 0 g fiber, 33 g pro.

Cajun Shrimp & Rice

Prep: 20 minutes   **Cook:** 5 hours (low)
or 3 hours (high) + 15 minutes (high)
Slow cooker size: $3\frac{1}{2}$- or 4-quart

2   14.5-ounce cans diced tomatoes,
     undrained
1   14-ounce can reduced-sodium
     chicken broth
1   cup chopped onion (1 large)
1   cup chopped green sweet pepper
     (1 large)
1   6-ounce package long grain and
     wild rice mix
$\frac{1}{4}$ cup water
$\frac{1}{2}$ teaspoon Cajun seasoning
2   cloves garlic, minced
1   pound cooked, peeled, and deveined
     shrimp
     Bottled hot pepper sauce (optional)

1. In a $3\frac{1}{2}$- or 4-quart slow cooker, stir together undrained tomatoes, chicken broth, onion, sweet pepper, rice mix (including seasoning packet), water, Cajun seasoning, and garlic.

2. Cover and cook on low-heat setting 5 to 6 hours or on high-heat setting 3 to $3\frac{1}{2}$ hours. If using low-heat setting, turn to high-heat setting. Stir in shrimp. Cover and cook 15 minutes more. If desired, serve with hot pepper sauce. Makes 6 servings.

Per serving: 219 cal., 1 g total fat (0 g sat. fat), 148 mg chol., 1,001 mg sodium, 32 g carbo., 4 g fiber, 21 g pro.

Cheesy Mexican-Style Vegetable Soup

Prep: 15 minutes
Cook: 6 hours (low) or 3 hours (high)
Slow cooker size: 3½- or 4-quart

2   cups chopped zucchini
1   medium red sweet pepper, chopped
1   medium onion, chopped
1   15-ounce can black beans, rinsed
    and drained
1   10-ounce package frozen whole
    kernel corn, thawed
1   14.5-ounce can diced tomatoes with
    green chiles, undrained
1   16-ounce jar cheddar cheese
    pasta sauce
1   cup reduced-sodium chicken broth
    or vegetable broth
    Coarsely crushed tortilla chips and
    sliced fresh jalapeño pepper
    (optional)

1. In a 3½- or 4-quart slow cooker, place
zucchini, sweet pepper, onion, drained beans,
and corn. Pour undrained tomatoes over
vegetables and beans. Combine cheese sauce
and broth; pour over all.
2. Cover and cook on low-heat setting for 6 to
8 hours or on high-heat setting for 3 to 4 hours.
Ladle soup into bowls and, if desired, top with
crushed tortilla chips and jalapeño slices.
Makes 5 to 6 servings.

Per serving: 289 cal., 14 g fat (5 g sat. fat), 35 mg
chol., 1,381 mg sodium, 36 g carbo., 7 g fiber, 12 g pro.

Barley Vegetable Soup

Prep: 25 minutes
Cook: 8 hours (low) or 4 hours (high)
Slow cooker size: 3½- to 5-quart

1   15-ounce can red beans, rinsed
    and drained
1   10-ounce package frozen whole
    kernel corn
½   cup medium pearl barley
1   14½-ounce can no-salt stewed
    tomatoes, undrained
2   cups sliced fresh mushrooms
1   cup chopped onion (2 medium)
½   cup coarsely chopped carrot
    (1 medium)
½   cup coarsely chopped celery (1 stalk)
3   cloves garlic, minced
2   teaspoons dried Italian seasoning,
    crushed
¼   teaspoon ground black pepper
5   cups reduced-sodium vegetable
    broth or chicken broth

1. In a 3½- to 5-quart slow cooker, place
drained beans, corn, barley, undrained
tomatoes, mushrooms, onion, carrot, celery,
garlic, Italian seasoning, and pepper. Pour broth
over the top.
2. Cover and cook on low-heat setting for 8 to
10 hours or on high-heat setting for 4 to 5 hours.
Makes 6 servings.

Per serving: 216 cal., 1 g total fat, 0 mg chol., 797 mg
sodium, 15 g carbo., 9.5 g fiber, 11 g pro.

mmm...
just like
mom's
{but quicker}

mmm ... just

Take the work out of your favorite comfort food recipes with these trusty shortcuts. But shhh ... don't tell Mom.

like mom's
{but quicker}

Easy Chicken & Dumplings

This speedy version of the down-home classic requires just six ingredients and only a few minutes to cook.

Prep: 25 minutes **Cook:** 15 minutes

1	2- to 2.5-pound purchased roasted chicken
1	16-ounce package frozen mixed vegetables
1¼	cups reduced-sodium chicken broth or water
1	10.75-ounce can reduced-fat, reduced-sodium condensed cream of chicken soup
⅛	teaspoon ground black pepper
1	11.5-ounce package refrigerated corn bread twists

1. Remove skin and bones from chicken and discard. Chop or shred chicken (you should have 3½ to 4 cups chopped chicken). In a large saucepan, stir together chicken, frozen vegetables, broth, soup, and pepper. Bring to boiling; reduce heat. Cover and simmer about 15 minutes or until vegetables are tender.

2. Meanwhile, remove corn bread twists from package; cut along perforations. Lay twists on a baking sheet; roll two twists together to make a spiral. Repeat with remaining twists. Bake according to package directions.

3. To serve, spoon chicken mixture into bowls and serve with corn bread spirals. Makes 4 to 6 servings.

Per serving: 650 cal., 30 g fat (8 g sat. fat), 107 mg chol., 1,399 mg sodium, 57 g carbo., 5 g fiber, 42 g pro.

mom's way:
dicing fresh vegetables, preparing made-from-scratch dumplings, and whisking together a homemade gravy

your way:
tossing in frozen veggies, popping open a package of refrigerated bread twists, and creating a gravy from a creamy canned soup

mom's way:
whipping together a concoction of bread crumbs and salt, then deep-frying chicken pieces on the stove

your way:
crushing scoops of cornflakes, mixing in herbs, then baking in the oven for a lower-fat variety

Oven-Fried Buttermilk Chicken

Cornflakes add crunch to this "fried" chicken without the mess and fat from actually frying it.

Prep: 20 minutes   **Bake:** 45 minutes

1	cup buttermilk or milk
2	eggs
½	teaspoon salt
2	cups crushed cornflakes
1	teaspoon dried oregano, crushed
3	pounds meaty chicken pieces (breast halves, thighs, and drumsticks), skinned, if desired
¼	cup butter, melted

1. Preheat oven to 400°F. In a shallow dish, beat together buttermilk, eggs, and salt with a fork until combined. In another dish, stir together crushed cornflakes and oregano. Dip chicken pieces, one at a time, into buttermilk mixture, then into cornflake mixture to coat. Arrange pieces in a lightly greased 13×9×2-inch baking pan so pieces do not touch. Drizzle with butter.

2. Bake, uncovered, for 45 to 50 minutes or until chicken pieces are tender and no longer pink (170°F for breast and 180°F for thighs or drumsticks). Makes 6 servings.

Per serving: 408 cal., 17 g fat (7 g sat. fat), 184 mg chol., 611 mg sodium, 26 g carbo., 36 g pro.

Mock Chicken Potpie

Prep: 15 minutes **Bake:** 6 minutes

Cook: 10 minutes

½ of a 15-ounce package rolled refrigerated unbaked piecrust (1 crust), room temperature

1 10.75-ounce can condensed cream of onion soup

1⅓ cups low-fat milk

3 ounces reduced-fat cream cheese, cut up

½ teaspoon dried sage, crushed

¼ teaspoon ground black pepper

1½ cups chopped cooked chicken

1 10-ounce package frozen mixed vegetables

½ cup uncooked instant rice

1. Preheat oven to 450°F. Unroll piecrust. Using a pizza cutter or sharp knife, cut piecrust into strips about ½ to 1 inch wide. Place strips on a baking sheet. Bake for 6 to 8 minutes or until golden.

2. Meanwhile, for filling, in a large saucepan, combine soup, milk, cream cheese, sage, and pepper. Cook and stir over medium-high heat until cream cheese melts. Stir in chicken, frozen vegetables, and rice. Bring to boiling; reduce heat. Cover; simmer 10 minutes or until vegetables and rice are tender. Transfer chicken mixture to a serving dish. Top with pastry strips. Makes 4 servings.

Per serving: 587 cal., 27 g fat (12 g sat. fat), 86 mg chol., 999 mg sodium, 58 g carbo., 2 g fiber, 25 g pro.

mom's way:

roasting her own chicken, making pastry and sauce from scratch, using fresh vegetables

your way:

starting with ready-made piecrust, using deli-roasted chicken and canned soup, adding frozen cut vegetables

Chicken & Noodles

Prep: 15 minutes   **Cook:** 30 minutes

1   12-ounce package frozen noodles
     (about 3 cups)
3   cups reduced-sodium chicken broth
2   cups sliced carrot (4 medium)
1   cup chopped onion (1 large)
½   cup sliced celery (1 stalk)
2   cups milk
1   cup frozen peas
3   tablespoons all-purpose flour
½   teaspoon salt
⅛   teaspoon ground black pepper
2   cups chopped cooked chicken
     Coarsely ground black pepper
     (optional)

1. In a 4-quart Dutch oven, combine noodles, broth, carrots, onion, and celery. Bring to boiling; reduce heat. Cover and simmer about 20 minutes or until noodles and vegetables are tender. Stir in 1½ cups of the milk and the peas.

2. In a small bowl, stir together the remaining ½ cup milk, the flour, salt, and ⅛ teaspoon pepper. Whisk until smooth; stir into noodle mixture along with chopped chicken. Cook and stir until thickened and bubbly. Cook and stir for 1 minute more. If desired, season each serving with coarsely ground pepper. Makes 8 servings.

Per serving: 269 cal., 5 g fat (2 g sat. fat), 86 mg chol., 36 g carbo., 3 g fiber, 19 g pro.

mom's way:
**making noodles
and chicken broth from
scratch and stewing on
the stove for hours**

your way:
**using store-bought
noodles and low-sodium
broth and cooking in a
large pot for a half hour**

mom's way:
simmering a hunk of roast beef in juices all afternoon with potatoes, carrots, and celery

your way:
roasting a cut of pork with chopped pineapple, cajun seasoning, and jalapeño pepper

Tropical Pot Roast

Prep: 20 minutes   **Roast:** 2 hours

1	3½- to 4-pound boneless pork shoulder roast
1	4-ounce can whole green chile peppers, drained
2	teaspoons chili powder
1	teaspoon sugar
½	teaspoon salt
½	teaspoon freshly ground black pepper
¼	teaspoon chipotle powder or cayenne pepper
1	fresh jalapeño chile pepper, seeded and chopped
1	20-ounce can crushed pineapple, undrained
2	tablespoons cornstarch

1. Preheat oven to 325°F. Trim fat from meat. Cut a pocket down the center of the roast. Stuff drained chile peppers down the center of the roast. Combine chili powder, sugar, salt, black pepper, and chipotle powder. Rub mixture over roast. Place the jalapeño pepper and half of the pineapple in a 6-quart Dutch oven. Place the roast on top, stuffed side up.

2. Cover and roast for 2 to 2½ hours or until meat is tender. Transfer meat to a platter. Skim fat from juices. Combine cornstarch and remaining pineapple; stir into juices in pan. Cook and stir over medium heat until thickened and bubbly. Cook for 1 minute more. Serve with meat. Makes 12 servings.

Per serving: 227 cal., 11 g fat (4 g sat. fat), 64 mg chol., 1,639 mg sodium, 12 g carbo., 1 g fiber, 19 g pro.

mom's way:
making bread crumbs,
mincing garlic, chopping
onion, making entire
recipe in one loaf pan

your way:
purchasing bread
crumbs, seasoning with
onion soup mix, baking
individual portions
as needed

Ketchup-Glazed Meat Loaves

Prep: 20 minutes   **Bake:** 20 minutes
Stand: 10 minutes

2   eggs
1   cup ketchup or hot and spicy ketchup
1   cup fine dry bread crumbs
1   envelope (½ of a 2.2-ounce package)
     onion soup mix
¼   teaspoon ground black pepper
1   tablespoon bottled minced garlic
     (6 cloves)
2   pounds lean ground beef

1. Preheat oven to 350°F. In a bowl, beat eggs; whisk in ½ cup of the ketchup. Stir in bread crumbs, soup mix, pepper, and garlic. Add meat; mix well. Form into eight 4-inch loaves. Arrange loaves in a foil-lined 15×10×1-inch baking pan.

2. Bake about 20 minutes or until internal temperature of loaves is 160°F.* Let stand 10 minutes. Spoon remaining ½ cup ketchup over meat loaves.

*****Note:** The internal color of a meat loaf is not a reliable doneness indicator. A meat loaf made with beef, veal, lamb, or pork cooked to 160°F is safe, regardless of color. To test the doneness of a meat loaf, insert an instant-read thermometer into the center of the meat loaf.

To Make Ahead: Wrap individual baked meat loaves in foil and freeze up to 3 months. Thaw overnight in refrigerator. Unwrap, place in a shallow baking pan, and reheat in a 350°F oven for 15 minutes. Or, store leftover baked meat loaves in a covered container in the refrigerator up to 3 days. Makes 8 servings.

Per serving: 296 cal., 13 g fat (5 g sat. fat), 124 mg chol., 1,091 mg sodium, 20 g carbo., 1 g fiber, 24 g pro.

Easy Shepherd's Pie

Prep: 20 minutes **Bake:** 20 minutes
Stand: 10 minutes

- 1 17-ounce package refrigerated cooked beef tips with gravy
- 2 cups frozen mixed vegetables
- 1 11-ounce can condensed tomato bisque soup
- 1 tablespoon Worcestershire sauce
- 1 teaspoon dried minced onion
- ½ teaspoon dried thyme, crushed
- ⅛ teaspoon ground black pepper
- 1 24-ounce package refrigerated mashed potatoes
- ½ cup shredded cheddar cheese

1. Preheat oven to 375°F. Lightly grease a 2-quart rectangular baking dish or four 16-ounce individual casseroles; set aside. In a large saucepan, combine beef tips, frozen vegetables, soup, Worcestershire sauce, onion, thyme, and pepper. Bring to boiling, stirring occasionally. Transfer to prepared baking dish.
2. Place potatoes in a large bowl; stir until nearly smooth. Spoon potatoes into mounds on top of meat mixture in baking dish.
3. Bake, uncovered, for 20 to 25 minutes or until bubbly around edges. Sprinkle with cheese. Let stand 10 minutes before serving. Makes 4 servings.

Per serving: 463 cal., 16 g fat (6 g sat. fat), 65 mg chol., 1,624 mg sodium, 53 g carbo., 6 g fiber, 26 g pro.

mom's way:
cooking beef tips, making pan gravy, cutting up fresh veggies, making mashed potatoes

your way:
using fully cooked beef tips in gravy, adding frozen veggies, calling on purchased refrigerated mashed potatoes

cooking 101

Mom made beef stew like a pro—but do you know how to re-create her savory one-pot supper? This quick-to-fix, slow-to-cook dish is easy to master with these step-by-step directions. The family's in for some mighty good spoonfuls!

TASTY TIP: Choose tougher cuts of beef for stew meat, because the long slow cooking tenderizes the meat. Look for stew meat in the store, or cut up beef chuck or round.

Beef Stew with Cornmeal Dumplings

Prep: 30 minutes   **Cook:** 1 hour 40 minutes

2	**pounds beef stew meat**
1	**tablespoon cooking oil**
1	**28-ounce can diced tomatoes, undrained**
1	**cup beef broth**
¼	**cup coarse-grain Dijon-style mustard**
1	**teaspoon dried thyme, crushed**
1	**teaspoon bottled minced garlic**
½	**teaspoon salt**
½	**teaspoon dried oregano, crushed**
½	**teaspoon ground black pepper**
1	**20-ounce package refrigerated diced potatoes with onion or 4 cups diced peeled potato**
1	**cup peeled baby carrots**
1	**9-ounce package frozen cut green beans**
1	**recipe Cornmeal Dumplings**

1. In a 4-quart Dutch oven, brown beef, half at a time, in hot oil over medium heat. Return all meat to pan. Add undrained tomatoes, broth, mustard, thyme, garlic, salt, oregano, and pepper. Bring to boiling; reduce heat. Cover; simmer for 1 hour.

2. Add potato and carrots. Return to boiling; reduce heat. Cover and simmer for 20 minutes. Stir in frozen green beans. Return to boiling; reduce heat.

3. Prepare batter for Cornmeal Dumplings. Drop batter from a tablespoon into mounds on simmering stew. Cover and cook about 20 minutes more or until a wooden toothpick inserted in a dumpling comes out clean.

Cornmeal Dumplings: Stir together one 8.5-ounce package corn muffin mix, ½ cup shredded cheddar cheese, and ¼ cup sliced green onion. Stir in one slightly beaten egg and ¼ cup dairy sour cream just until moistened (batter will be thick). Makes 12 cups stew + dumplings.

Per 1½ **cups stew + dumplings :** 446 cal., 13 g fat (4 g sat. fat), 104 mg chol., 1,092 mg sodium, 47 g carbo., 4 g fiber, 33 g pro.

Before you brown the meat, test the pan to make sure the oil is hot. To test, add one chunk of meat to the hot oil. If the meat sizzles, you can begin browning. But only brown half of the meat at a time; when too much meat is added at once, the food steams instead of browning.

Stewing simply means to simmer food in liquid in a covered pot for a long time. The long, slow, moist cooking softens the tough fibers of meat, making it tender, juicy, and delicious. While your stew simmers, you should see a few bubbles form slowly and burst just before reaching the surface.

When dropping the dumpling dough on top of the stew, the stew should be boiling so that the bottoms of the dumplings cook evenly. Once you've dropped the dumplings, keep the pan covered for the minimum cooking time. (Don't even peek.)

Shortcut Lasagna

Prep: 30 minutes **Bake:** 40 minutes
Stand: 5 minutes

8	ounces ground beef
8	ounces bulk Italian sausage
1	26-ounce jar tomato-basil pasta sauce
1	egg
1	15-ounce carton low-fat ricotta cheese
1	2.25-ounce can sliced pitted ripe olives
9	no-boil lasagna noodles
1	8-ounce package sliced mozzarella cheese
¼	cup grated Parmesan cheese (1 ounce)

1. Preheat oven to 350°F. In a large saucepan, cook beef and sausage over medium heat until brown. Drain off fat. Stir pasta sauce into browned meat in saucepan; bring to boiling.

2. Meanwhile, in a bowl, beat egg slightly with a fork. Stir in ricotta cheese and olives.

3. To assemble lasagna, spread about 1 cup of hot meat mixture in bottoms of two 9×5-inch loaf pans or dishes. Cover with three noodles, breaking noodles as necessary to fit in pans and making sure noodles do not touch edges of pans. Cover with one-third of the ricotta mixture, one-third of the remaining meat mixture, and one-third of the mozzarella cheese. Repeat with two more layers of noodles, meat mixture, ricotta mixture, and mozzarella. (Make sure noodles are covered with sauce.) Sprinkle with Parmesan.

4. Cover pans with foil. Bake for 30 minutes. Uncover; bake for 10 to 15 minutes more or until top is golden and noodles are tender. Let stand for 5 minutes. Makes 8 servings.

To Make Ahead: Prepare as directed. Cool lasagnas slightly; chill in pans for at least 1 hour. Using two spatulas, carefully remove lasagnas from pans. Transfer to large resealable plastic bags. Seal; freeze for up to 3 months. Thaw in the refrigerator for 1 to 2 days. Carefully return lasagnas to the loaf pans. Bake in a 350°F oven for 40 to 45 minutes or until heated through.

Per serving: 492 cal., 26 g fat (12 g sat. fat), 109 mg chol., 987 mg sodium, 34 g carbo., 2 g fiber, 31 g pro.

mom's way:
chopping fresh herbs, making homemade spaghetti sauce, cooking noodles on the stovetop

your way:
using ready-made spaghetti sauce with seasonings added, relying on no-boil lasagna noodles

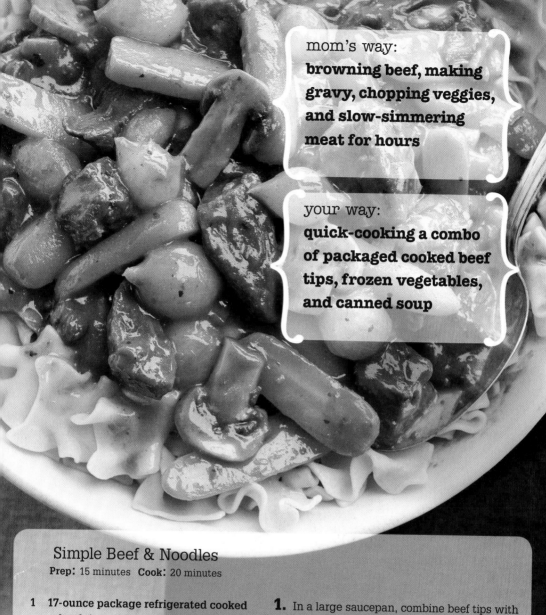

mom's way:
browning beef, making gravy, chopping veggies, and slow-simmering meat for hours

your way:
quick-cooking a combo of packaged cooked beef tips, frozen vegetables, and canned soup

Simple Beef & Noodles

Prep: 15 minutes **Cook:** 20 minutes

1	17-ounce package refrigerated cooked beef tips with gravy
½	teaspoon dried basil, crushed
¼	teaspoon ground black pepper
1	10.75-ounce can condensed golden mushroom soup
½	cup beef broth
1½	cups sliced fresh mushrooms
1	cup packaged peeled baby carrots, halved lengthwise
1	cup loose-pack frozen small whole onions
12	ounces dried wide egg noodles (6 cups)

1. In a large saucepan, combine beef tips with gravy, basil, and pepper. Stir in soup and broth. Bring to boiling. Add mushrooms, carrots, and onions. Return to boiling; reduce heat to low. Cover and simmer for 20 to 25 minutes or until vegetables are tender, stirring frequently.

2. Meanwhile, cook noodles according to package directions; drain. Serve meat mixture over noodles. Makes 6 servings.

Per serving: 364 cal., 8 g fat (2 g sat. fat), 87 mg chol., 903 mg sodium, 51 g carbo., 4 g fiber, 22 g pro.

cooking 101

Add some olé to the old favorite of spaghetti! This zippy dish combines two kid-approved favorites—tacos and spaghetti—into one peppy pasta that will please everyone.

Taco Spaghetti

This is the ultimate fusion food!

Prep: 25 minutes   **Bake:** 15 minutes

5   ounces packaged spaghetti, broken
1   pound ground beef
1   large onion, chopped
¾   cup water
½   of a 1.25-ounce envelope
       (2 tablespoons) taco seasoning mix
1   11-ounce can whole kernel corn with
       sweet peppers, drained
1   cup sliced, pitted ripe olives
1   cup shredded Colby and Monterey Jack
       cheese or cheddar cheese (4 ounces)
½   cup salsa
1   4-ounce can diced green chile peppers,
       drained
6   cups shredded lettuce
1   medium tomato, seeded and chopped
       Tortilla chips (optional)
       Dairy sour cream (optional)

1. Preheat oven to 350°F. Cook pasta according to package directions; drain. Set aside.

2. In a large skillet, cook beef and onion over medium heat until meat is brown. Drain off fat. Stir in water and taco seasoning. Bring to boiling; reduce heat. Simmer, uncovered, for 2 minutes, stirring occasionally. Stir in cooked pasta, drained corn, olives, half of the shredded cheese, the salsa, and drained chile peppers.

3. Transfer mixture to a lightly greased 2-quart casserole dish. Cover and bake for 15 to 20 minutes or until heated through. Sprinkle with remaining cheese. Serve with shredded lettuce, chopped tomato, and, if desired, tortilla chips and sour cream. Makes 6 servings.

Per serving: 424 cal., 22 g fat (8 g sat. fat), 65 mg chol., 978 mg sodium, 38 g carbo., 3 g fiber, 26 g pro.

Cook spaghetti until done. What's the best way to test pasta for doneness? Taste it. Swirl a few strands around a fork, cool them with cold water, and take a bite. They should be tender enough to bite through cleanly—neither hard nor squishy.

Once the spaghetti is ready, brown beef and onion in a skillet. Stir in water and taco seasoning and bring to boiling before reducing heat. Simmer, uncovered, and stir in cooked pasta, corn, olives, half of the shredded cheese, salsa, and chile peppers.

Lightly grease a 2-quart casserole dish. Transfer mixture to dish, cover, and bake for 15 to 20 minutes. Sprinkle with remaining cheese and serve! (For extra fun: Top with your favorite taco add-ons like lettuce and sour cream.)

Speedy, Spicy Tuna & Noodles

Mac 'n' cheese meets tuna noodle casserole in a kickin' dinnertime dish.

Start to Finish: 25 minutes

- 8 ounces dried elbow macaroni (2⅔ cups)
- 1 10.75-ounce can condensed fiesta nacho cheese soup
- ½ cup fat-free milk
- 1 12-ounce can solid white tuna (water pack), drained and broken into chunks
- 1 4-ounce can or jar diced green chile peppers, drained
- Rich round crackers (optional)

1. Cook pasta in lightly salted water according to package directions; drain well. Return pasta to saucepan.

2. Add soup and milk to cooked pasta and stir until pasta is coated and creamy. Gently fold in tuna and drained chile peppers. Heat through. If desired, serve with crackers. Makes 4 servings.

Per serving: 414 cal., 9 g fat (4 g sat. fat), 44 mg chol., 905 mg sodium, 51 g carbo., 2 g fiber, 31 g pro.

mom's way:

making a sauce, adding gobs of cheese and crackers, and baking for an hour

your way:

using canned soup, spicing things up with diced peppers, and preparing it all in one pot

No-Hassle Pork Ribs

These boneless country-style ribs offer more meat with less mess. Skip the grill and cook these all day in a slow cooker.

Prep: 15 minutes
Cook: 8 hours (low) or 4 hours (high)

3½ pounds boneless pork country-
      style ribs
1   cup bottled barbecue sauce
1   8-ounce jar honey mustard
2   teaspoons zesty herb grill
      seasoning blend

1. Place ribs in a 3½- to 4-quart slow cooker. In a small bowl, stir together barbecue sauce, honey mustard, and seasoning blend. Pour over ribs in cooker. Stir to coat.

2. Cover and cook on low-heat setting for 8 to 10 hours or on high-heat setting for 4 to 5 hours.

3. Transfer ribs to a serving platter. Strain sauce; skim fat from sauce. Drizzle some of the sauce over the ribs and pass remaining sauce. Makes 6 to 8 servings.

Per serving: 322 cal., 12 g fat (4 g sat. fat), 94 mg chol., 497 mg sodium, 18 g carbo., 1 g fiber, 29 g pro.

mom's way:
making barbecue sauce from scratch, tending to long-cooking ribs on the grill all afternoon

your way:
tossing boneless country-style ribs and bottled barbecue sauce into a slow cooker

TIP: Resist the temptation to peek under the lid. Uncovering the grill lets heat escape and can add as much as 15 minutes to the grilling time.

cooking 101

Okay, some things just have to be made the old-fashioned way—like ribs on the grill. Yet this recipe is so easy, there's no doubt you'll get them right (first time, every time).

Sweet & Spicy BBQ Ribs

Prep: 35 minutes   **Grill:** 1½ hours

- 1½ cups ketchup
- ⅓ cup white wine vinegar
- ½ cup packed brown sugar
- 2 tablespoons curry powder
- 1 tablespoon Worcestershire sauce
- 2 or 3 cloves garlic, minced
- 1 teaspoon hickory-flavor salt or salt
- 1 teaspoon ground black pepper
- 3½ to 4 pounds pork loin back ribs

1. For sauce, in a medium bowl, combine the ketchup, vinegar, brown sugar, curry powder, Worcestershire sauce, garlic, hickory-flavor salt, and pepper. Cover and let stand at room temperature for 30 minutes or in the refrigerator for up to 5 days.

2. For a charcoal grill, arrange medium-hot coals around edge of grill. Test for medium heat where ribs will cook. Place ribs, bone sides down, in a foil-lined roasting pan*. (To protect the pan, cover the outside with foil too.) Set pan on center of grill rack. (For a gas grill, preheat grill. Set heat to medium and adjust grill for indirect cooking. Place pan with ribs on grill rack over unlit burner.)

3. Cover and grill for 1½ to 2 hours or until ribs are very tender, brushing generously with sauce the last 15 minutes of grilling. Cut ribs into serving-size pieces. Heat remaining sauce and pass with ribs. Makes 4 to 6 servings.

*Note: If you don't have a pan that you want to put on a grill, you can grill the ribs directly on the grill rack. If using a charcoal grill, place a foil drip pan under the ribs to catch the drippings.

Per serving: 607 cal., 18 g fat (6 g sat. fat), 118 mg chol., 1,730 mg sodium, 53 g carbo., 1 g fiber, 57 g pro.

For rib sauce, combine ketchup, vinegar, brown sugar, curry powder, Worcestershire sauce, garlic, hickory-flavor salt, and pepper. Cover and let stand at room temperature for 30 minutes.

Arrange medium-hot coals around edge of grill. Test for medium heat where ribs will cook. Heat is "medium" if you can hold your hand over the grill for 4 seconds before needing to pull it away. Set pan on center of grill rack. (For a gas grill, set heat to medium and adjust grill for indirect cooking. Place pan over unlit burner.)

Place ribs, bone sides down, in roasting pan on grill rack. Cover and grill for 1½ to 2 hours, or until ribs are very tender, brushing generously with sauce the last 15 minutes of grilling.

mom's way:
there's no way around it—Mom's way is perfect. Canned beans and soup with fried onions. Yum!

your way:
what's to change? Frozen beans to cut sodium, a new canned soup, and crunchy water chestnuts. Excellent!

Golden Green Bean Crunch

Prep: 15 minutes   **Bake:** 30 minutes

1   16-ounce package frozen French-cut green beans
1   10.75-ounce can condensed golden mushroom soup
1   8-ounce can sliced water chestnuts, drained (optional)
½   of a 2.8-ounce can french-fried onions (about ¾ cup) or 1 cup chow mein noodles

1. Preheat oven to 350°F. Cook frozen beans according to package directions; drain well. In a 1½-quart casserole, stir together the beans, soup, and, if desired, drained water chestnuts.

2. Bake, uncovered, about 25 minutes or until bubbly around edges. Sprinkle with the onions. Bake about 5 minutes more or until heated through. Makes 4 to 6 servings.

Per serving: 188 cal., 6 g fat (1 g sat. fat), 3 mg chol., 719 mg sodium, 27 g carbo., 5 g fiber, 5 g pro.

Speedy Potato Salad

Prep: 20 minutes   **Chill:** 4 hours

1	24-ounce package frozen loose-pack diced hash brown potatoes with onions and peppers
1½	cups thinly sliced celery
1	8-ounce container light dairy sour cream chive dip
⅔	cup light mayonnaise or salad dressing
1	tablespoon sugar
1	tablespoon white wine vinegar
1	tablespoon prepared mustard
½	teaspoon salt
3	hard-cooked eggs, coarsely chopped
	Celery leaves (optional)
	Cracked black pepper

1. In a covered saucepan, cook potatoes in boiling water for 6 to 8 minutes or until tender; drain well. In a large bowl, combine potatoes and celery. Set aside.

2. In a bowl, combine sour cream dip, mayonnaise, sugar, vinegar, mustard, and salt. Add mayonnaise mixture to potato mixture; toss lightly to coat. Gently fold in hard-cooked eggs. Cover and refrigerate 4 to 24 hours.

3. Before serving, garnish with celery leaves (if desired) and sprinkle with black pepper. Makes 20 servings.

Per serving: 98 cal., 5 g fat (2 g sat. fat), 43 mg chol., 265 mg sodium, 10 g carbo., 1 g fiber, 2 g pro.

mom's way:
peeling, boiling, and chopping potatoes and preparing everything from scratch

your way:
using precooked potatoes with peppers included, stirring together a quick dressing of sour cream dip and mayo

24-Hour Layered Vegetable Salad

Prep: 10 minutes   **Chill:** 2 hours

2   cups purchased torn mixed salad
    greens
1   cup broccoli florets
¾   cup packaged fresh crinkle-cut
    carrot coins
3   slices packaged ready-to-serve cooked
    bacon, chopped
¾   cup shredded smoked cheddar cheese
    (3 ounces)
½   cup bottled creamy Italian salad
    dressing
    Thinly sliced green onion

1. In a 1½-quart (medium) glass bowl, place the greens. Top with broccoli, carrot, bacon, and ½ cup of the cheese. Spoon dressing over top, spreading to cover. Sprinkle with remaining ¼ cup cheese. Sprinkle with green onion. Cover and chill for 2 to 24 hours.

2. To serve, toss mixture until combined. Makes 4 servings.

Per serving: 226 cal., 19 g total fat (7 g sat. fat), 26 mg chol., 467 mg sodium, 7 g carbo., 2 g fiber, 8 g pro.

mom's way:
chopping vegetables, shredding cheese, using a bland, high-fat salad dressing

your way:
using prechopped veggies, packaged shredded cheese, and flavor-packed dressing

mom's way:
boiling glass jars, preparing pickling mixture, and tediously canning cucumbers

your way:
slicing cucumbers, peppers, and onions; mixing vinegar and spice; marinating in the fridge

Quick Pickles
Start to Finish: 30 minutes

- 2   tablespoons white wine vinegar
- 1   teaspoon sugar
- ⅛   teaspoon salt
- 1   medium cucumber, thinly sliced
- ¼   cup chopped green sweet pepper
- ¼   cup chopped onion

1. In a medium bowl, stir together vinegar, sugar, and salt until dissolved. Add cucumber slices, green pepper, and onion. Toss to combine. Let stand for 10 minutes. Store in refrigerator up to 24 hours. Makes 3 to 4 servings.

Per serving: 26 cal., 0 g fat (0 g sat. fat), 0 mg chol., 99 mg sodium, 6 g carbo., 1 g fiber, 1 g pro.

cooking 101

Oh, was it tedious to make a pie before purchased piecrust—making the crust, rolling the crust, crimping the crust. Now just toss the crust in the pan and fold it over the filling for an irresistible, can't-tell-the-difference indulgence.

Easy as Peach Pie

No experience necessary! It's a piece of cake ... or pie.

Prep: 20 minutes **Bake:** 60 minutes
Stand: 45 minutes

½ of a 15-ounce package rolled refrigerated unbaked piecrust (1 crust)
1 cup sugar
3 tablespoons cornstarch
4 cups sliced, peeled peaches or one 16-ounce package frozen unsweetened peach slices
1 cup fresh or frozen red raspberries
Vanilla ice cream (optional)

1. Bring piecrust to room temperature according to package directions. Preheat oven to 350°F. Meanwhile, in a large mixing bowl, combine sugar and cornstarch. Add peaches and raspberries; toss to coat. (For frozen fruit, let stand for 15 to 30 minutes or until partially thawed.)

2. Ease crust into a 9-inch disposable foil pie pan, allowing edges of crust to hang over edges of pan. (Or use a 9-inch glass pie plate.) Spoon peach mixture into pastry-lined pan. Fold crust edges over filling (crust will not totally cover fruit mixture).

3. Place pie pan in a foil-lined shallow baking pan. Bake on the bottom rack of the oven for 60 to 70 minutes or until pastry is golden brown and filling is bubbly.

4. Remove pan from oven and let stand for 45 minutes before serving. If desired, serve with ice cream. Makes 6 to 8 servings.

Per serving: 401 cal., 11 g fat (2 g sat. fat), 0 mg chol., 205 mg sodium, 76 g carbo., 5 g fiber, 4 g pro.

Pick a large mixing bowl and toss in sugar and cornstarch with peaches and frozen raspberries. Let stand a few minutes to thaw. Then stir sugar and cornstarch until totally dissolved. The mixture should have a syrupy consistency.

After the piecrust has been brought to room temperature, place it in the bottom of a pie pan and pour the fruit/sugar mixture on top. Spread the mixture evenly across the piecrust, being careful not to tear it.

Fold over the edges of the piecrust (crust won't totally cover the fruit mixture) and pop it in the oven on the bottom rack for 60–70 minutes or until crust is golden brown and filling is bubbly. Serve with ice cream and enjoy a taste of summer anytime.

TASTY TIP: Frozen fruit is a great way to experience your favorite summertime produce in any season. This pie recipe will also taste great with frozen blueberries, blackberries, strawberries, or rhubarb.

Rhubarb Raspberry Pie

Prep: 30 minutes   **Bake:** 55 minutes

1	15-ounce package rolled refrigerated unbaked piecrust (2 crusts)
1½	cups sugar
⅓	cup all-purpose flour
3½	cups sliced fresh rhubarb or one 16-ounce package frozen unsweetened sliced rhubarb*
1	medium cooking apple, peeled, cored, and coarsely shredded
1	cup fresh raspberries

1. Let piecrusts stand according to package directions. Preheat oven to 375°F. Unroll one of the piecrusts; transfer to a 9-inch pie plate. Trim pastry to ½ inch beyond edge of pie plate. Fold under extra pastry. Crimp edge. Set aside.

2. In a large mixing bowl, stir together the sugar and flour. Stir in rhubarb and apple until coated. Gently fold in raspberries. Transfer to pastry-lined pie plate. Unroll remaining piecrust. Cut out desired shapes using small cutters or a fluted pastry wheel. Place shapes on top of filling. Place a foil-lined baking sheet on the oven rack below the rack the pie will bake on.

3. To prevent overbrowning, cover edge of pie with foil. Bake for 25 minutes. Remove foil. Bake for 30 minutes more or until filling is bubbly and bottom crust is golden. Cool. Makes 8 servings.

***Note:** If using frozen rhubarb, toss the frozen rhubarb with the sugar and flour mixture. Let stand about 30 minutes or until the rhubarb is partially thawed but still icy and beginning to juice out. Stir well. Gently fold in the apple and raspberries. Transfer rhubarb mixture to the pastry-lined pie plate. Continue as directed except bake pie with the edges covered with foil for 50 minutes. Remove foil and bake for 25 to 30 minutes more or until fruit is bubbly.

Per slice: 421 cal., 14 g fat (6 g sat. fat), 10 mg chol., 219 mg sodium, 72 g carbo., 3 g fiber, 2 g pro.

mom's way:
making piecrust from scratch, chopping orchard-fresh fruit, and topping with piecrust

your way:
using store-bought piecrust and frozen, precut fruit (if desired), and topping with fun piecrust shapes

Easy Fruit Cobbler
Prep: 15 minutes   **Bake:** 25 minutes

3   cups desired frozen fruit, such as
     sliced peaches, raspberries, and/or
     blueberries, thawed*
3   tablespoons sugar
1   tablespoon quick-cooking tapioca
1   cup packaged biscuit mix
¼   cup milk
     Cinnamon-sugar (optional)

1. Preheat oven to 400°F. In a medium bowl, stir together undrained fruit, 2 tablespoons of the sugar, and the tapioca. Divide fruit mixture between two 10-ounce ramekins or custard cups. In a small bowl, stir together biscuit mix, the remaining 1 tablespoon sugar, and the milk until combined. Spoon batter over fruit mixture. If desired, sprinkle tops with cinnamon-sugar. Place ramekins in a shallow baking pan.

2. Bake in the preheated oven about 25 minutes or until filling is bubbly and topping is golden. Serve warm. Makes 2 servings.

*Note: Thaw fruit overnight in the refrigerator.

Per serving: 457 cal., 10 g fat (3 g sat. fat), 2 mg chol., 755 mg sodium, 92 g carbo., 5 g fiber, 7 g pro.

mom's way:
peeling and cutting up fresh fruit and making biscuits from scratch for the topping

your way:
using packaged frozen fruit and starting with purchased biscuit mix for the topping

Quick Fruit Crisp

Granola is a simple topper compared with the streusel Mom used to put together.

Start to Finish: 30 minutes

- 2   21-ounce cans apple pie filling
- ¼   cup dried cherries, cranberries, or mixed dried fruit bits
- 1½   cups granola
  Vanilla ice cream (optional)

1. Preheat oven to 375°F. Stir together the pie filling and dried fruit in a 2-quart square baking dish; sprinkle with granola. Bake, uncovered, 20 to 25 minutes or until heated through. Serve warm with ice cream, if desired. Makes 6 servings.

Per serving: 334 cal., 5 g fat (2 g sat. fat), 101 mg sodium, 73 g carbo., 4 g fiber, 3 g pro.

mom's way:
peeling and chopping fruit, boiling a sweet sauce, and topping with a mixture of oats and sugar

your way:
opening canned fruit, stirring in dried cherries, and topping with a cup of granola straight from the box

cooking 101

Growing up, nothing said summer like strawberry shortcake with whipped cream billows. Here's your chance to bring back that warm-weather bliss with this simplified individual-size version.

Stir 'n' Bake Strawberry Shortcakes

Prep: 20 minutes **Bake:** 10 minutes

6 cups sliced strawberries
½ cup sugar
2 cups all-purpose flour
2 teaspoons baking powder
½ cup cold butter
1 egg, lightly beaten
⅔ cup milk
1 recipe Sweetened Whipped Cream

1. Preheat oven to 450°F. In a bowl, stir together strawberries and ¼ cup of the sugar. In a medium bowl, stir together the remaining ¼ cup sugar, the flour, and baking powder. Cut in the butter until mixture resembles coarse crumbs. Combine egg and milk; add to flour mixture. Stir just to moisten.

2. Drop dough into 8 mounds on an ungreased baking sheet; flatten each mound with the back of a spoon until about ¾ inch thick. Bake about 10 minutes or until golden. Transfer to a wire rack and let cool about 10 minutes.

3. Prepare Sweetened Whipped Cream. Cut shortcakes in half horizontally. Spoon half of the strawberries and Sweetened Whipped Cream over bottom halves. Replace top halves of shortcakes. Top with remaining whipped cream and strawberries.

Sweetened Whipped Cream: In a large chilled mixing bowl, beat 1 cup whipping cream, 1 tablespoon sugar, and 1 teaspoon vanilla with an electric mixer on medium speed until soft peaks form (tips curl).

Per shortcake: 427 cal., 24 g fat (15 g sat. fat), 100 mg chol., 172 mg sodium, 48 g carbo., 3 g fiber, 6 g pro.

In a medium bowl, stir together sugar, flour, and baking powder. Cut in the butter using a pastry blender (if you don't have one, use two knives) until mixture resembles coarse crumbs.

Combine the egg and milk; add to flour mixture. Stir just to moisten (you should still see some clumps of dough, and the dough should stick to the sides of the bowl).

Drop dough into 8 mounds on an ungreased baking sheet. Flatten each mound with the back of a spoon. Bake in a 450°F oven about 10 minutes or until golden.

TASTY TIP: For an extra-special treat, substitute vanilla-bean ice cream for the whipped cream.

Shortcut Malted Chocolate Cake

Prep: 10 minutes **Bake:** 30 minutes

1   2-layer-size package dark chocolate fudge or devil's food cake mix
⅓   cup vanilla malted milk powder
1   16-ounce can whipped chocolate frosting
¼   cup vanilla malted milk powder
1½   cups coarsely crushed malted milk balls

1. Preheat oven to 350°F. Prepare cake mix according to package directions, adding the ⅓ cup malted milk powder to batter. Pour batter into a greased 13×9-inch baking pan. Bake for 30 to 35 minutes or until a toothpick inserted near the center comes out clean. Place pan on a wire rack and cool completely.

2. In a bowl, stir together frosting and the ¼ cup malted milk powder. Spread evenly over cake. Top with crushed malted milk balls. Makes 20 servings.

Per serving: 231 cal., 7 g fat (2 g sat. fat), 2 mg chol., 281 mg sodium, 41 g carbo., 1 g fiber, 3 g pro.

{ mom's way:
making chocolate cake from scratch and mixing together sugar, butter, and milk for frosting }

{ your way:
adding some flair to packaged cake mix, topping with a can of store-bought frosting }

Easy Boston Cream Pie

Prep: 30 minutes **Bake:** 30 minutes
Cool: 5 minutes

1 package 2-layer-size yellow cake mix
½ of a 4-serving-size package
   (5 tablespoons) vanilla instant
   pudding mix
1¼ cups milk
1 cup semisweet chocolate pieces
   Whipped cream (optional)
   Maraschino cherries (optional)

1. Preheat oven to 350°F. Grease and flour two 9-inch round baking pans. Prepare cake mix according to package directions; spoon batter into prepared pans. Bake according to package directions. Cool in pans on a wire rack for 10 minutes; remove from pans. Cool completely.

2. Meanwhile, in a small bowl, stir together instant pudding mix and 1 cup of the milk. Whisk for 2 minutes or until pudding starts to set.

3. For chocolate glaze, in a small saucepan, combine chocolate and the remaining ¼ cup milk. Heat over low heat until melted and smooth. Cool for 5 minutes.

4. To assemble, place one cake layer on a serving plate. Spoon pudding over layer on plate. Top with remaining cake layer. Spoon chocolate glaze over top, allowing it to drip down the sides. Serve immediately, or cover and chill for up to 24 hours. If desired, serve with whipped cream and top with maraschino cherries. Store in refrigerator. Makes 12 servings.

Per serving: 258 cal., 8 g fat (4 g sat. fat), 2 mg chol., 349 mg sodium, 49 g carbo., 1 g fiber, 3 g pro.

mom's way:
**making everything
from scratch, including
cake, chocolate glaze,
and pudding filling**

your way:
**using instant everything,
but relying on your
creativity to make it
your own**

One-Rise Caramel-Pecan Rolls

Prep: 25 minutes **Rise:** 60 minutes
Bake: 20 minutes **Stand:** 5 minutes

1¼   cups powdered sugar
⅓   cup whipping cream
1   cup coarsely chopped pecans
½   cup packed brown sugar
1   tablespoon ground cinnamon
2   16-ounce loaves frozen white bread
      dough or sweet roll dough, thawed*
3   tablespoons butter or margarine,
      melted

1. Preheat oven to 375°F. Generously grease two 9×1½-inch round baking pans. Line bottoms with parchment paper or nonstick foil. Stir together powdered sugar and cream. Divide sugar mixture between prepared baking pans; gently spread to edges. Sprinkle with pecans.

2. Stir together brown sugar and cinnamon; set aside. On a lightly floured surface, roll each loaf of dough into a 12×8-inch rectangle. Brush rectangles with melted butter; sprinkle evenly with sugar-cinnamon mixture.

3. Roll up each rectangle, starting from a long side. Pinch seams to seal. Slice each roll into 12 pieces; place pieces cut sides down in pans. Cover rolls; let rise in a warm place until nearly double (60 minutes). Break surface bubbles with a greased toothpick.

4. Bake in a 375°F oven 20 to 25 minutes or until rolls sound hollow when gently tapped (to prevent overbrowning, cover rolls with foil the last 10 minutes of baking). Cool for 5 minutes. Loosen edges of rolls and carefully invert rolls onto serving plate. Serve warm. Makes 24 rolls.

* Note: Thaw dough in the refrigerator overnight.
To Make Ahead: Prepare through Step 3. Cover with greased waxed paper, then with plastic wrap. Chill for 2 to 24 hours. Before baking, let rolls stand, covered, at room temperature for 60 minutes. Uncover; bake rolls for 25 to 30 minutes or until golden brown. Continue as directed.

Per roll: 183 cal., 6 g fat (2 g sat. fat), 8 mg chol., 13 mg sodium, 27 g carbo., 1 g fiber, 3 g pro.

mom's way:
making dough from scratch, kneading, and waiting for dough to rise two times before baking

your way:
grabbing a roll of frozen bread dough, spreading with sugar and spice, and waiting for dough to rise once

No-Fry French Toast

Prep: 15 minutes   **Bake:** 13 minutes

Nonstick cooking spray
1   slightly beaten egg
⅓   cup milk
¼   teaspoon vanilla
    Dash ground cinnamon
4   slices Texas toast
½   cup orange juice
1   tablespoon honey
1   teaspoon cornstarch
⅛   teaspoon ground cinnamon
1   tablespoon sifted powdered sugar
    (optional)

1. Preheat oven to 450°F. Line a large baking sheet with foil; coat with cooking spray. In a pie plate, combine the egg, milk, vanilla, and dash cinnamon. Cut each bread slice vertically into 3 sticks. Dip bread sticks in egg mixture, turning to coat. Place on the prepared baking sheet.

2. Bake about 8 minutes or until bread is lightly browned. Turn bread; bake for 5 to 8 minutes more or until golden brown.

3. Meanwhile, for orange syrup, in a saucepan, stir together orange juice, honey, cornstarch, and the remaining ⅛ teaspoon cinnamon. Cook and stir over medium heat until thickened and bubbly. Reduce heat. Cook and stir for 2 minutes more.

4. If desired, sprinkle the French toast with powdered sugar. Serve the toast with orange syrup. Makes 4 servings.

Per serving: 178 cal., 4 g fat (0 g sat. fat), 103 mg chol., 267 mg sodium, 29 g carbo., 0 g fiber, 9 g pro.

mom's way:

preparing homemade white bread, soaking slices in egg mixture, and frying each piece individually in a skillet

your way:

coating purchased Texas toast in egg mixture, tossing pieces in the oven, and serving with a quick-fix sauce

{
mom's way:
mixing, kneading, baking, and cooling homemade bread; toasting; and coating with cinnamon sugar

{
your way:
soaking French bread in an egg and cinnamon mixture, topping with granola, and frying

Cinnamon Toast

To make this recipe even quicker, skip the Cinnamon Yogurt Sauce and drizzle with maple syrup instead.

Start to Finish: 40 minutes

- 1 **recipe Cinnamon Yogurt Sauce**
- 3 **eggs, lightly beaten**
- ¾ **cup fat-free milk**
- 1 **tablespoon sugar**
- 1 **tablespoon finely shredded orange peel**
- ½ **teaspoon vanilla**
- ¼ **teaspoon ground cinnamon**
- 12 **½-inch thick bias-slices baguette-style French bread**
- 2 **tablespoons butter**
- 1 **cup granola, coarsely crushed**

1. Prepare Cinnamon Yogurt Sauce. In a shallow bowl, beat together eggs, milk, sugar, 1½ teaspoons of the orange peel, vanilla, and cinnamon with a whisk. Dip bread slices into egg mixture, coating both sides.

2. In a skillet or on a griddle, melt 1 tablespoon of the butter over medium heat; add half of the bread slices. Sprinkle some of the granola on top of each slice of bread in the skillet, pressing in gently with spatula so granola sticks. Cook for 2 to 3 minutes or until bottom is golden brown. Flip each slice, pressing lightly with the spatula. Cook for 2 minutes more or until golden brown. When removing from pan, flip each slice so granola side is on top. Repeat with remaining butter, bread slices, and granola. Serve immediately with Cinnamon Yogurt Sauce and remaining 1½ teaspoons orange peel. If desired, sprinkle with additional ground cinnamon. Makes four 3-slice servings.

Cinnamon Yogurt Sauce: In a small bowl combine one 8-ounce container plain nonfat yogurt; 1 tablespoon honey; ¼ teaspoon ground cinnamon, if desired; and ¼ teaspoon vanilla. Makes about ¾ cup.

Per serving: 781 cal., 14 g fat (6 g sat. fat), 176 mg chol., 775 mg sodium, 125 g carbo., 6 g fiber, 29 g pro.

sunday dinner together

menu #1

kids can help

{easy tasks:}

❊ Stir together ingredients for New Potato Bake

❊ Toss Greens & Berries Salad ingredients with dressing

❊ Stir ingredients for Root Beer Float Cake; pour batter into cake pan

❊ Frost Root Beer Float Cake

Sirloin with Mustard & Chives

If you end up with leftovers of the sour cream mixture, try it on baked potatoes or with fresh steamed vegetables.
Start to Finish: 20 minutes

4	boneless beef sirloin or ribeye steaks, cut about ¾ inch thick (about 1½ pounds)
2	teaspoons garlic-pepper seasoning
½	cup light dairy sour cream
2	tablespoons Dijon-style mustard
1	tablespoon snipped fresh chives

1. Sprinkle both sides of steaks with 1½ teaspoons of the seasoning. Grill steaks on the rack of an uncovered grill directly over medium coals to desired doneness, turning once halfway through grilling. (Allow 9 to 11 minutes for medium rare and 11 to 13 minutes for medium.) Transfer steaks to a serving platter.

2. Meanwhile, in a small bowl, combine sour cream, mustard, chives, and remaining ½ teaspoon seasoning. Spoon sour cream mixture on top of steaks. Serve any leftover sour cream mixture on baked potatoes. Makes 4 servings.

Per serving: 256 cal., 9 g fat (4 g sat. fat), 112 mg chol., 421 mg sodium, 2 g carbo., 0 g fiber, 37 g pro.

New Potato Bake

Prep: 15 minutes   **Cook:** 10 minutes
Bake: 25 minutes   **Stand:** 10 minutes

1½   **pounds tiny new potatoes, quartered**
5   **cups fresh baby spinach**
4   **green onions, chopped**
1   **tablespoon butter**
1   **tablespoon all-purpose flour**
¼   **teaspoon salt**
⅛   **teaspoon cayenne pepper**
   Dash ground nutmeg
1   **cup milk**
1   **cup shredded Swiss cheese (4 ounces)**
   Nonstick cooking spray
1   **tablespoon fine dry bread crumbs**

1. Preheat oven to 375°F. In a large saucepan, cook the potatoes, covered, in lightly salted boiling water for 8 minutes. Stir in spinach. Drain.

2. In a small saucepan, cook green onion in hot butter over medium heat for 3 minutes or until softened. Stir in flour, salt, cayenne pepper, and nutmeg. Stir in milk. Cook and stir over medium heat until thickened and bubbly. Add ½ cup of the cheese; stir until melted.

3. Lightly coat a 2-quart square baking dish with cooking spray. Layer half of the potato mixture in the dish; spoon half of the sauce over the potato mixture. Sprinkle with ¼ cup of the remaining cheese. Top with remaining potato mixture and remaining sauce. Sprinkle with remaining ¼ cup cheese. Top with bread crumbs.

4. Bake, uncovered, for 25 to 30 minutes or until potatoes are tender and crumbs are browned. Let stand for 10 to 15 minutes before serving. Makes 6 to 8 servings.

Tip: Need more? Make 12 to 16 servings by doubling all ingredients and assembling in a 3-quart rectangular baking dish.

Per serving: 223 cal., 9 g fat (6 g sat. fat), 29 mg chol., 229 mg sodium, 25 g carbo., 3 g fiber, 11 g pro.

Greens & Berries Salad

Start to Finish: 15 minutes

1	8-ounce package torn mixed greens (about 8 cups)
½	cup crumbled blue cheese (optional)
2	¼-inch-thick slices red onion, separated into rings
1	cup fresh raspberries or sliced fresh strawberries
1	2-ounce package slivered almonds, toasted (⅓ cup)
¼	cup bottled balsamic vinaigrette salad dressing
1	teaspoon Dijon-style mustard

1. In a large salad bowl, combine the greens, blue cheese (if desired), red onion, raspberries, and almonds.

2. In a small bowl, whisk together the salad dressing and mustard. Pour dressing over the salad ingredients. Toss well to combine and serve immediately. Makes 4 to 6 servings.

Per serving: 157 cal., 12 g fat (1 g sat. fat), 0 mg chol., 215 mg sodium, 11 g carbo., 5 g fiber, 5 g pro.

Root Beer Float Cake

Prep: 25 minutes

1	2-layer-size caramel or yellow cake mix
	Root beer
1½	teaspoons vanilla
1	teaspoon finely shredded lemon peel
1	recipe Root Beer Frosting

1. Preheat oven to 350°F. Prepare cake mix according to package directions except substitute root beer for the liquid called for and add vanilla and lemon peel. Pour batter into a greased 13×9×2-inch baking pan. Bake according to package directions. Cool in pan for 10 minutes. Remove from pan; cool completely.

2. Prepare Root Beer Frosting. Cut cooled cake in half crosswise. Frost top of one cake half with some frosting. Top with remaining cake half; frost top layer of cake. Makes 12 servings.

Root Beer Frosting: In a medium mixing bowl, beat ⅓ cup softened butter with an electric mixer until smooth. Gradually add 1 cup powdered sugar, beating well. Slowly beat in 3 tablespoons root beer and 1 teaspoon vanilla. Gradually beat in 2 cups more powdered sugar. Beat in more root beer or powdered sugar to make spreadable.

Per serving (with icing): 347 cal., 8 g fat (4 g sat. fat), 14 mg chol., 321 mg sodium, 69 g carbo., 0 g fiber, 2 g pro.

menu #2

kids can help

{easy tasks:}

* Stir together ingredients for Plum-Easy Mustard Sauce and heat through
* Spoon cream mixture into Volcano Potatoes casserole
* Make topping for Vegetable Medley au Gratin
* Scoop ice cream into serving bowls and top with Orange-Praline Sauce

Spiral-Sliced Ham with Plum-Easy Mustard Sauce

You can prepare the sauce and chill it for up to 24 hours. Before serving, reheat sauce over low heat, stirring constantly.

Prep: 10 minutes   **Bake:** 2 hours
Stand: 20 minutes

1   7- to 8-pound fully cooked spiral-sliced ham
1   18-ounce jar red plum jam
2   tablespoons honey mustard
⅛   teaspoon ground black pepper

1. Preheat oven to 300°F. Place ham in a roasting pan according to package directions (discard flavor or seasoning packet). Roast about 2 hours or until an instant-read thermometer reads 140°F.
2. Meanwhile, in a small saucepan, heat red plum jam over medium-low heat until jam is melted and bubbly, stirring occasionally. Stir in honey mustard and pepper. Serve warm. Makes about 1½ cups.
3. Remove ham from oven; cover with foil and let stand for 20 minutes before serving. Pass sauce with ham. Makes 12 to 16 servings.

Per 3 ounces ham + 2 tablespoons sauce: 261 cal.,
7 g total fat (3 g sat. fat), 49 mg chol., 1,125 mg sodium,
34 g carbo., 2 g fiber, 14 g pro.

Volcano Potatoes

Make rich, flavorful mashed potatoes with no need for gravy in a fraction of the time it would take from scratch.

Prep: 15 minutes   **Bake:** 65 minutes

3   20-ounce packages refrigerated mashed potatoes
¾   cup whipping cream
¾   cup shredded Gruyère, Havarti, or American cheese (3 ounces)
   Freshly cracked black pepper

1. Preheat oven to 300°F. Spoon potatoes into a 2-quart casserole. Bake, covered, for 50 minutes.
2. Meanwhile, in a medium mixing bowl, beat cream to soft peaks (tips curl); fold in cheese.
3. Remove casserole from oven. Increase oven temperature to 375°F. Uncover potatoes. With a large spoon, make a well in the center of the potatoes by pushing from the center to the sides. Spoon the whipping cream mixture into the well. Sprinkle top with pepper.
4. Bake, uncovered, for 15 to 20 minutes more or until top is golden. Makes 10 servings.

Per serving: 243 cal., 13 g fat (6 g sat. fat), 37 mg chol.,
300 mg sodium, 24 g carbo., 1 g fiber, 7 g pro.

Vegetable Medley au Gratin

Prep: 20 minutes **Bake:** 65 minutes

1 10.75-ounce can condensed cream of chicken and mushroom soup

½ cup dairy sour cream

½ teaspoon dried dillweed

2 16-ounce packages loose-pack frozen broccoli, cauliflower, and carrots, thawed

⅔ cup crushed stone-ground wheat crackers (about 15 crackers)

⅓ cup finely chopped walnuts

¼ cup finely shredded Parmesan cheese

2 tablespoons butter, melted

1. Preheat oven to 300°F. In a large mixing bowl, stir together soup, sour cream, and dillweed; stir in thawed vegetables. Transfer vegetable mixture to a 2-quart rectangular baking dish. Cover with foil.

2. Bake, covered, for 50 minutes. In a small bowl, stir together crushed crackers, walnuts, Parmesan cheese, and melted butter. Uncover baking dish and sprinkle crumb mixture over top. Increase oven temperature to 375°F. Bake, uncovered, about 15 minutes more or until topping is browned. Makes 10 servings.

Per serving: 160 cal., 11 g fat (4 g sat. fat), 15 mg chol., 440 mg sodium, 11 g carbo., 3 g fiber, 5 g pro.

Ice Cream with Orange-Praline Sauce

Start to Finish: 15 minutes

1   12-ounce jar caramel ice
    cream topping
½   cup orange marmalade
⅔   cup coarsely chopped
    pecans, toasted
½   gallon vanilla, cinnamon,
    pumpkin, or eggnog
    ice cream

1. In a small saucepan, stir together caramel ice cream topping and orange marmalade; cook over medium-low heat until marmalade is melted, stirring occasionally. Stir in pecans; heat through. Spoon warm sauce over scoops of ice cream. Makes 10 servings.

Make-Ahead Tip: Cover and chill sauce up to 24 hours. Just before serving, in a small saucepan, reheat sauce over low heat, stirring occasionally.

Per serving: 484 cal., 24 g fat (13 g sat. fat), 109 mg chol., 156 mg sodium, 61 g carbo., 1 g fiber, 7 g pro.

kids can help

{easy tasks:}

❋ Measure and combine ingredients for Fruit and Broccoli Salad

❋ Shape and roll dough for Parmesan Dinner Rolls

❋ Scoop ice cream to serve with Brownie-Walnut Pie

menu #3

MENU #3 HANDS-ON PREP PLAN

{DAY BEFORE}
* Bake Brownie-Walnut Pie
* Prepare Creamy Cheddar Dip; chill

{2 HOURS BEFORE}
* Toss together Fruit and Broccoli Salad; chill
* Prepare Parmesan Dinner Rolls

{30 MINUTES BEFORE}
* Prepare Maple Chicken Fettuccine

Creamy Cheddar Dip

Prep: 10 minutes   **Chill:** 4 hours

1   16-ounce container dairy sour cream
1   1.4-ounce envelope dry vegetable soup mix
½   cup shredded cheddar cheese (2 ounces)
    Assorted vegetable dippers (such as blanched asparagus spears, cherry tomatoes, pea pods, red sweet pepper strips, radishes, zucchini slices, and/or cauliflower florets)

1. In a medium bowl, stir together sour cream and soup mix. Stir in cheddar cheese. Cover and chill for at least 4 hours or up to 48 hours. Serve with vegetable dippers. Makes 1¾ cups dip.

Per 2 tablespoons dip: 94 cal., 8 g fat (5 g sat. fat), 19 mg chol., 248 mg sodium, 3 g carbo., 0 g fiber, 2 g pro.

Maple Chicken Fettuccine

Prep: 10 minutes   **Cook:** 20 minutes

10 ounces dried fettuccine
5 skinless, boneless chicken breast
   halves (1½ pounds total)
   Salt and ground black pepper
1 tablespoon olive oil
1 16-ounce package frozen stir-fry
   vegetables
¾ cup chicken broth
1 tablespoon cornstarch
1 teaspoon snipped fresh rosemary
⅛ teaspoon ground black pepper
¼ cup maple syrup

1. Cook pasta according to package directions; drain. Set aside and keep warm. Meanwhile, season chicken with salt and black pepper. In a large skillet, cook chicken in hot oil over medium heat for 10 to 12 minutes or until an instant-read thermometer inserted in chicken registers 170°F, turning once. Remove from skillet; keep warm. Increase heat to medium-high. Add frozen vegetables; cook and stir 6 to 8 minutes or until crisp-tender.

2. In a small bowl, combine broth, cornstarch, rosemary, and black pepper. Add to skillet. Cook and stir until thickened and bubbly. Cook and stir for 1 minute more. Stir in maple syrup. To serve, arrange hot pasta in shallow bowls. Top with chicken. Spoon vegetables and sauce over chicken. Makes 5 servings.

Per serving: 465 cal., 6 g fat (1 g sat. fat), 79 mg chol., 285 mg sodium, 60 g carbo., 2 g fiber, 40 g pro.

Fruit and Broccoli Salad

Prep: 15 minutes **Chill:** 1 hour

½ of a 16-ounce package broccoli slaw
   mix (about 2½ cups)
1 cup seedless red and/or green grapes,
   halved
1 medium apple, cored and chopped
⅓ to ½ cup bottled poppy seed salad
   dressing
2 medium oranges, peeled, seeded,
   and sectioned*
½ cup coarsely chopped pecans or
   walnuts, toasted if desired**
Red Bibb lettuce

1. In a large bowl, combine broccoli slaw, grapes, and apple. Pour salad dressing over broccoli mixture; add oranges and toss gently to coat. Cover and chill for 1 to 4 hours. Sprinkle with nuts; toss again. Spoon salad into lettuce-lined dishes.

*To section oranges: Hold peeled oranges over a bowl to catch the juices. Cut down against inside membrane of one segment on both sides and release segment. Repeat with remaining segments, removing any seeds.

**To toast nuts: Preheat oven to 350°F. Spread nuts in a single layer in a shallow baking pan. Bake for 5 to 10 minutes or until light golden brown, watching carefully and stirring once or twice. Makes 6 to 8 servings.

Per serving: 234 cal., 16 g fat (2 g sat. fat), 6 mg chol., 17 mg sodium, 22 g carbo., 3 g fiber, 3 g pro.

Parmesan Dinner Rolls

Prep: 25 minutes **Rise:** 30 minutes
Bake: 12 minutes

1   **16-ounce package hot roll mix**
¼   **cup finely shredded Parmesan cheese**
2   **tablespoons snipped fresh basil or**
    1 teaspoon dried basil, crushed
2   **tablespoons sugar**
1   **tablespoon milk**
2   **tablespoons finely shredded Parmesan**
    cheese

1. In a large mixing bowl, prepare hot roll mix according to package directions through the resting step, stirring the ¼ cup Parmesan, the basil, and sugar into the flour mixture. Divide dough in half.

2. Grease twenty-four 1¾-inch muffin cups. Using a knife, divide each dough half into 12 portions (24 portions total). Gently pull each dough portion into a ball, tucking edges beneath. Arrange balls, smooth side up, in the prepared muffin cups. Cover; let rise in a warm place until nearly double in size (about 30 minutes).

3. Preheat oven to 400°F. Using a pastry brush, brush roll tops with milk; sprinkle with the 2 tablespoons Parmesan cheese. Bake rolls for 12 to 15 minutes or until tops are golden brown. Remove rolls from muffin cups and serve warm. Makes 24 rolls.

To Make Ahead: Prepare and bake the rolls up to 2 days in advance, wrap them in foil packets, and freeze. Just before dinner, reheat the frozen rolls in a 350°F oven for about 20 minutes.

Per roll: 89 cal., 2 g fat (0 g sat. fat), 9 mg chol., 145 mg sodium, 15 g carbo., 0 g fiber, 3 g pro.

Brownie-Walnut Pie

Prep: 10 minutes **Bake:** 50 minutes
Cool: 20 minutes + 1 hour

½ of a 15-ounce package rolled refrigerated unbaked piecrust (1 crust)
½ cup butter or margarine
3 ounces unsweetened chocolate, cut up
3 eggs, lightly beaten
1½ cups sugar
½ cup all-purpose flour
1 teaspoon vanilla
1 cup chopped walnuts
Vanilla or coffee ice cream
Caramel ice cream topping

1. Bring piecrust to room temperature according to package directions. Preheat oven to 350°F. Unroll piecrust; transfer to a 9-inch pie plate. Trim piecrust to ½ inch beyond edge of pie plate. Fold under extra pastry. Crimp edge; set aside.

2. For filling, in a heavy, small saucepan, melt butter and chocolate over low heat, stirring frequently. Cool for 20 minutes.

3. In a large bowl, combine eggs, sugar, flour, and vanilla. Stir in chocolate mixture and nuts; pour into pastry shell. Bake for 50 to 55 minutes or until knife inserted in center comes out clean. Cool 1 hour on wire rack. Serve warm with ice cream and caramel topping. Makes 10 to 12 servings.

Per serving with ½ cup ice cream: 655 cal., 42 g fat (19 g sat. fat), 156 mg chol., 193 mg sodium, 65 g carbo., 3 g fiber, 10 g pro.

kids can help

{easy tasks:}

❉ Tear washed salad greens into bite-size pieces

❉ Arrange ingredients on the platter for Salad Sampler

❉ Roll and cut out biscuits, then top with milk and poppy seeds

❉ Spoon pumpkin filling into tartlets and top each with a pecan half

menu #4

Salad Sampler

This salad packs a variety of toppings. When kids get to make their own, it encourages them to try new things.

Start to Finish: 20 minutes

5   cups torn washed greens or spinach
2   cups grape tomatoes
2   cups broccoli florets
1   small cucumber, cut into 2×½-inch strips
8   ounces bacon, cooked until crisp and crumbled
2   hard-cooked eggs, peeled and quartered
⅓   cup bottled salad dressing (desired flavor)

1. On a large serving platter, arrange greens, tomatoes, broccoli, cucumber, bacon, and eggs. Serve with dressing. Makes 4 main-dish or 8 side-dish servings.

Per main-dish serving: 359 cal., 25 g fat (7 g sat. fat), 132 mg chol., 655 mg sodium, 14 g carbo., 3 g fiber, 13 g pro.

Cranberry-Glazed Pork Roast

Any leftover pork roast can be made into delicious
sandwiches and served with reheated leftover sauce.

Prep: 15 minutes **Roast:** 1½ hours
Stand: 15 minutes

¼	teaspoon salt
¼	teaspoon ground black pepper
½	teaspoon ground sage
1	2½- to 3-pound boneless pork top loin roast
1	16-ounce can whole or jellied cranberry sauce
½	teaspoon finely shredded orange peel
⅓	cup orange juice

1. Preheat oven to 325°F. For rub, in a small bowl, stir together salt, pepper, and ¼ teaspoon of the sage. Sprinkle rub evenly over all sides of pork roast; rub in mixture with your fingers. Place roast on rack in a shallow roasting pan. Roast, uncovered, for 1 hour.

2. For sauce, in a medium saucepan, stir together cranberry sauce, orange peel, orange juice, and the remaining ¼ teaspoon sage. Bring to boiling; reduce heat. Simmer, uncovered, about 10 minutes or until mixture has thickened slightly.

3. Spoon about ¼ cup of the sauce over meat. Roast, uncovered, for 30 to 45 minutes more or until internal temperature is 155°F. Remove from oven. Cover meat loosely with foil; let stand for 15 minutes before slicing. (The temperature of the meat will rise 5°F during standing.) Serve remaining warm sauce with meat. Makes 8 to 10 servings.

Per serving: 290 cal., 7 g fat (2 g sat. fat), 77 mg chol., 132 mg sodium, 23 g carbo., 1 g fiber, 31 g pro.

Roasted Root Vegetables

Prep: 20 minutes   **Roast:** 60 minutes

1¼   **pounds Yukon gold potatoes, peeled
      and cut into 1-inch chunks (3½ cups)**
2   **cups packaged peeled baby carrots**
2   **medium yellow onions, cut into
      1-inch-wide wedges**
8   **fresh sage leaves, slivered**
3   **tablespoons olive oil**
1½   **teaspoons salt**
¼   **teaspoon freshly ground black pepper**
2   **tablespoons honey**

1. Preheat oven to 325°F.* In a large greased roasting pan, combine potato, carrot, onion, and sage. Drizzle oil over vegetable mixture; sprinkle with salt and pepper. Toss lightly to coat.

2. Roast, uncovered, for 50 to 55 minutes or until vegetables are just tender, stirring occasionally. Increase oven temperature to 425°F; roast for 10 to 15 minutes more or until vegetables are lightly browned, stirring once. Drizzle honey over vegetables. Stir gently to coat. Makes 4 to 6 servings.

*Note: Vegetables can be roasted alongside the pork roast. When roast is removed from oven, increase oven temperature to finish vegetables while roast stands.

Per serving: 284 cal., 11 g fat (1 g sat. fat), 0 mg chol., 653 mg sodium, 46 g carbo., 5 g fiber, 4 g pro.

Save time
by roasting
the vegetables
alongside the
pork roast.

Honey & Poppy Seed Biscuits

Prep: 15 minutes **Bake:** 10 minutes

½   cup cream-style cottage cheese
¼   cup milk
2   tablespoons honey
2¼ cups packaged biscuit mix
    Poppy seeds

1. Preheat oven to 450°F. In a food processor or blender, combine cottage cheese, milk, and honey. Cover and process or blend until nearly smooth.

2. Prepare biscuit mix according to package directions for rolled biscuits, except substitute the pureed cottage cheese mixture for the liquid called for on package. Lightly brush with additional milk and sprinkle with poppy seeds.

3. Bake for 10 to 12 minutes or until bottoms are lightly browned.* Makes 10 to 12 biscuits.

***Note:** Like hot biscuits? Instead of baking them too far in advance, try popping them in the oven while the roast stands before slicing. They'll be hot from the oven at the same time the pork is ready to serve.

Per biscuit: 148 cal., 5 g fat (1 g sat. fat), 3 mg chol., 394 mg sodium, 21 g carbo., 1 g fiber, 4 g pro.

Feel free to make these the night before if you're pressed for time; they store well.

Pecan Pumpkin Tartlets

Prep: 20 minutes **Bake:** 25 minutes

1	15-ounce package rolled refrigerated unbaked piecrust (2 crusts)
1	egg, slightly beaten
1	cup canned pumpkin
2	tablespoons half-and-half, light cream, or milk
1/3	cup sugar
1 1/2	teaspoons all-purpose flour
1/2	teaspoon finely shredded lemon peel
1/2	teaspoon pumpkin pie spice
1/2	teaspoon vanilla
1/8	teaspoon salt
24	pecan halves

1. Preheat oven to 375°F. Let piecrust stand according to package directions. Unroll crusts; using a 2½-inch round cutter, cut out 24 circles. (Reserve scraps to repair any tears.) Press circles into twenty-four 1¾-inch muffin cups; set aside.

2. In a medium bowl, stir together egg, pumpkin, and half-and-half. Stir in sugar, flour, lemon peel, spice, vanilla, and salt. Spoon about 1 tablespoon pumpkin mixture into each pastry-lined cup. Place a pecan half on top of each tartlet.

3. Bake about 25 minutes or until crust is browned and filling is set. Cool on a wire rack. Store in an airtight container in the refrigerator within 2 hours of baking. Makes 24 tartlets.

Per tartlet: 63 cal., 1 g fat (0 g sat. fat), 9 mg chol., 144 mg sodium, 12 g carbo., 0 g fiber, 2 g pro.

menu #5

Winter Salad

Raspberry Cranbe Sauce

Roasted Potatoes & Vegetables

Pantry Pot Roast

RεCiPES

kids can help

{easy tasks:}

❊ Season veggies and toss to coat

❊ Section orange and grapefruit and help stir in dressing for Winter Salad

❊ Slice pound cake with a butter knife

Pantry Pot Roast

Prep: 15 minutes

Cook: 8 hours (low) or 4 hours (high)

1   3-pound boneless beef chuck pot roast
1   tablespoon cooking oil
1   7- to 8-ounce package mixed dried fruit
2   medium onions, cut into thin wedges
      (2 cups)
¼   teaspoon ground allspice
1   5.5-ounce can apple juice

1. Trim fat from meat. In a Dutch oven, brown meat in hot oil over medium-high heat until brown on all sides. Sprinkle with *salt* and *ground black pepper*. Set aside.

2. Cut up dried fruit pieces. Place fruit and onion wedges in slow cooker; top with meat. Sprinkle with allspice. Add apple juice.

3. Cover and cook on low-heat setting for 8 to 10 hours or on high-heat setting for 4 to 5 hours. Makes 6 servings.

Per serving: 428 cal., 11 g fat (3 g sat. fat), 134 mg chol., 371 mg sodium, 33 g carbo., 1 g fiber, 50 g pro.

Balsamic-Roasted Vegetables

Prep: 10 minutes   **Bake:** 30 minutes

1½   pounds tiny new potatoes, halved
½   of an 16-ounce package peeled baby
      carrots
1   medium red onion, cut into wedges
3   tablespoons olive oil or cooking oil
1   teaspoon dried rosemary, crushed
¾   teaspoon salt
¼   teaspoon ground black pepper
3   tablespoons balsamic vinegar

1. Preheat oven to 425°F. In a lightly greased shallow baking pan, combine potato, carrots, and onion. In a bowl, mix oil, rosemary, salt, and pepper. Drizzle over vegetables; toss to coat.

2. Roast, uncovered, 30 to 35 minutes or until potatoes and onion are tender; stir once. Drizzle vinegar over vegetables and toss to coat; serve immediately. Makes 6 servings.

Per serving: 179 cal., 7 g fat (1 g sat. fat), 0 mg chol., 327 mg sodium, 27 g carbo., 3 g fiber, 3 g pro.

Winter Salad

Prep: 25 minutes **Chill:** 30 minutes

- 3 tablespoons salad oil
- 3 tablespoons orange juice
- 2 tablespoons red wine vinegar
- 1 tablespoon honey
- ⅛ teaspoon cracked black pepper
- 2 medium pink grapefruit
- 1 medium orange
- 2 apples and/or pears, cored and sliced
- ¾ cup green and/or red seedless grapes

1. For dressing, in a screw-top jar, combine oil, orange juice, vinegar, honey, and pepper. Cover and shake well. Refrigerate dressing for 30 minutes.

2. Meanwhile, use a small, sharp knife to peel grapefruit and orange, removing as much of the white pith as possible. Cut sections from grapefruit and orange and place in a bowl with apples and/or pears, and grapes. Shake dressing and drizzle over fruit mixture. Makes 6 servings.

To Make Ahead: Refrigerate dressing for up to 3 days. Section grapefruit and oranges; cover and chill for up to 24 hours. Drain before using.

Per serving: 165 cal., 7 g fat (1 g sat. fat), 0 mg chol., 1 mg sodium, 27 g carbo., 4 g fiber, 1 g pro.

Raspberry-Cranberry Sauce

Start to Finish: 15 minutes

- 2 tablespoons sugar
- 1 tablespoon cornstarch
- ½ of a 16-ounce can whole cranberry sauce
- 1 10-ounce package frozen red raspberries (in syrup), thawed
- 2 tablespoons brandy (optional)
    Pound cake, brownies, or vanilla ice cream

1. In a medium saucepan, combine sugar and cornstarch. Stir in cranberry sauce and raspberries. Cook and stir over medium heat until thickened and bubbly. Cook and stir for 2 minutes more. Remove from heat. If desired, stir in brandy.

2. Serve warm or cold over slices of pound cake, brownies, or ice cream. Makes 2 cups sauce.

Per ¼ cup sauce: 119 cal., 0 g fat (0 g sat. fat), 0 mg chol., 13 mg sodium, 29 g carbo., 1 g fiber, 0 g pro.

kids
in the
kitchen

top 5 nutrition issues for teens

What they're doing, what they should be doing, and what you can do to help.

focus on the sexes:

The teen years are a critical time for proper nutrition, yet teens are notorious for poor eating habits. Don't worry! Here are some quick fixes.

#1 Issue for Teen Girls: Unhappiness with weight

Teenagers may strive to look like the fashion models they see on television and in magazines—but this isn't a realistic goal. However, maintaining a healthy weight and activity level is a goal that every teen girl can strive toward. Keep plenty of nutritious foods around the house and encourage teens to get outside and move around.

#1 Issue for Teen Boys: Eating to build muscle

Teenage boys can have just as many issues with their body images as girls. Where girls want to lose weight, boys often want to bulk up and build strong muscles. While there's nothing wrong with lifting weights and working out, it is important to do so safely. Diets that are extremely high in protein should be avoided, as well as dietary supplements that might not be safe.

THE PROBLEM: Low levels of calcium and other nutrients
THE SOLUTION: Eat 3 to 4 servings of dairy each day
Try 3 to 4 servings of low-fat or fat-free milk (flavored milk is fine on occasion), low-fat yogurt, and cheese each day. When you factor in one serving with each meal, this is simple.

THE PROBLEM: High-fat foods when dining out
THE SOLUTION: Trim the fat, keep the flavor
Go for lean meats, such as turkey or ham, when ordering sandwiches, and instead of mayonnaise, opt for mustard. Avoid fattening fried foods (for example, try grilled chicken instead of its fried counterpart) or order the smallest size possible (for must-have favorites like french fries).

THE PROBLEM: Huge portions
THE SOLUTION: Pay attention to food labels
In a nation that loves big portions, it can be hard to tell what an appropriate serving size is. Encourage teens to read the labels on their favorite foods—such as cookies and chips—so they know how much they're actually consuming. Restaurant meals often contain more food than diners need to eat during one meal, so suggest that teens (and you) set a portion of the meal aside in a doggy bag to eat for lunch the following day.

THE PROBLEM: Too little variety, especially in fruits and vegetables
THE SOLUTION: Eat fruits or vegetables with every meal and snack
Eating fruits or vegetables several times a day—for a total of about 2 cups of fruit and 2½ cups of vegetables—supplies important nutrients, such as fiber and vitamins A and C, without piling on the calories. Start with fruit salad or a banana at breakfast, suggest a visit to the salad bar at lunch, and include cooked or raw veggies at dinner.

THE PROBLEM: Fad dieting
THE SOLUTION: Eat healthfully and be physically active each day
Consuming a variety of nutritious foods while not overindulging is the best plan for keeping weight on track. Certain diets that are featured in magazines and online can be too low in nutrients and calories—not a good plan for growing teenagers. Exercise is important for a healthy lifestyle, so encourage physical activity every day. Walking, biking, or shooting hoops in the driveway are teen-friendly choices.

{teens can cook}

breakfast for

{ Give Mom a neededbreak on Mother's Day— serve her this simple breakfast in bed for guaranteed brownie points. }

Orange Dream Fruit Salad
Start to Finish: 15 minutes

1   cup sliced strawberries and/or chopped, peeled, seeded mango or papaya
1   11-ounce can mandarin orange sections, drained
1   cup seedless red and/or green grapes, halved
1   6-ounce container orange-flavor yogurt
¼   teaspoon poppy seeds (optional)

1. In a medium bowl, combine the strawberries, oranges, and grapes. If desired, in a small bowl, stir together yogurt and poppy seeds. Gently stir yogurt into the fruit mixture until combined. Makes 4 to 6 side-dish servings.

Per serving: 119 cal., 1 g fat (0 g sat. fat), 2 mg chol., 26 mg sodium, 28 g carbo., 2 g fiber, 2 g pro.

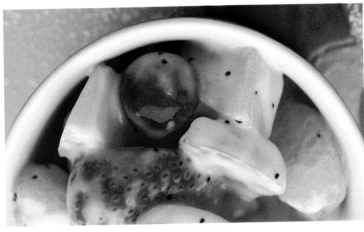

mother's day

Croissant French Toast

Prep: 20 minutes   **Bake:** 15 minutes

Nonstick cooking spray
4   purchased croissants, split
1   8-ounce tub light cream cheese spread with strawberries
2   eggs, lightly beaten
½   cup milk
½   teaspoon ground cinnamon
    Powdered sugar
    Fresh strawberries
    Maple syrup, warmed

1. Preheat oven to 375°F. Line a shallow baking pan with foil. Coat foil with cooking spray; set aside.

2. Spread cut sides of croissants with cream cheese. Place cut sides back together. In a shallow dish, beat together the eggs, milk, and cinnamon with a fork. Dip each filled croissant in the egg mixture for 30 seconds, turning once. Place in prepared baking pan.

3. Bake about 15 minutes or until browned and heated through. Sprinkle with powdered sugar. Serve warm with fresh strawberries and warm maple syrup. Makes 4 servings.

Per serving: 522 cal., 29 g fat (17 g sat. fat), 209 mg chol., 454 mg sodium, 53 g carbo., 3 g fiber, 13 g pro.

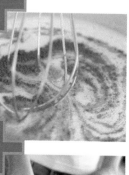

{teens can cook}
pizza!

Forget the delivery guy—nothing's faster than these homemade pizzas. The crust is already made and the assembly couldn't be easier. Let teens customize their pizzas by picking their favorite toppings, such as green peppers, onions, and more!

Pepperoni Pizza

Prep: 15 minutes **Bake:** 10 minutes

- 4 6-inch Italian bread shells or two 12-inch Italian bread shells (such as Boboli brand)
- 1 8-ounce can pizza sauce
- ½ teaspoon dried Italian seasoning, crushed
- 1 8-ounce package shredded four-cheese pizza cheese (2 cups)
- 1 3.5-ounce package sliced pepperoni
- 1 2.25-ounce can sliced pitted ripe olives, drained (optional)

1. Preheat oven to 425°F. Place bread shells on an ungreased baking sheet. In a small bowl, stir together pizza sauce and Italian seasoning. Spread pizza sauce mixture over bread shells.

2. Sprinkle bread shells with the cheese. Top with pepperoni and, if desired, olives. Bake about 10 minutes or until cheese is melted and bubbly. Makes 4 to 8 servings.

Per individual pizza: 1,167 cal., 66 g fat (36 g sat. fat), 192 mg chol., 2,811 mg sodium, 63 g carbo., 0 g fiber, 74 g pro.

Pizza Alfredo: Prepare as above except substitute ⅔ cup refrigerated Alfredo pasta sauce for pizza sauce and 1½ cups shredded cooked chicken breast for pepperoni. Omit olives. If desired, garnish with fresh snipped Italian (flat-leaf) parsley. Makes 4 to 8 servings.

Per individual pizza: 695 cal., 34 g fat (9 g sat. fat), 107 mg chol., 1,169 mg sodium, 54 g carbo., 0 g fiber, 43 g pro.

{teens can cook}
fast food

{ Whipping up savory sandwiches and smoothies is a supersimple way for teens to feed themselves. These goodies are not only tasty but much more nutritious than real fast food. }

Focaccia Turkey Sandwiches

Start to Finish: 15 minutes

1   8- to 9-inch Italian flatbread (focaccia)
¼   to ½ cup reduced-calorie Thousand
     Island dressing
4   ounces sliced cooked turkey breast
¼   cup thinly sliced red onion
1   small tomato, sliced
4   romaine lettuce leaves and/or ½ cup
     fresh spinach leaves

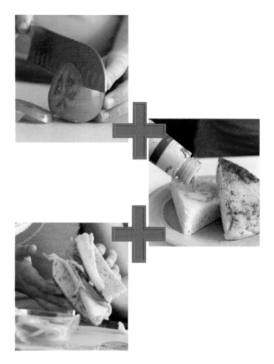

1. Cut focaccia into four wedges. Slice each wedge in half horizontally. Spread cut sides of bread with Thousand Island dressing. Layer bottom half of each focaccia wedge with turkey, onion, tomato, and lettuce. Add top half of each focaccia wedge. Makes 4 servings.

Per serving: 355 cal., 10 g fat (3 g sat. fat), 14 mg chol., 472 mg sodium, 53 g carbo., 5 g fiber, 16 g pro.

Tropical Smoothies

Chill: 1 hour   **Prep:** 10 minutes

2   medium bananas
½   cup fresh or canned pineapple, drained
1   mango
1   cup refrigerated jarred papaya
¼   cup apple juice
1   tablespoon honey
1   cup ice cubes

1. Chill the bananas, drained pineapple, and mango in the refrigerator for 1 hour. Peel and slice bananas and mango. Place bananas, pineapple, mango, and papaya in a blender. Add apple juice and honey. Cover and blend until smooth. With blender running, add ice cubes, one at a time, through opening in lid. Blend until smooth. Makes four 8-ounce servings.

Per serving: 172 cal., 1 g fat (0 g sat. fat), 0 mg chol., 4 mg sodium, 44 g carbo., 4 g fiber, 1 g pro.

{teens can cook}
lasagna

Young cooks will love the ease and convenience of this speedy lasagna recipe. Simply roll up the tasty fillings, pour on the sauce, and pop the whole thing in the oven. When it's done, teens can be proud of the home-cooked meal they made for the family.

Chicken Lasagna Rolls with Chive-Cream Sauce

Prep: 40 minutes   **Bake:** 35 minutes

  6   dried lasagna noodles
  1   8-ounce package reduced-fat cream
       cheese (Neufchâtel), softened
 ½   cup milk
 ¼   cup grated Romano or Parmesan cheese
  1   tablespoon snipped fresh chives
1½ cups chopped cooked chicken*
 ½   of a 10-ounce package frozen chopped
       broccoli, thawed and drained (1 cup)
 ½   cup bottled roasted red sweet peppers,
       drained and sliced
 ⅛   teaspoon ground black pepper
  1   cup purchased marinara or pasta sauce

1. Preheat oven to 350°F. Cook lasagna noodles according to package directions. Drain noodles, rinsing with cold water. Cut each in half crosswise; set aside.

2. For white sauce, in a mixing bowl, beat cream cheese with an electric mixer on medium for 30 seconds. Slowly add milk, beating until smooth. Stir in Romano cheese and chives.

3. For filling, in a mixing bowl, stir together ½ cup of the white sauce, chicken, broccoli, roasted red sweet pepper, and ground black pepper. Place ¼ cup filling at one end of each cooked noodle and roll. Place rolls, seam sides down, in a 3-quart rectangular baking dish.

4. Spoon the marinara sauce over the rolls. Spoon remaining white sauce over marinara sauce. Cover with foil. Bake for 35 to 40 minutes or until heated through. Makes 6 servings.

*Tip: If you need cooked chicken for a recipe but don't have any leftovers, use a purchased deli-roasted chicken.

Per serving: 288 cal., 13 g fat (7 g sat. fat), 65 mg chol., 412 mg sodium, 22 g carbo., 2 g fiber, 19 g pro.

{teens can cook}
quesadillas

Ooey, gooey, and packed with cheese—
this dish is the perfect indulgence for a
Saturday night with friends. Let your
teen invite the gang over for quesadillas,
movies, and laugh-out-loud fun.

BBQ Chicken Quesadillas

Dip quesadilla wedges into salsa and sour cream. Or top the quesadillas with condiments and eat them with a knife and fork.

Prep: 20 minutes
Cook: 4 minutes per batch

4   7- or 8-inch flour tortillas
1   18-ounce tub refrigerated
    shredded chicken with
    barbecue sauce (2 cups)
1   cup shredded extra-sharp
    cheddar cheese or Mexican-
    blend cheese (4 ounces)
1   4-ounce can diced green chile
    peppers, drained
    Nonstick cooking spray
1   cup bottled salsa
$^1/_4$ cup dairy sour cream
$^1/_4$ cup sliced green onion

1. Place tortillas on cutting board. Spread half of each tortilla with $^1/_2$ cup of the barbecue chicken. Sprinkle $^1/_4$ cup of the cheese over chicken. Top with drained chile peppers. Fold tortillas in half, pressing gently.
2. Spray a 10-inch nonstick skillet with nonstick cooking spray. Heat skillet over medium heat. Cook quesadillas, two at a time, in hot skillet for 4 to 6 minutes or until light brown, turning once. Remove quesadillas from skillet; place on a baking sheet. Keep warm in a 300°F oven. Repeat with remaining quesadillas. To serve, cut each quesadilla into 3 wedges. Serve with salsa, sour cream, and green onion. Makes 4 main-dish servings.

Per serving: 469 cal., 21 g fat (10 g sat. fat), 86 mg chol., 1,629 mg sodium, 46 g carbo., 1 g fiber, 25 g pro.

{kids can cook}
mac & cheese

Make cooking fun and kids will learn to love it! This cheesy macaroni recipe is a made-from-scratch version that tastes better than boxed and is just as easy to make. With a little encouragement, your budding chef will catch on quickly.

Macaroni & Cheese

Start to Finish: 35 minutes

8   ounces dried elbow macaroni and/or
    desired fun-shape pasta (2 cups)
1   12-ounce package sliced reduced-fat
    process American cheese, torn
2   tablespoons butter or margarine
2   tablespoons all-purpose flour
⅛   teaspoon ground black pepper
1½ cups fat-free milk

1. Follow the package directions to cook macaroni. While the macaroni is cooking, tear cheese slices. Drain the macaroni in a colander.

2. For the cheese sauce, in a saucepan, melt butter over medium heat. Stir in flour and pepper. Add milk all at once. Cook and stir until sauce is slightly thickened and bubbly. Add cheese; stir until cheese is melted and mixed in.

3. Carefully stir the cooked macaroni into the saucepan full of cheese sauce. Be sure to coat all macaroni with the sauce. Cook over low heat for 2 to 3 minutes or until heated through, stirring frequently. Let stand 10 minutes before serving. Makes 4 servings.

Oven Macaroni and Cheese: Preheat oven to 350°F. Prepare as above, except increase milk to 2 cups. Transfer mixture from the saucepan to a 2-quart casserole dish. Bake, uncovered, for 25 to 30 minutes or until bubbly and heated through. Let stand for 10 minutes before serving.

Per serving: 507 calories, 20 g total fat (11 g sat. fat), 2 g fiber, 54 g carbo, 62 mg chol., 1,245 mg sodium, 29 g pro.

{three easy steps:}

{kids can cook}
quick snacks

{ Whether it's an after-school bite, a Saturday afternoon treat, or a sleepover snack, these recipes are both fun and nutritious. Perfect for little cooks to make on their own. }

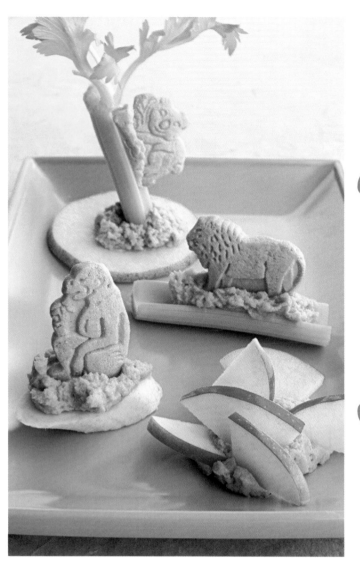

> **Try this:**
> For a choco-licious spin on this tasty treat, stir in chocolate-hazelnut spread instead of peanut butter.

Safari Snacks

Start to Finish: 10 minutes

½ of an 8-ounce package reduced-fat cream cheese (Neufchâtel), softened
½ cup creamy peanut butter
2 to 3 tablespoons milk
2 teaspoons honey
Celery sticks, banana slices, animal crackers, and/or assorted dippers, such as carrot sticks, sliced apples, pear wedges, or graham crackers

1. For dip, in a small mixing bowl, beat cream cheese with an electric mixer on medium speed until smooth. Beat in peanut butter, milk, and honey until well combined and smooth. If desired, chill before serving.

2. To serve, spread dip on celery sticks and garnish with animal crackers. Or serve with assorted dippers. Makes twenty 1-tablespoon servings (1¼ cups).

Per 1 tablespoon dip with dippers: 65 cal., 5 g fat (2 g sat. fat), 4 mg chol., 59 mg sodium, 4 g carbo., 1 g fiber, 2 g pro.

Kickin' Cheesy Popcorn

Start to Finish: 10 minutes

8   cups popped popcorn
2   tablespoons butter or
    margarine, melted
1   teaspoon chili powder
⅛   teaspoon garlic powder
2   tablespoons grated
    Parmesan
    cheese

1. Place popcorn in a large bowl. In a small bowl, stir together melted butter, chili powder, and garlic powder. Drizzle over popcorn; toss to coat. Sprinkle with Parmesan cheese; toss to coat. Store in a tightly covered container at room temperature up to 3 days. Makes 10 servings (about 8 cups).

Per serving: 51 cal., 3 g fat (2 g sat. fat), 7 mg chol., 46 mg sodium, 5 g carbo., 1 g fiber, 1 g pro.

Double Dippin' Fruit
Start to Finish: 15 minutes

1   4-ounce container vanilla pudding
      (prepared pudding cup)
3   tablespoons caramel ice cream topping
½   teaspoon vanilla
¼   of an 8-ounce container frozen light
      whipped dessert topping, thawed
¾   cup low-fat granola
      Assorted fresh fruit, such as
      sliced apples, banana chunks,
      and/or strawberries

1. For caramel dip, in a medium bowl, combine pudding, caramel topping, and vanilla; stir until smooth. Fold in whipped topping.

Try this:
Make this fruit dip a buffet of textures and flavors. Add bowls of raisins, sunflower seeds, chocolate chips, or rice cereal.

2. Spoon caramel dip into a serving bowl. Place granola in another serving bowl. Serve with fruit. (To serve, dip fruit in caramel dip, then in granola.) Makes 6 servings.

Per serving: 129 cal., 3 g fat (2 g sat. fat), 0 mg chol., 86 mg sodium, 24 g carbo., 1 g fiber, 1 g pro.

after-school munchies

It's 3:00, school's out, and the kids are hungry! What to do? Stock up on some healthful ingredients and serve them something that's as good for them as it is delicious. (And try Indoor S'mores for a special treat). The best part is, these recipes are easy enough for most kids to make. Just provide a little assistance as needed, and the snacking's on.

peanut butter who?

Whipped cream cheese and apple butter are a perfect creamy PB substitute.

Apple Butter & Banana Sandwiches

Start to Finish: 10 minutes

3 tablespoons apple butter or applesauce
3 tablespoons whipped cream cheese
4 slices whole wheat bread
1 small banana, peeled and sliced
2 tablespoons raisins (optional)

1. In a small bowl, whisk together the apple butter and cream cheese until smooth. Spread mixture over 2 of the bread slices. Top with banana slices and, if desired, raisins. Top with remaining bread. Cut in half to serve. Makes 2 servings.

Tip: For open-face sandwiches, cut bread slices into desired shapes and spread with apple butter mixture. Top with desired fruit.

Per serving: 477 cal., 10 g fat (4 g sat. fat), 16 mg chol., 670 mg sodium, 92 g carbo., 9 g fiber, 9 g pro.

Carrot-Raisin Peanut Butter Sandwiches

Sneak some veggies into their favorite sweet sandwich by topping peanut butter with shredded carrots.

Start to Finish: 15 minutes

8   slices white, whole wheat, or
     cinnamon bread
½ to ⅔ cup peanut butter
¼   cup raisins
¼   cup shredded carrot

1. Preheat broiler. Spread half of the bread slices with peanut butter; top with the raisins, carrot, and remaining bread slices. Broil 4 inches from heat for 1 to 2 minutes. Turn sandwiches. Broil for 1 to 2 minutes more or until toasted. Cut into triangles or squares. Makes 4 sandwiches.

Per sandwich: 354 cal., 18 g fat (4 g sat. fat), 1 mg chol., 422 mg sodium, 39 g carbo., 4 g fiber, 13 g pro.

Indoor S'mores

*Enjoy easy s'mores any time of year. Fudge topping keeps
the marshmallows in place until they melt.*
Start to Finish: 10 minutes

   4   graham crackers, quartered
   4   teaspoons fudge ice cream topping
  64   miniature marshmallows
       (about ¾ cup)
   4   teaspoons strawberry jam

1. Place 8 graham cracker quarters on
a microwave-safe plate. Spread ice
cream topping evenly on the crackers.
Top evenly with marshmallows (about
8 each). Microwave on 100-percent
power (high) for 30 seconds.

2. Spoon jam evenly over
marshmallows and quickly top with
the remaining graham cracker
quarters. Serve immediately. Makes
8 s'mores.

Peanut Butter S'mores: Prepare as
directed, except use chocolate
graham crackers and substitute
peanut butter for ice cream topping.
Omit jam, if desired.

   Per s'more: 52 cal., 0 g fat (0 g sat. fat),
0 mg chol., 32 mg sodium, 12 g carbo., 0 g fiber,
0 g pro.

Pretzel Pets

Start to Finish: 15 minutes

½ of an 8-ounce container
    whipped cream cheese
1 tablespoon honey
1 15-ounce can pear halves
    in light syrup, drained
    Small pretzel twists
    Desired dried fruit, snipped
    Pretzel sticks, broken

1. In a bowl, mix cream cheese and honey. Fill pear halves with cream cheese mixture. Top each with pretzels and fruit to create pet. Makes 5 pets.

Per pet: 200 cal., 7 g fat (4 g sat.), 22 mg chol., 391 mg sodium, 33 g carbo., 2 g fiber, 3 g pro.

Fruit Kabobs with Creamy Dipping Sauce

Start to Finish: 15 minutes

2   fresh kiwifruits, peeled and quartered
8   fresh pineapple chunks
8   fresh strawberries
16 large fresh blueberries
1   6-ounce carton strawberry or
    blueberry low-fat yogurt
½   cup light dairy sour cream
2   tablespoons strawberry or
    blueberry spread

1. Alternately thread fruit on each of eight 6-inch skewers.
2. In a small bowl, stir together yogurt, sour cream, and strawberry spread. Serve kabobs with sauce. Makes 8 kabobs.

Per 2 kabobs: 142 cal., 3 g fat (2 g sat. fat), 11 mg chol., 51 mg sodium, 27 g carbo., 2 g fiber, 3 g pro.

Salad-to-Go

Start to Finish: 10 minutes

- 1 cup dried apples, coarsely chopped
- 1 cup seedless red or green grapes
- ½ cup purchased sliced crinkle-cut carrot
- ¼ cup raisins, dried cranberries, or mixed dried fruit bits
- ¼ cup honey-roasted cashews or peanuts

1. In a medium bowl, toss together apples, grapes, carrot, raisins, and nuts. Divide among 4 plastic bags or cups. Makes 4 servings.

Per serving: 251 cal., 3 g fat (1 g sat. fat), 3 mg chol., 152 mg sodium, 51 g carbo., 3 g fiber, 9 g pro.

Pretzel Snack Mix

Start to Finish: 5 minutes

- 3 cups pretzel sticks
- 2 cups puffed corn cereal
- 2 cups honey graham cereal

1. In a mixing bowl, combine pretzels and cereals. Store, covered, in an airtight container for up to 3 days. Makes 6 cups.

Per serving: 157 cal., 1 g fat (0 g sat. fat), 0 mg chol., 547 mg sodium, 33 g carbo., 1 g fiber, 1 g pro.

picky eater pleasers

You want your children to eat adequate amounts of nutritious food, but just how much is one serving?

{ pint-size portions for kids 6–12 years old }

Here are some recommendations for serving sizes, but remember that one size doesn't necessarily fit every child. Adjust portions according to age, weight, and activity level.

grains
6 or more servings a day

CEREAL:
An amount of cold cereal the size of a tennis ball equals one serving.

PASTA OR RICE:
An amount half the size of a baseball equals one serving.

BAGEL:
Half of a large bagel, about the size of a hockey puck, equals one serving.

fruits & veggies
5 or more servings a day

MIXED VEGETABLES:
An amount half the size of a baseball equals one serving.

APPLE:
Any fresh fruit that is about the size of a baseball is one serving.

FRUIT JUICE:
One 4-ounce glass of fruit juice equals one serving.

dairy
2 or more servings a day

MILK:
One 8-ounce glass of milk equals one serving.

CHEESE:
Three slices of cheese, each about the size of a domino, equals one serving.

YOGURT:
An amount of yogurt the size of a tennis ball equals one serving.

meat/ protein
3 or more servings a day

PEANUT BUTTER:
An amount the size of a golf ball equals one serving.

CHICKEN BREAST:
A chicken breast the size of a deck of cards is one serving.

PINTO BEANS:
An amount of legumes the size of a baseball equals one serving.

Veggie Nuggets

Prep: 20 minutes **Bake:** 15 minutes

Nonstick cooking spray
1 egg yolk
¼ cup milk
½ cup seasoned fine dry bread crumbs
¼ cup grated Parmesan cheese
4 cups vegetables, such as ¼-inch-thick
    slices zucchini, peeled baby carrots,
    broccoli florets, and/or green beans
2 tablespoons butter, melted (optional)
¾ cup bottled ranch salad dressing
    Shredded cheddar cheese

1. Lightly coat a baking sheet with cooking spray; set aside. Preheat oven to 400°F. In a shallow dish, whisk together the egg yolk and milk. In another shallow dish, stir together the bread crumbs and Parmesan cheese. Dip vegetables in egg mixture, then in bread crumb mixture to coat. Arrange vegetable pieces on the prepared baking sheet. If desired, drizzle with melted butter.

2. Bake for 15 to 20 minutes or until vegetables are tender and golden. Serve warm with ranch dressing that has been sprinkled with cheddar cheese. Makes 5 to 6 servings.

Per serving: 271 cal., 22 g fat (4 g sat. fat), 51 mg chol., 662 mg sodium, 14 g carbo., 1 g fiber, 5 g pro.

Chicken & Biscuit Pockets

Kids will be so busy munching on these pockets, they'll never know summer squash loaded with vitamins A and C is hidden inside.

Prep: 20 minutes **Bake:** 10 minutes

- 1 6-ounce package (5) refrigerated buttermilk biscuits
- $1/2$ cup finely chopped cooked chicken
- $1/3$ cup coarsely shredded yellow summer squash
- $1/4$ cup shredded Monterey Jack or cheddar cheese
- $1/2$ cup mayonnaise dressing
- 1 tablespoon honey mustard
- $1/2$ cup bottled ranch salad dressing

1. Preheat oven to 400°F. Separate biscuits and flatten each with the palm of your hand to a $3^{1}/_{2}$-inch circle. Divide chicken, squash, and cheese evenly among dough circles, placing filling on one side of each dough circle. Fold the other sides of dough circles over filling; pinch edges well to seal.* Arrange filled biscuits on an ungreased baking sheet. Bake about 10 minutes or until golden.

2. Meanwhile, in a small bowl, stir together mayonnaise and mustard. Serve mayonnaise mixture and ranch dressing as dipping sauces for warm biscuits. Makes 5 servings.

*__Tip:__ For a tighter seal, press edges with the tines of a fork.

Per pocket: 414 cal., 34 g fat (7 g sat. fat), 30 mg chol., 663 mg sodium, 19 g carbo., 0 g fiber, 8 g pro.

Turkey & Tomato Wraps
Start to Finish: 15 minutes

4   butterhead lettuce leaves (Bibb
     or Boston)
4   ounces very thinly sliced cooked
     turkey breast
2   teaspoons honey mustard or low-fat
     mayonnaise or salad dressing
1   small roma tomato, halved and
     very thinly sliced

1. Place lettuce leaves on a flat surface. Cut leaves in half lengthwise; remove center vein.
2. Place ½ ounce turkey onto each leaf just below the center. Spread honey mustard over turkey. Top with tomato slices. Roll up, starting from a short side. Secure with wooden toothpicks. Makes 8 wraps.

Per 2 wraps: 35 cal., 1 g fat (0 g sat. fat), 11 mg chol., 338 mg sodium, 3 g carbo., 0 g fiber, 5 g pro.

Shape Sandwiches

*Teach your tots a lesson about different shapes while
you make these whole wheat cutouts.*

Start to Finish: 10 minutes

1. Using small cutters, cut two slices whole wheat bread into desired shapes
(squares, circles, triangles, or rectangles). Spread ¼ cup spreadable cream
cheese evenly on shapes. Let children top sandwiches with fruit toppings,
such as sliced strawberries, apple slices, banana slices, or raspberries. Makes
2 servings.

Per serving: 174 cal., 11 g fat (7 g sat. fat), 32 mg chol., 204 mg sodium, 14 g carbo.,
2 g fiber, 6 g pro.

Fruit-Topped Tostadas
Start to Finish: 25 minutes

2 7- to 8-inch multigrain or regular
   flour tortillas
Light spreadable plain or flavored
   cream cheese
Desired chopped fruit, such as bananas,
   strawberries, raspberries, kiwifruits,
   and/or blueberries
Chopped nuts, such as toasted
   almonds, flavored sliced almonds,
   and/or toasted pecans (optional)

1. Preheat broiler. Cut tortillas into quarters or use desired-shape cutters. Broil 2 to 3 minutes or until toasted. Cool slightly. Spread cream cheese on wedges and top with desired fruit and nut toppings. Makes 8 tostadas.

Per 2 tostadas: 133 cal., 4 g fat (2 g sat. fat), 8 mg chol., 236 mg sodium, 18 g carbo., 6 g fiber, 6 g pro.

Double-Decker Fruit Stacks

Start to Finish: 20 minutes

½   **of an 8-ounce tub light cream cheese, softened**
½   **teaspoon finely shredded orange peel**
2   **to 3 teaspoons fat-free milk**
3   **8-inch whole wheat or plain flour tortillas**
1   **medium apple, pear, and/or banana**
¼   **cup chopped almonds, pecans, or walnuts, toasted (optional)**

1. In a small bowl, stir together cream cheese, orange peel, and enough milk to make spreading consistency; set aside.

Spread tortillas with cream cheese mixture; set aside. If using apple or pear, core and thinly slice crosswise. If using banana, peel and slice.

2. On 1 tortilla, arrange half of the fruit slices, cream cheese side up. If desired, sprinkle with half of the almonds. Top with another tortilla, cream cheese side up. Top with remaining fruit slices and, if desired, remaining almonds. Top with remaining tortilla, cream cheese side down. Cut into wedges to serve. Makes 4 to 6 wedges.

Per wedge: 177 cal., 6 g fat (3 g sat. fat), 13 mg chol., 419 mg sodium, 26 g carbo., 2 g fiber, 6 g pro.

Pumpkin Cream Cheese Spread

Look for flavored bagels (cinnamon, apple, or raisin) or use mini bagels, which are even more appealing to kids.

Start to Finish: 15 minutes

1   8-ounce package cream cheese, softened
½   cup canned pumpkin
2   tablespoons sugar
½   teaspoon pumpkin pie spice or ground cinnamon
    Bagels or English muffins, split and toasted
    Roasted shelled sunflower seeds (optional)

1. In a mixing bowl, beat cream cheese, pumpkin, sugar, and pumpkin pie spice with an electric mixer on medium speed until smooth. Cover and chill for up to 1 week.

2. To serve, quarter the bagels or muffin halves. Spread desired amount of the pumpkin cream cheese on the toasted sides of bagel pieces. Sprinkle with sunflower seeds, if desired. Makes 1½ cups spread.

Per 2-tablespoon serving: 39 cal., 3 g fat (2 g sat. fat), 10 mg chol., 28 mg sodium, 2 g carbo., 0 g fiber, 1 g pro.

*VITAMIN SNEAK ATTACK!
Pumpkin is packed with vitamin A—each serving of this spread contains 18 percent of the recommended daily value!

✱ DID YOU KNOW?
If you don't have oat bran, place 2 cups regular rolled oats in a food processor. Cover and process until finely ground.

Banana Oat Muffins

Start to Finish: 30 minutes

Nonstick cooking spray
1½ cups oat bran
1 cup all-purpose flour
2 teaspoons baking powder
½ teaspoon salt
¼ teaspoon baking soda
1 egg, slightly beaten
¾ cup mashed ripe banana
½ cup fat-free milk
¼ cup honey
2 tablespoons cooking oil
½ cup semisweet chocolate pieces
   or raisins

1. Preheat oven to 400°F. Lightly coat the bottoms of twelve 2½-inch muffin cups with cooking spray; set aside. In a bowl, stir together oat bran, flour, baking powder, salt, and baking soda. Make a well in the center of the flour mixture; set aside.

2. In a small bowl, stir together egg, banana, milk, honey, and oil. Add banana mixture to well in flour mixture. Stir just until moistened (batter should be lumpy). Fold in chocolate pieces. Spoon batter into the prepared muffin cups.

3. Bake 14 to 16 minutes or until golden and a wooden toothpick inserted in centers comes out clean. Cool on a wire rack. Serve warm. Makes 12 muffins.

Per muffin: 167 cal., 6 g fat (2 g sat. fat), 18 mg chol., 175 mg sodium, 30 g carbo., 3 g fiber, 4 g pro.

Yam & Jam Muffins

Sweet potatoes pump vitamin A into these sweet and spicy, low-fat muffins. They're great as an after-school snack or even for dessert.

Prep: 20 minutes **Bake:** 18 minutes
Cool: 25 minutes

1³/₄ **cups all-purpose flour**
¹/₃ **cup packed brown sugar**
1¹/₂ **teaspoons baking powder**
¹/₂ **teaspoon baking soda**
1 **teaspoon apple pie spice or ground cinnamon**
¹/₄ **teaspoon salt**
¹/₂ **of a 17-ounce can sweet potatoes, drained (about 1 cup)**
1 **egg, beaten**
¹/₂ **cup milk**
¹/₃ **cup fruit jam or preserves (such as plum, strawberry, peach, or apricot)**
¹/₄ **cup cooking oil**

1. Preheat oven to 400°F. Lightly grease twelve 2¹/₂-inch muffin cups or line with paper bake cups; set aside.

2. In a large bowl, stir together flour, brown sugar, baking powder, baking soda, apple pie spice, and salt. Make a well in center of flour mixture; set aside.

3. In another bowl, mash the drained sweet potatoes with a fork. Stir in egg, milk, jam, and oil. Add sweet potato mixture all at once to flour mixture. Stir just until moistened (batter should be lumpy). Spoon batter into prepared muffin cups, filling each about three-fourths full.

4. Bake for 18 to 20 minutes or until golden and a wooden toothpick inserted in centers comes out clean. Cool in muffin cups on a wire rack for 5 minutes. Remove from muffin cups. Cool slightly. If desired, top with additional jam or preserves. Makes 12 muffins.

Per muffin: 215 cal., 6 g fat (1 g sat. fat), 19 mg chol., 174 mg sodium, 39 g carbo., 1 g fiber, 3 g pro.

PICKY TIP
When baking these muffins, canned sweet potatoes are used in place of oil to add vitamins and decrease fat.

No-Nuts Cereal Snack

Start to Finish: 35 minutes

2   cups puffed corn cereal
2   cups round toasted oat cereal
1   cup small fish-shape cheese crackers
1   cup chow mein noodles
3   tablespoons cooking oil
1   0.4-ounce envelope dry buttermilk
    salad dressing mix (1 tablespoon)

1. Preheat oven to 350°F. In a 13 × 9 × 2-inch baking pan, combine cereals, crackers, and chow mein noodles. Drizzle oil over mixture; toss to coat. Sprinkle with dressing mix; toss to coat.

2. Bake for 10 minutes, stirring once. Cool in pan for 15 minutes. Store in an airtight container at room temperature for up to 1 week. Makes 6 servings.

Per serving: 236 cal., 12 g fat (2 g sat. fat), 1 mg chol., 449 mg sodium, 28 g carbo., 2 g fiber, 4 g pro.

Bear-y Good Snack Mix

Start to Finish: 5 minutes

1½   cups cinnamon-flavor bear-shape
     graham snack cookies
½   cup raisins
½   cup dried tart cherries
½   cup candy-coated milk chocolate
     pieces or semisweet chocolate
     pieces
¼   cup chopped dried pineapple

1. In a large bowl, stir together all ingredients. Transfer to an airtight container; cover and store at room temperature for up to 24 hours or store in the refrigerator for up to 2 days. Makes 3¼ cups (4 to 6 servings).

Per serving: 351 cal., 8 g fat (3 g sat. fat), 2 mg chol., 125 mg sodium, 68 g carbo., 3 g fiber, 3 g pro.

Sweet 'n' Nutty Popcorn
Start to Finish: 10 minutes

1¼	cups sugar
¼	cup water
2	tablespoons butter
⅛	teaspoon ground cinnamon
6	cups popped popcorn
2	cups bite-size wheat square cereal
1	cup salted cashews
1	cup golden raisins

1. In a 5- to 6-quart Dutch oven, combine sugar, water, butter, and cinnamon. Bring to boiling over medium heat, stirring constantly. Continue to cook for 4 minutes more, stirring occasionally. Remove syrup from heat.

2. Add the popcorn, cereal, cashews, and raisins to the syrup; stir quickly to coat all ingredients evenly. Spread mixture in a single layer on 1 or 2 large baking sheets lined with waxed paper or parchment paper. Cool completely. Break up any large pieces. Store in an airtight container at room temperature for up to 3 days. Makes 12 cups.

Per ½ cup: 117 cal., 4 g fat (1 g sat. fat), 3 mg chol., 48 mg sodium, 20 g carbo., 1 g fiber, 2 g pro.

Crunchy Cracker Mix
Start to Finish: 35 minutes

4	cups bite-size cheese crackers
5	cups wheat stick crackers
3	cups pretzel twists
2	cups mixed nuts
½	cup butter or margarine, melted
1	0.6- to 0.7-ounce envelope cheese-garlic or Italian-flavor dry salad dressing mix

1. Preheat oven to 300°F. Place cheese crackers and wheat crackers in a large roasting pan. Bake about 5 minutes or until warm.

2. Add pretzel twists and nuts to pan. Pour melted butter over mixture. Sprinkle with salad dressing mix; stir well to coat. Bake for 20 minutes more, stirring once. Spread mixture on foil to cool. Store in an airtight container at room temperature for up to 1 week. Makes 13 cups.

Per ¼ cup: 80 cal., 6 g fat (2 g sat. fat), 5 mg chol., 165 mg sodium, 5 g carbo., 1 g fiber, 2 g pro.

Goldfish Trail Mix

Start to Finish: 10 minutes

1 cup bite-size fish-shape crackers
1 cup round toasted-oat cereal with
   nuts and honey
1 cup pretzel sticks or twists
1 cup raisins, dried tart cherries, dried
   cranberries, and/or chopped dried
   pineapple

1. In a large bowl, combine all ingredients. Divide mix among 8 snack-size resealable bags. Store at room temperature for up to 2 weeks. Makes 4 cups.

Per ½ cup: 121 cal., 2 g fat (0 g sat. fat), 2 mg chol., 173 mg sodium, 26 g carbo., 1 g fiber, 2 g pro.

Nutty Corn and Fruit Mix

Start to Finish: 15 minutes

1	package (6- to 7-cup yield) plain microwave popcorn
	Nonstick cooking spray
2	to 3 tablespoons grated Parmesan cheese
2	cups potato sticks
1½	cups peanuts or almonds
1	cup mixed dried fruit

1. Pop popcorn according to package directions. Pour popcorn into a very large bowl; coat with cooking spray.
2. Sprinkle popcorn with Parmesan cheese; toss gently to coat. Stir in potato sticks, peanuts, and dried fruit. Makes about 12 cups.

Per 1 cup: 190 cal., 13 g fat (2 g sat. fat), 1 mg chol., 125 mg sodium, 16 g carbo., 2 g fiber, 6 g pro.

picky strategies

Ever wonder how to get picky eaters to try new things? Get 'em involved with four of their senses:

✳ Smell it—teach kids to use their noses when trying new food. Ask what the scent makes them think of.

✳ Feel it—encourage kids to describe the texture of new food. Is it crunchy? Soft?

✳ Look at it—color and shape are great ways to engage kids.

✳ Taste it—of course! Coax a little nibble and talk about the flavor. Is it sour? Sweet?

Dried Fruit Snack Mix

This snack mix has a nice combo of sweet and salty flavors. Store it in the freezer so the cereal and pretzels stay crisp.

Start to Finish: 10 minutes

½ cup dried tart red cherries or raisins
½ cup dried pineapple, chopped
½ cup small pretzel twists
½ cup round toasted oat cereal or puffed corn cereal

1. Stir together all ingredients in a large bowl. Place in an airtight container. Seal; store in freezer up to 1 week. Makes four ½-cup servings.

Per serving: 162 cal., 1 g fat (0 g sat. fat), 0 mg chol., 120 mg sodium, 38 g carbo., 2 g fiber, 2 g pro.

Granola-Topped Pudding

No time for fancy chocolate curls? Instead, sprinkle with semisweet chocolate pieces.

Start to Finish: 15 minutes

1   4-serving-size package fat-free, sugar-free, reduced-calorie chocolate instant pudding mix
2   cups milk
½   of an 8-ounce package reduced-fat cream cheese (Neufchâtel), softened
¼   cup peanut butter
1   cup granola cereal
    Milk chocolate curls* (optional)

1. In a large bowl, whisk together the pudding mix and 1¾ cups of the milk for 2 minutes or until thickened; set aside. In a medium bowl, whisk together the cream cheese, peanut butter, and the remaining ¼ cup milk until smooth.

2. Spoon pudding mixture evenly into 4 dessert dishes. Top evenly with cream cheese mixture. Sprinkle each serving with granola before serving. If desired, garnish with chocolate curls. Makes 4 servings.

*Tip: To make milk chocolate curls, draw a vegetable peeler across a thick bar of milk chocolate. It helps if the chocolate is at room temperature.

Per serving: 374 cal., 22 g fat (9 g sat. fat), 31 mg chol., 577 mg sodium, 33 g carbo., 3 g fiber, 14 g pro.

Easy Peach-Blueberry Crisp

The cookie topping provides the "crisp" in this stovetop dessert. Shortbread cookies are yummy, but you could use another favorite, such as gingersnaps or pecan sandies.
Start to Finish: 20 minutes

2 cups frozen unsweetened peach slices
2 tablespoons packed brown sugar
1 tablespoon water
½ teaspoon pumpkin pie spice
¼ cup fresh or frozen blueberries
8 shortbread cookies or other crisp
   cookies, coarsely crushed

1. In a medium saucepan, stir together peach slices, brown sugar, water, and spice. Bring to boiling, stirring to combine; reduce heat. Simmer, uncovered, for 4 to 5 minutes or until peach mixture is thickened. Gently stir in blueberries. Remove from heat. Cover and let stand for 5 minutes. Spoon peach mixture into dessert dishes. Sprinkle each serving with cookies. Makes 4 servings.

Per serving: 208 cal., 8 g fat (0 g sat. fat), 10 mg chol., 133 mg sodium, 35 g carbo., 2 g fiber, 4 g pro.

Goin' Bananas Malts

Start to Finish: 5 minutes

1 pint vanilla ice cream
1 ripe banana, peeled and sliced
½ cup milk
2 tablespoons instant malted
   milk powder

1. In a blender, combine ice cream, banana, milk, and malted milk powder. Cover and blend until smooth. Pour into glasses. Makes 2 cups.

Per ⅔ cup: 359 cal., 18 g fat (11 g sat. fat), 98 mg chol., 146 mg sodium, 43 g carbo., 1 g fiber, 7 g pro.

Fantastic, frosty, and fruity! The Goin' Bananas Malts offer kids a flavor twist on one of their favorite snacks.

storing bananas

Store bananas at room temperature until ripe. When bananas are the right color for your desired use, place them in the refrigerator until you need them. The peel turns black when the fruit is refrigerated, but the pulp stays at the desired ripeness for a few days.

{ Make this Banana Dip a supereasy snack with cut-up fresh fruit found in your supermarket's produce department. }

Fruit with Banana Dip

Prep: 20 minutes **Chill:** up to 2 hours

1 medium banana, peeled and sliced
½ cup low-fat lemon yogurt
1 tablespoon sugar
1 teaspoon lemon juice
4 cups cut-up fresh fruit, such as papaya, banana, strawberries, pineapple, cantaloupe, honeydew melon, mango, kiwifruit, and/or blueberries

1. For dip, in a blender, combine banana, yogurt, sugar, and lemon juice. Cover and blend until smooth. Transfer to a small bowl. Cover and chill dip for up to 2 hours. To serve, arrange fruit on a platter. Serve with dip. Makes 4 servings.

Per serving: 139 cal., 1 g fat (0 g sat. fat), 2 mg chol., 30 mg sodium, 32 g carbo., 3 g fiber, 2 g pro.

Rocky Road Malts

Start to Finish: 10 minutes

1   **quart chocolate ice cream**
⅓   **to ½ cup milk**
⅓   **cup chocolate instant
     malted milk powder**
¼   **cup creamy peanut butter**
     Marshmallow cream (optional)
     Coarsely chopped peanuts (optional)
     Miniature sandwich cookies (optional)

1. Place half of the ice cream, ⅓ cup of the milk, the malted milk powder, and the peanut butter in a blender. Cover; blend until smooth. Spoon in remaining ice cream; blend until smooth. If necessary, add additional milk until malts are desired consistency.
2. To serve, spoon into glasses. If desired, top malts with marshmallow cream, chopped peanuts, and miniature sandwich cookies. Makes 4 servings.

Per serving: 493 cal., 24 g fat (11 g sat. fat), 47 mg chol., 252 mg sodium, 66 g carbo., 4 g fiber, 11 g pro.

Tropical Treat
Start to Finish: 10 minutes

1   single-serving container vanilla or banana pudding, applesauce, or vanilla yogurt
1   tablespoon tropical-blend dried fruit bits
1   tablespoon chopped almonds or macadamia nuts (optional)
1   teaspoon toasted coconut, toasted wheat germ, or granola cereal

1. In a bowl, stir together the pudding, fruit bits, and, if desired, nuts. Top with toasted coconut. Makes 1 serving.

Per serving: 201 cal., 6 g fat (3 g sat. fat), 0 mg chol., 183 mg sodium, 33 g carbo., 1 g fiber, 2 g pro.

⑤ ways to outsmart picky eaters

{1} Serve a variety of kid-pleasing foods at each meal. Expect that your child will eat some and leave others.

{2} Place a new food in front of your child at mealtime without making a big deal about it. Chances are your child will go for at least one bite.

{3} Introduce new foods one at a time and in small amounts. At mealtime, offer one or two favorite foods along with something new.

{4} Wait until your child is hungry to introduce something new, such as sliced mango.

{5} Realize that some children's palates are more sensitive than others, and they simply won't like the texture, color, or taste of some foods. Maybe toast reminds them of a time when they were sick. Or perhaps the mere thought of biting into a strawberry makes them pucker up.

we like, they like

Tired of making two meals each night—one for the kids and one for the adults? Instead, try this: one meal tweaked two different ways so everyone wins!

Great Grilled Burgers
Prep: 20 minutes   **Grill:** 14 minutes

- 1½ pounds lean ground beef
- 1 teaspoon dried Italian seasoning, crushed
- ½ teaspoon salt
- ½ teaspoon ground black pepper
- ¼ cup finely chopped onion
- 2 slices cheddar or Edam cheese (2 ounces)
- 2 hamburger buns, split and toasted
  Desired toppers, such as sliced tomato, sliced onion, lettuce, and pickles

1. Combine beef, Italian seasoning, salt, and pepper. Transfer half of the mixture to another bowl for the Mini Cheddar Burgers. Add onion to the remaining beef mixture; mix well. Shape into two ¾-inch-thick patties.

2. For a charcoal grill, grill patties directly over medium coals for 12 to 16 minutes (160°F), turning once halfway through grilling. Top each burger with a slice of cheese. Grill about 1 minute more or until cheese is just melted. (For a gas grill, preheat grill. Reduce heat to medium. Place patties on grill rack over heat. Cover and grill as above.) Place burgers in buns; top with desired toppers. Makes 2 burgers.

Per burger: 540 cal., 25 g fat (11 g sat. fat), 131 mg chol., 945 mg sodium, 31 g carbo., 2 g fiber, 44 g pro.

for the grown-ups
Adults will drool over these flavorful burgers with Edam cheese.

Mini Cheddar Burgers

Prep: 20 minutes   **Grill:** 11 minutes

½ recipe Great Grilled Burgers (see
    recipe, page 354)
4 slices cheddar cheese (4 ounces)
8 ½-inch-thick slices baguette-style
    French bread, toasted, or 4 small
    round dinner rolls (such as potato
    rolls or dollar rolls), split and toasted,
    if desired
Ketchup and/or yellow mustard
Desired garnishes, such as pimiento-
    stuffed olives, small pickles, and/or
    cherry tomatoes (optional)

1. Using reserved beef mixture from Great Grilled Burgers, shape mixture into four ¾-inch-thick patties.

2. For a charcoal grill, grill patties directly over medium coals for 10 to 12 minutes (160°F), turning once halfway through grilling. Top each burger with a slice of cheese, trimming cheese as needed to cover burger. Grill about 1 minute more or until cheese is just melted. (For a gas grill, preheat grill. Reduce heat to medium. Place patties on grill rack over heat. Cover and grill as above.) Place burgers on 4 bread slices. Top with remaining bread and desired garnishes. Makes 4 burgers.

Per mini burger: 376 cal., 16 g fat (8 g sat. fat), 76 mg chol., 732 mg sodium, 28 g carbo., 2 g fiber, 27 g pro.

for the kids
Tiny hands will love these simple pint-size cheeseburgers.

Grilled Vegetables with Herbs

Prep: 25 minutes **Grill:** 25 minutes

Nonstick cooking spray
½ recipe Grilled Veggie Foil Packet
  (see recipe, page 357)
½ cup chopped red, green, yellow,
  or orange sweet pepper
½ cup 2- to 3-inch pieces fresh asparagus
2 tablespoons chopped fresh chives
1 teaspoon snipped fresh oregano or
  ½ teaspoon dried oregano, crushed
1 teaspoon snipped fresh rosemary or
  ¼ teaspoon dried rosemary, crushed
1 teaspoon snipped fresh thyme or
  ½ teaspoon dried thyme, crushed
  Salt
  Ground black pepper
1 tablespoon butter

1. Fold a 24×18-inch piece of heavy-duty foil in half to make a 12×18-inch rectangle. Coat the foil with cooking spray.

2. Place the vegetables from the Grilled Veggie Foil Packet in the center of the foil. Add the sweet pepper and asparagus. Sprinkle with chives, oregano, rosemary, thyme, salt, and black pepper. Dot with butter. Bring up two opposite edges of foil and seal with double fold. Fold remaining ends to enclose the vegetables, leaving space for steam to build.

3. For a charcoal grill, grill foil packet directly over medium coals for 25 minutes or until vegetables are tender, turning packet 3 to 4 times during grilling. (For a gas grill, preheat grill. Reduce heat to medium. Place foil packet on grill rack over heat. Cover and grill as above.) Makes 2 servings.

Per serving: 152 cal., 9 g fat (6 g sat. fat), 23 mg chol., 525 mg sodium, 16 g carbo., 4 g fiber, 3 g pro.

for the grown-ups
A heap of fresh herbs and extra veggies will please adults.

Grilled Veggie Foil Packet

Prep: 25 minutes   **Grill:** 25 minutes

Nonstick cooking spray
1 cup sliced red potato
1 cup sliced carrot
½ cup sliced red onion
1 tablespoon bottled minced garlic
1 tablespoon butter
Salt
Ground black pepper

1. Fold a 24×18-inch piece of heavy-duty foil in half to make a 12×18-inch rectangle. Coat the foil with cooking spray. Toss together potato, carrot, onion, and garlic. Place half of the mixture in the center of the foil. (Reserve remaining half for Grilled Vegetables with Herbs.) Dot with butter; sprinkle with salt and pepper. Bring up two opposite edges of foil; seal with double fold. Fold remaining ends to enclose the vegetables, leaving space for steam to build.

2. For a charcoal grill, grill foil packet directly over medium coals for 25 minutes or until vegetables are tender, turning packet 3 to 4 times during grilling. (For a gas grill, preheat grill. Reduce heat to medium. Place foil packet on grill rack over heat. Cover and grill as above.) Makes 2 servings.

Per serving: 80 cal., 3 g fat (2 g sat. fat), 8 mg chol., 191 mg sodium, 13 g carbo., 2 g fiber, 2 g pro.

for the kids
Children will leap for this fresh mix of their fave veggies.

Puttanesca Sauce

Start to Finish: 25 minutes

Makes: 2 servings

½ recipe 20-Minute Marinara
    Sauce (see recipe, page 359)
½ of a 4-ounce can (drained weight)
    sliced mushrooms, drained
¼ cup sliced pitted ripe olives
2 tablespoons dry red wine
1 anchovy fillet, drained and mashed, or
    ½ teaspoon anchovy paste (optional)
    Dash crushed red pepper
4 ounces dried pasta, cooked and drained
    Shaved Parmesan cheese (optional)

1. Place sauce in a medium saucepan over low heat. Stir in mushrooms, olives, wine, anchovy (if desired), and the crushed red pepper. Heat through. Serve over hot pasta. If desired, top with cheese. Makes 2 servings.

Per serving: 555 cal., 11 g fat (1 g sat. fat), 0 mg chol., 672 mg sodium, 96 g carbo., 6 g fiber, 17 g pro.

This spaghetti dinner is a winner for all! Pair the two sauce versions with the bread recipes on pages 360 and 361.

for the grown-ups

A basic marinara sauce is transformed into a savory Puttanesca Sauce—flavored with olives and red wine—and marries well with penne pasta. Grown-ups will think it's divine.

20-Minute Marinara Sauce

Start to Finish: 20 minutes

1   28-ounce can whole tomatoes, undrained
3   tablespoons snipped fresh basil
½   teaspoon bottled minced garlic
2   tablespoons olive oil
¼   teaspoon salt
¼   teaspoon ground black pepper
4   ounces dried spaghetti, cooked and drained
    Grated Parmesan cheese (optional)

1. Puree undrained tomatoes in a food processor or blender. Stir in the basil; set aside. In a large skillet, cook garlic in hot olive oil over medium heat until garlic is lightly browned. Add pureed tomatoes, salt, and pepper. Bring to boiling; reduce heat. Simmer, uncovered, for 10 minutes. Remove from heat. (Reserve half of the sauce for Puttanesca Sauce.)

2. To serve, spoon remaining sauce over the hot cooked pasta. If desired, top each serving with grated Parmesan cheese. Makes 2 servings.

Tip: If desired, add frozen cooked meatballs to sauce. Heat as directed on package.

Per serving: 306 cal., 8 g fat (1 g sat. fat), 0 mg chol., 402 mg sodium, 51 g carbo., 3 g fiber, 9 g pro.

for the kids

Half of the rich 20-Minute Marinara Sauce goes over hot cooked pasta. Kids will slurp it up!

Garlic Bread

Prep: 10 minutes **Broil:** 2 minutes

½ of a 1-pound loaf French bread, halved
    horizontally
2 tablespoons butter, softened
1 tablespoon snipped fresh Italian
    (flat-leaf) parsley
½ teaspoon bottled minced garlic
½ teaspoon dried Italian seasoning,
    crushed
¼ cup finely shredded Parmesan cheese

1. Preheat broiler. Place bread, cut sides up, on a baking sheet. In a small bowl, stir together butter, parsley, garlic, and Italian seasoning. Spread butter mixture over cut sides of bread. Broil 3 to 4 inches from the heat for 1 to 2 minutes or until browned. Sprinkle with cheese. Broil for 1 to 2 minutes more or until cheese melts and is lightly browned. Cut crosswise into slices to serve. Serve warm. Makes 4 servings.

Per serving: 229 cal., 9 g fat (5 g sat. fat), 19 mg chol., 472 mg sodium, 30 g carbo., 2 g fiber, 7 g pro.

for the grown-ups

Parsley and garlic make this bread more sophisticated.

Cheese Bread

Prep: 10 minutes **Broil:** 2 minutes

- 2 tablespoons butter, softened
- ½ of a 1-pound loaf French bread, halved horizontally
- ¾ cup shredded provolone or mozzarella cheese (3 ounces)

1. Preheat broiler. Spread butter over cut sides of bread. Place bread, cut sides up, on a baking sheet. Broil 3 to 4 inches from the heat for 1 to 2 minutes or until browned. Sprinkle with cheese. Broil for 1 to 2 minutes more or until cheese melts. Cut crosswise into slices to serve. Serve warm. Makes 4 servings.

Per serving: 281 cal., 13 g fat (8 g sat. fat), 30 mg chol., 572 mg sodium, 30 g carbo., 2 g fiber, 10 g pro.

for the kids
Keep it simple with cheese, cheese, and more cheese!

Ramen Noodles with Mushrooms & Shallots

Start to Finish: 30 minutes

6 ounces assorted mushrooms, stemmed, if necessary, and sliced

¼ cup finely chopped shallots (2 medium)

2 tablespoons butter

¼ cup dry white wine or reduced-sodium chicken broth

2 tablespoons soy sauce

½ recipe Ramen Noodles with Vegetables (see recipe, page 363)

1. In a large skillet, cook mushrooms and shallots in butter over medium heat about 4 minutes or until tender. Remove from heat. Stir in wine and soy sauce. Return to heat. Cook, uncovered, about 5 minutes or until most of the liquid evaporates. Add reserved Ramen Noodles with Vegetables mixture and toss to coat. Makes 2 servings.

Per serving: 440 cal., 26 g fat (8 g sat. fat), 31 mg chol., 1,276 mg sodium, 40 g carbo., 2 g fiber, 12 g pro.

meal for the vegetarian family

for the grown-ups
Adults will love the robust flavor of rich mushrooms and shallots in an easy-to-prepare wine-soy sauce.

Ramen Noodles with Vegetables

Start to Finish: 15 minutes

2   3-ounce packages ramen noodles (any flavor)
1   cup purchased shredded carrot
12 ounces fresh asparagus, trimmed and cut into 1-inch pieces (2 cups)
1   tablespoon cooking oil
¼   cup light teriyaki sauce

1. Cook noodles according to package directions (discard seasoning packet). Drain and keep warm.

2. Meanwhile, in a large skillet, cook carrot and asparagus in hot oil over medium-high heat for 3 to 5 minutes or until asparagus is crisp-tender. Stir in noodles. (Reserve half the mixture for Ramen Noodles with Mushrooms & Shallots.) In remaining half, stir in teriyaki sauce; toss to coat. Makes 2 to 3 servings.

Per serving: 281 cal., 14 g fat (4 g sat. fat), 0 mg chol., 269 mg sodium, 34 g carbo., 3 g fiber, 6 g pro.

for the kids

Kids will grin for slick ramen noodles swirled with sweet teriyaki sauce and tangy asparagus spears. You'll love its ease.

Chicken & Pepper Stir-Fry

Prep: 10 minutes   **Cook:** 8 minutes

1½ **cups frozen stir-fry vegetables**
     (green, red, and yellow sweet
     peppers and onions)
  1 **tablespoon cooking oil**
  2 **tablespoons snipped fresh cilantro**
  ½ **recipe Snappy Chicken Stir-Fry**
     (see recipe, page 365)
  1 **tablespoon finely chopped peanuts**

1. In a medium skillet, cook frozen vegetables in hot oil over medium heat about 4 minutes or until tender. Stir in cilantro and Snappy Chicken Stir-Fry. Heat through. Top with peanuts. Makes 2 servings.

Per serving: 296 cal., 14 g fat (2 g sat. fat), 66 mg chol., 388 mg sodium, 29 g carbo., 2 g fiber, 30 g pro.

meal for the meat lovin' family

for the grown-ups
The mixed-veggie stir-fry is packed with color, crunch, and a flavorful shot of cilantro.

for the kids
Simpler tastes will prefer sweet and subtle chicken and peas.

Snappy Chicken Stir-Fry

Start to Finish: 20 minutes

1	**pound skinless, boneless chicken breast halves**
¼	**cup orange juice**
2	**tablespoons water**
2	**tablespoons light soy sauce**
2	**teaspoons cornstarch**
1	**tablespoon cooking oil**
1	**cup fresh sugar snap peas or snow pea pods, trimmed and halved crosswise**
	Toasted sesame seeds (optional)

1. Cut chicken into 1-inch pieces. In a small bowl, stir together orange juice, water, soy sauce, and cornstarch. Set aside.

2. Heat a wok or large skillet over high heat. Add cooking oil. Stir-fry chicken, half at a time, for 2 to 3 minutes or until no longer pink. (Add more oil as necessary.) Return all chicken to wok. Push chicken to the sides of the wok. Stir orange juice mixture and add to center of wok. Cook and stir until thickened and bubbly.

3. Add sugar snap peas to wok; stir until chicken and sugar snap peas are coated with sauce. Cover and simmer for 1 minute. Reserve half the mixture for Chicken & Pepper Stir-Fry. If desired, sprinkle remaining half with sesame seeds. Makes 2 to 3 servings.

Per serving: 189 cal., 5 g fat (1 g sat. fat), 66 mg chol., 368 mg sodium, 5 g carbo., 1 g fiber, 27 g pro.

Curry Burritos

Prep: 15 minutes

1 tablespoon cooking oil
½ cup purchased shredded carrot
½ cup snow pea pods, cut into thin strips
½ recipe filling from Turkey & Bean Burritos (about 2 cups) (see recipe, page 367)
¼ cup unsweetened coconut milk
2 teaspoons curry powder
Reserved tortillas (see recipe, page 367)
¼ cup finely chopped peanuts
Chutney (optional)

1. In a skillet, heat oil over medium-high heat. Add carrots; cook and stir 4 to 5 minutes or until crisp-tender; add pea pods for the last minute. Add reserved turkey filling, coconut milk, and curry powder. Bring to boil; reduce heat. Simmer, uncovered, for 2 minutes.

2. Divide mixture among tortillas. Top with peanuts. Fold bottom edge over filling until covered. Fold in opposite sides. Roll up, tucking in sides. If desired, serve with chutney. Makes 4 burritos.

Per serving: 306 cal., 16 g fat (5 g sat. fat), 22 mg chol., 378 mg sodium, 30 g carbo., 5 g fiber, 14 g pro.

for the grown-ups
This sweet 'n' spicy curry burrito brings together the best flavors of New Delhi and Cancun (minus the hassle of passports and airfare).

Turkey & Bean Burritos

Prep: 25 minutes   **Bake:** 10 minutes

8	8-inch flour tortillas
12	ounces uncooked ground turkey
1	cup chopped onion (2 medium)
2	cloves garlic, minced
1	15-ounce can black beans or pinto beans, rinsed and drained
½	cup salsa
2	teaspoons chili powder
¼	cup shredded cheddar cheese (1 ounce)
¼	cup shredded lettuce
	Salsa (optional)
	Dairy sour cream (optional)

1. Preheat oven to 350°F. Stack tortillas; wrap in foil. Heat in the oven for 10 minutes to soften.

2. Meanwhile, for filling, in a large skillet, cook turkey, onion, and garlic over medium heat until meat is brown and onion is tender. Drain off fat. Stir in drained beans, the ½ cup salsa, and the chili powder. Heat through. Reserve half of filling mixture (about 2 cups) and 4 of the tortillas for Curry Burritos.

3. Spoon about ⅓ cup of the remaining filling onto each remaining tortilla and top each with 1 tablespoon cheese and 1 tablespoon lettuce. Fold bottom edge up and over filling, just until covered. Fold in opposite sides. Roll up, tucking in sides.

4. If desired, serve burritos with additional salsa and dairy sour cream. Makes 4 burritos.

Per serving: 238 cal., 10 g fat (4 g sat. fat), 37 mg chol., 427 mg sodium, 26 g carbo., 4 g fiber, 15 g pro.

for the kids

Kids will love the familiar hearty, cheesy flavor of their favorite Mexican roll-ups, and parents will love that these burritos are low in fat and high in fiber.

for the grown-ups

Flavor-packed stir-ins will have any saucy rice connoisseur begging for more.

Picadillo Rice

Start to Finish: 10 minutes

½   recipe Mexican Rice (about 3 cups)
     (see recipe, page 369)
½   cup raisins
½   cup sliced pimiento-stuffed olives
1   tablespoon dry sherry (optional)
½   teaspoon paprika
     Dairy sour cream (optional)
     Fresh cilantro sprigs (optional)

1. In a saucepan, stir together Mexican Rice, raisins, olives, dry sherry (if using), and paprika. Heat through over medium-low heat, stirring occasionally. If desired, garnish with sour cream and cilantro. Makes 4 to 6 servings.

Per serving: 234 cal., 3 g fat (0 g sat. fat), 1 mg chol., 640 mg sodium, 49 g carbo., 2 g fiber, 4 g pro.

DID YOU KNOW? This rice dish tastes great with any veggie. Try green beans, sweet peppers, or broccoli.

Mexican Rice

Prep: 10 minutes   **Cook:** 15 minutes
Stand: 5 minutes

1½	cups uncooked long grain white rice
1	14.5-ounce can Mexican-style stewed tomatoes, undrained and cut up finely
1	14-ounce can chicken broth
½	cup water
½	cup chopped carrot (1 medium)
½	cup frozen peas or chopped zucchini
	Lime wedges (optional)

for the kids
Simpler tastes will live the subtle flavors of tried-and-true rice with veggies.

1. In a large saucepan, stir together rice, undrained tomatoes, broth, water, and carrot. Bring to boiling; reduce heat. Cover and simmer for 15 to 20 minutes or until rice is tender and most of the liquid is absorbed. Stir in peas. Let stand, covered, for 5 minutes. Fluff with a fork before serving. If desired, garnish with lime wedges. Makes 8 servings.

Per serving: 155 cal., 0 g fat (0 g sat. fat), 1 mg chol., 391 mg sodium, 33 g carbo., 1 g fiber, 4 g pro.

Zesty Tomato-Zucchini Soup

*Use Red Tomato Soup as the base
for this veggie-packed soup that adults
(and maybe some kids) are sure to love.*

Prep: 15 minutes **Cook:** 10 minutes

2   cups Red Tomato Soup
     (see recipe, page 371)
½   cup chopped zucchini
¼   to ½ teaspoon bottled hot pepper sauce
½   cup frozen artichoke hearts, thawed
     and chopped
2   tablespoons sliced pitted ripe olives
¼   cup water
     Italian-style croutons
     (optional)
     Finely shredded Parmesan cheese
     (optional)

1. In a medium saucepan, combine soup, zucchini, and hot pepper sauce. Bring to boiling, stirring occasionally. Reduce heat; simmer, uncovered, for 10 to 15 minutes or until zucchini is tender. Stir in artichoke hearts, olives, and water. Heat through. If desired, top each serving with croutons and Parmesan cheese. Makes two 1¼-cup servings.

Per serving: 159 cal., 5 g fat (2 g sat. fat), 8 mg chol., 769 mg sodium, 26 g carbo., 5 g fiber, 4 g pro.

**for the
grown-ups**
Adults will love
this surprisingly
fresh tomato soup
that spruces up
the kids' plain
version with
chopped zucchini,
artichokes, and
a splash of
hot sauce.

Red Tomato Soup

Better than canned, this homemade soup explodes with flavor. Top it with crisp cheese puffs for fun.

Prep: 15 minutes **Cook:** 15 minutes

½ cup chopped carrot (1 medium)
¼ cup chopped onion
¼ cup chopped celery
1 tablespoon butter or margarine
1 28-ounce can diced tomatoes, undrained
1 5½-ounce can vegetable juice (⅔ cup)
2 teaspoons sugar
½ teaspoon dried Italian seasoning, crushed
¼ teaspoon salt
⅛ teaspoon ground black pepper
1 to 1¼ cups water
 Crisp cheese puffs or corn chips (optional)

1. In a medium saucepan, cook carrot, onion, and celery in hot butter over medium heat for 5 to 8 minutes or until tender. Add tomatoes, vegetable juice, sugar, Italian seasoning, salt, and pepper. Bring to boiling; reduce heat. Simmer, uncovered, for 10 minutes. Remove from heat.

2. Cool slightly. In a blender or food processor, place half of the tomato mixture. Cover and blend until smooth. Repeat with remaining tomato mixture. Return all of the soup to the saucepan. Add enough water to reach desired consistency. Heat through. Reserve 2 cups of soup for Zesty Tomato-Zucchini Soup. If desired, top remaining soup with cheese puffs. Makes 4 servings.

Per serving: 125 cal., 3 g fat (2 g sat. fat), 8 mg chol., 661 mg sodium, 21 g carbo., 2 g fiber, 2 g pro.

for the kids

For the less adventurous, stick with tried-and-true tomato soup that comes together in less than 30 minutes. Plus, the kids will love to top it off with crunchy cheese curls.

Grilled Corned Beef Sandwich

This Reuben-type sandwich adds adult-friendly spark to plain grilled cheese.

Prep: 5 minutes   **Cook:** 4 minutes

1   tablespoon butter, softened
2   slices white or whole wheat bread
2   slices process Swiss cheese (2 ounces)
1   tablespoon low-calorie Thousand
      Island salad dressing
2   tablespoons sauerkraut, drained
1   ounce thinly sliced corned beef

1. Spread butter on one side of one slice of bread. Place bread, buttered side down, in a skillet. Place cheese slices on top of bread, cutting cheese to fit so all bread is covered (overlap as necessary). Spread salad dressing over cheese; top with sauerkraut and corned beef.

2. Spread butter on one side of the remaining bread slice. Place bread on sandwich, buttered side up.

3. Cook sandwich over medium heat about 3 to 5 minutes or until bottom slice of bread is toasted and cheese begins to melt; turn sandwich.* Cook for 1 to 2 minutes more or until bottom slice of bread is toasted and cheese is melted. Makes 1 sandwich.

Grilled Provolone and Pepperoni Sandwich: Prepare as directed, except substitute provolone cheese for the Swiss cheese, 1 tablespoon pizza sauce for the salad dressing, and 5 to 6 slices ($\frac{1}{2}$ ounce) thinly sliced pepperoni for the corned beef. Omit sauerkraut.

*Note: If you are making an additional sandwich, carefully add the assembled sandwich to the hot skillet. Cooking times may be slightly less.

Per serving: 500 cal., 35 g fat (18 g sat. fat), 98 mg chol., 1,051 mg sodium, 29 g carbo., 2 g fiber, 21 g pro.

for the grown-ups
Go Reuben-style with corned beef and Swiss cheese. Pair it with Zesty Tomato-Zucchini Soup (page 370) for dinner or lunch.

Grilled Ham & Cheese Sandwich

There is no wrong way to make this sandwich:
Personalize this recipe by substituting your child's
favorite cheese and lunch meat.

Prep: 5 minutes **Cook:** 5 minutes

- 1 tablespoon butter, softened
- 2 slices white or whole wheat bread
- 2 slices process American or
     Swiss cheese (2 ounces)
- 1 ounce thinly sliced cooked ham

1. Spread butter on one side of one slice of bread. Place bread, buttered side down, in a skillet. Place cheese slices on top of bread, cutting cheese to fit so all bread is covered (overlap as necessary); top with ham.

2. Spread butter on one side of the remaining bread slice. Place bread on sandwich, buttered side up.

3. Cook sandwich over medium heat about 3 to 5 minutes or until bottom slice of bread is toasted and cheese begins to melt; turn sandwich.* Cook for 1 to 2 minutes more or until bottom slice of bread is toasted and cheese is melted. Makes 1 sandwich.

Grilled Cheddar & Salami Sandwich: Prepare as directed, except substitute cheddar or Colby and Monterey Jack cheese for the American cheese and thinly sliced salami for the ham.

***Note:** If you are making an additional sandwich, carefully add the assembled sandwich to the hot skillet. Cooking times may be slightly less.

Per serving: 494 cal., 33 g fat (20 g sat. fat), 100 mg chol., 1,636 mg sodium, 27 g carbo., 2 g fiber, 21 g pro.

for the kids

Ooey-gooey grilled cheese with some ham for protein. Pair it with Red Tomato Soup (page 371) for a tummy-warming meal.

Two-Way Tuna Melt

Prep: 10 minutes **Bake:** 14 minutes
Broil: 2 minutes

1	10.2-ounce package (5) refrigerated large flaky biscuits
1	pint deli tuna salad (2 cups)
¼	teaspoon Cajun seasoning
2	tablespoons chopped pimiento-stuffed olives
1	cup shredded cheddar and/or Swiss cheese (4 ounces)

1. Bake biscuits according to package directions; cool. Use a fork to split each biscuit in half. Remove 1 cup of the tuna salad from container and place it in a bowl. Stir the Cajun seasoning and chopped olives into the tuna salad in bowl.

2. For the adult version, spread the tuna salad with Cajun seasoning and olives evenly onto 5 of the biscuit halves. Sprinkle with ½ cup of the cheese; set aside.

3. For the kid version, spread the remaining plain tuna salad on the remaining biscuit halves. Sprinkle with the remaining ½ cup cheese. Arrange all of the biscuits on a baking sheet.

4. Preheat broiler. Place baking sheet under broiler with biscuits 4 to 5 inches from heat. Broil for 2 to 3 minutes or until cheese is melted and slightly browned. Makes 5 servings of the adult version and 5 servings of kid version.

Per serving for adult version: 222 cal., 13 g fat (4 g sat. fat), 17 mg chol., 568 mg sodium, 16 g carbo., 0 g fiber, 11 g pro.

Per serving for kid version: 217 cal., 12 g fat (4 g sat. fat), 17 mg chol., 509 mg sodium, 16 g carbo., 0 g fiber, 11 g pro.

for the grown-ups

Stir a little Cajun seasoning and a few chopped pimiento-stuffed olives into the tuna salad.

for the kids

Add their favorite kind of cheese to the top.

"throw a party" food

from pantry

to party table

These whip-together party appetizers start
as simple ingredients from the pantry (or
refrigerator or freezer) and end up nothing less
than spectacular. Everyone will rave about your
culinary skills, and no one will suspect each
recipe took only a few minutes to make.
Beware: You might get requests to make
these treats again and again!

Devilicious Eggs

Prep: 20 minutes **Cook:** 15 minutes

7 **Hard-Cooked Eggs**
¼ **cup mayonnaise or salad dressing**
1 **to 2 teaspoons Dijon-style mustard, honey mustard, or other favorite mustard**
½ **teaspoon dry mustard**
  Salt and ground black pepper
  Paprika (optional)
  Parsley leaves (optional)

1. Cut 6 eggs in half lengthwise; gently remove yolks; set whites aside. Coarsely chop the remaining egg.

2. In a sturdy, resealable plastic bag, combine egg yolks, chopped egg, mayonnaise, Dijon-style mustard, and dry mustard. Seal bag. Gently knead bag to combine ingredients. Season to taste with salt and pepper.

3. Snip a hole in one corner of the bag. Squeeze yolk mixture into egg white halves. If desired, top with paprika and parsley leaves. Cover and chill for up to 12 hours. Makes 12 servings.

Hard-Cooked Eggs: Place eggs in a single layer in a large saucepan. Add enough cold water to cover eggs by 1 inch. Bring to a full boil over high heat. Reduce heat so water just simmers; cover and cook 15 minutes. Transfer eggs to a colander; run cold water over eggs until cool enough to handle. To peel, gently tap eggs on the counter. Roll eggs between palms of your hands; remove shells. Cover; chill eggs for at least 1 hour.

Per serving: 72 cal., 6 g fat (1 g sat. fat), 109 mg chol., 63 mg sodium, 0 g carbo., 0 g fiber, 3 g pro.

I'm-So-Stuffed Mushrooms

Prep: 25 minutes **Bake:** 8 minutes

24	large fresh mushrooms, 1½ to 2 inches in diameter (1½ to 2 pounds total)
¼	cup sliced green onion (2)
1	clove garlic, minced
¼	cup butter or margarine
⅔	cup fine dry bread crumbs
½	cup shredded cheddar cheese (2 ounces)*

1. Preheat oven to 425°F. Rinse and drain mushrooms. Remove stems; reserve caps. Chop enough stems to make 1 cup; discard any remaining stems.

2. In a saucepan, cook the chopped stems, green onion, and garlic in butter over medium heat until tender. Stir in bread crumbs and cheese. Spoon crumb mixture into mushroom caps. Arrange mushrooms in a 15×10×1-inch baking pan. Bake for 8 to 10 minutes or until heated through. Makes 24 mushrooms.

*Note: Save a few bucks by buying a block of cheese and shredding it yourself.

Per mushroom: 42 cal., 3 g fat (2 g sat. fat), 7 mg chol., 97 mg sodium, 2 g carbo., 0 g fiber, 2 g pro.

Chile-Stuffed Mushrooms

Prep: 25 minutes   **Bake:** 10 minutes

24   large fresh mushrooms, 1½ to
      2 inches in diameter
      (1½ to 2 pounds total)
¼   cup canned diced green chile
      pepper, undrained
¼   cup finely chopped green onion (2)
1   clove garlic, minced
¼   cup butter or margarine
⅔   cup finely crushed corn chips
½   cup shredded Monterey Jack
      cheese (2 ounces)
¼   teaspoon salt

1. Preheat oven to 450°F. Clean mushrooms.
Remove stems. Chop enough stems to make
1 cup. Discard remaining stems, if desired.
Arrange mushroom caps, stem sides up, in a
15×10×1-inch baking pan; set aside.
2. In a saucepan, cook mushroom stems,
chile pepper, green onion, and garlic in butter
over medium heat about 5 minutes or until
stems are tender. Remove from heat. Stir in
corn chips, cheese, and salt. Spoon into
mushroom caps.
3. Bake 10 to 12 minutes or until filling is
heated through and caps are lightly browned.
Makes 24 mushrooms.

Per mushroom: 41 cal., 4 g fat (2 g sat. fat), 7 mg
chol., 68 mg sodium, 2 g carbo., 0 g fiber, 2 g pro.

Chile-Lime Chicken Skewers

Prep: 20 minutes   **Broil:** 10 minutes

1   pound skinless, boneless chicken
      breast halves
2   limes
1½   teaspoons ground ancho chile
      pepper
1   teaspoon garlic-herb seasoning

1. Cut chicken into 1-inch strips. Place strips
in a shallow dish; set aside. Finely shred
enough peel from one of the limes to measure
1 teaspoon (chill lime and use for juice another
time). Cut remaining lime into wedges and
set aside. For rub, combine lime peel, chile
pepper, and garlic-herb seasoning. Sprinkle
over chicken; rub in with fingers.
2. Preheat broiler. Thread chicken accordion-
style on 4 long metal skewers, leaving a
¼-inch space between pieces. Place chicken
skewers on the unheated rack of a broiler pan.
Broil 4 to 5 inches from the heat for 10 to
12 minutes or until chicken is no longer pink
(170°F). Serve with lime wedges. Makes
4 servings.

Per serving: 137 cal., 2 g fat (0 g sat. fat), 66 mg
chol., 75 mg sodium, 4 g carbo., 1 g fiber, 26 g pro.

Cranberry-Sauced Franks

Choose your favorite barbecue sauce for a spicy, sweet, or smoky flavor.

Prep: 10 minutes
Cook: 4 hours (low) or 2 hours (high)

1   cup bottled barbecue sauce
1   16-ounce can jellied cranberry sauce
2   1-pound packages cocktail wieners
      and/or small cooked smoked
      sausage links

1. In a 3½- or 4-quart slow cooker, stir together the barbecue sauce and cranberry sauce until combined. Stir in the wieners and/or sausages.
2. Cover and cook on low-heat setting for 4 to 5 hours or on high-heat setting for 2 to 2½ hours. Serve immediately or keep warm on low-heat setting for up to 2 hours. Serve with toothpicks. Makes 32 servings.

Per serving: 118 cal., 8 g fat (4 g sat. fat), 15 mg chol., 275 mg sodium, 8 g carbo., 0 g fiber, 3 g pro.

start with ...
frozen crab cakes

... end with
crab cakes
with garlic mayo

Crab Cakes with Garlic Mayo

Prep: 15 minutes

1 6- to 9-ounce package frozen crab cakes (about 6 regular-size or 12 miniature)
⅓ cup mayonnaise dressing
½ to 1 teaspoon bottled minced garlic
1 teaspoon water
½ teaspoon lemon juice
⅛ teaspoon kosher salt or coarse sea salt
¼ to ⅓ cup extra virgin olive oil
2 teaspoons snipped fresh basil
   Snipped fresh basil
   Lemon wedges (optional)

1. Heat crab cakes according to package directions. Meanwhile, combine mayonnaise and garlic. Whisk in the water, lemon juice, and salt until smooth. Whisk in oil until mayonnaise mixture is desired thickness. (If too thick, whisk in more water to reach desired consistency.) Stir in the 2 teaspoons basil.

2. Serve garlic mayo with hot crab cakes. Sprinkle with basil. If desired, serve with lemon wedges. Makes 6 appetizer servings.

Per serving: 236 cal., 22 g fat (4 g sat. fat), 9 mg chol., 254 mg sodium, 7 g carbo., 0 g fiber, 2 g pro.

Skewered Shrimp & Pineapple

Prep: 15 minutes **Marinate:** 30 minutes

- 8 6-inch wooden skewers
- 8 frozen cooked, peeled, and deveined large shrimp (tails intact), thawed
- 8 pineapple wedges (peeled, if desired)
- ¼ cup lime juice
- ¼ cup olive oil
- 2 tablespoons red onion slivers
- 2 tablespoons snipped fresh cilantro
- ⅛ teaspoon salt

1. On each skewer, thread 1 shrimp and 1 pineapple wedge. Arrange in a shallow dish. In a small bowl, stir together lime juice, olive oil, onion, cilantro, and salt. Pour mixture over skewers in dish, turning to coat. Cover and marinate in the refrigerator for 30 minutes, turning occasionally. To serve, place skewers in individual bowls. Spoon some of the marinade over each. Makes 8 appetizer servings.

Per serving: 58 cal., 2 g fat (0 g sat. fat), 37 mg chol., 53 mg sodium, 6 g carbo., 1 g fiber, 4 g pro.

start with ...
frozen cooked
shrimp

... end with
skewered shrimp
& pineapple

{ start with ...
frozen pizza

... end with
shrimp-topped
pizza squares }

Shrimp-Topped Pizza Squares

Prep: 10 minutes **Broil:** 1 minute

1   **12-inch frozen cheese pizza**
16 **cooked, peeled, deveined
    large shrimp**
1   **cup finely shredded Asiago cheese
    (4 ounces)**
2   **tablespoons snipped fresh basil**

1. Heat pizza according to package directions. Preheat broiler. Cut pizza into sixteen 2½-inch squares. If desired, butterfly shrimp. Top each pizza square with a shrimp. Sprinkle with cheese. Arrange squares on a baking sheet. Broil 3 to 4 inches from heat for 1 to 2 minutes or until cheese melts. Arrange squares on a platter. To serve, sprinkle with snipped basil. Makes 16 appetizer servings.

Per serving: 125 cal., 5 g fat (3 g sat. fat), 45 mg chol., 277 mg sodium, 11 g carbo., 0 g fiber, 10 g pro.

Vegetable Pizza

Have kids help top this pizza by "planting"
the vegetables in rows just like a garden.

Prep: 25 minutes   **Bake:** 12 minutes

- 1   8-ounce package (8) refrigerated crescent-roll dough
- 1   8-ounce container desired-flavor vegetable dip (1 cup)
- 1½   cups chopped raw vegetables (such as broccoli, cauliflower, sweet pepper, and/or carrot)
- ½   cup shredded cheddar cheese (2 ounces)

1. Preheat oven to 375°F. Line a 13×9×2-inch baking pan with foil, allowing ends of foil to hang over edge of pan. For crust, unroll dough (do not separate). Press dough into the bottom of the prepared pan, pressing perforations to seal.

2. Bake about 12 minutes or until golden. Cool crust in the pan on a wire rack. Using the foil to lift, remove crust from pan; remove and discard foil. Transfer crust to a serving tray.

3. Spread vegetable dip over the cooled crust to within ½ inch of the edges. Arrange assorted vegetables and cheese on top of the dip. Serve immediately or cover and chill for up to 1 hour. Cut into squares to serve. Store any leftovers in the refrigerator. Makes 8 servings.

To Make Ahead: Wrap cooled crust tightly with plastic wrap and store at room temperature for up to 24 hours. Add toppings before serving.

Per serving: 197 cal., 14 g fat (6 g sat. fat), 19 mg chol., 492 mg sodium, 15 g carbo., 1 g fiber, 5 g pro.

Tomato, Basil & Mozzarella Crostini

Start to Finish: 20 minutes

1   **8-ounce loaf baguette-style French bread**
2   **to 3 tablespoons olive oil**
    Ground black pepper
4   **ounces fresh mozzarella, thinly sliced**
24 **red and/or yellow cherry tomatoes, halved**
    Snipped or shredded fresh basil
    Olive oil
    Salt
    Fresh basil leaves (optional)

1. Preheat oven to 425°F. For crostini, cut French bread into ½-inch-thick slices. Lightly brush both sides of each bread slice with oil; sprinkle with pepper. Place on an ungreased baking sheet. Bake for 5 to 7 minutes or until crisp and light brown, turning once.

2. Top crostini with mozzarella slices, tomato halves, and basil. Drizzle with additional oil; sprinkle with salt and additional pepper. If desired, garnish with additional basil leaves. Makes 16 servings.

Per serving: 87 cal., 5 g fat (1 g sat. fat), 6 mg chol., 168 mg sodium, 9 g carbo., 1 g fiber, 3 g pro.

start with ...
frozen egg rolls

... end with
Asian
appetizer
salad

Asian Appetizer Salad

Start to Finish: 20 minutes

8 frozen egg rolls
4 cups torn romaine lettuce
1 red sweet pepper, stemmed, seeded,
   and cut into thin, bite-size strips
1 11-ounce can mandarin orange
   sections, drained
   Soy-Ginger Dressing

1. Heat egg rolls according to package directions. Arrange lettuce, sweet pepper, and orange slices in 8 martini glasses.

2. To serve, cut egg rolls crosswise into 1-inch pieces. Arrange egg roll pieces on top of vegetable and fruit mixture. Drizzle with dressing. If desired, sprinkle with sliced *green onion*.

Soy-Ginger Dressing: In a screw-top jar, combine 3 tablespoons salad oil, 2 tablespoons lime juice, 2 tablespoons soy sauce, 1 teaspoon grated fresh ginger, and ½ teaspoon bottled minced garlic. Cover and shake well. Chill until served. Shake before using. Makes 8 appetizer servings.

Per serving: 98 cal., 6 g fat (1 g sat. fat), 1 mg chol., 290 mg sodium, 10 g carbo., 2 g fiber, 2 g pro.

Spiky Cucumber Salad

Prep: 20 minutes   **Chill:** 2 hours

½   cup rice vinegar
¼   cup olive oil
1   tablespoon finely shredded
       lemon peel
2   tablespoons lemon juice
1   tablespoon grated fresh ginger
1   tablespoon sugar
1½ teaspoons coarsely ground
       black pepper
1   teaspoon toasted sesame oil
1   teaspoon salt
¼   teaspoon crushed red pepper
8   medium cucumbers, cut into
       bite-size strips
1   red onion, thinly sliced and
       separated into rings

1. In a screw-top jar, combine vinegar, olive oil, lemon peel and juice, ginger, sugar, black pepper, sesame oil, salt, and crushed red pepper. Close jar; shake to combine.
2. In a large bowl, toss dressing with cucumber and onion. Cover; refrigerate 2 hours or up to 12 hours, tossing occasionally. Drain to serve. Makes 24 to 26 servings.

Per serving: 27 cal., 1 g fat (0 g sat. fat), 0 mg chol., 51 mg sodium, 3 g carbo., 1 g fiber, 1 g pro.

Too-Easy Guacamole

Prep: 15 minutes   **Chill:** up to 8 hours

2   ripe avocados, halved, seeded,
       and peeled
2   tablespoons dairy sour cream
2   tablespoons snipped fresh cilantro
1   tablespoon lime juice
⅛   teaspoon salt
       Tortilla chips
       Sliced green onion
       Chopped tomato

1. Place avocado halves, sour cream, cilantro, lime juice, and salt in a sturdy, resealable plastic bag. Seal bag. Knead with your hands to combine ingredients. Place in the refrigerator until ready to use (up to 8 hours).
2. To serve, arrange chips on a serving platter. Snip a hole in one corner of the bag. Squeeze avocado mixture onto chips. Sprinkle with onion and tomato. Makes about 1 cup.

Per 1 tablespoon: 39 cal., 4 g fat (1 g sat. fat), 1 mg chol., 21 mg sodium, 2 g carbo., 1 g fiber, 0 g pro.

Basil Guacamole

Basil gives this guacamole a fresh,
balanced flavor.

Start to Finish: 25 minutes

- 2 medium ripe avocados, halved, seeded, and peeled
- ½ cup snipped fresh basil
- ½ cup chopped seeded tomato
- 1 tablespoon lime juice
- ¼ to ½ teaspoon salt
- ¼ to ½ teaspoon garlic powder
  Assorted dippers, such as pita chips, sliced radishes, sweet pepper strips, and/or tortilla chips

1. In a bowl, mash avocados with a fork. Stir in basil, tomato, lime juice, salt, and garlic powder. Serve immediately with assorted dippers or cover surface with plastic wrap and chill up to 2 hours. Makes 16 servings.

Per 2-tablespoon serving: 47 cal., 4 g fat (1 g sat. fat), 0 mg chol., 37 mg sodium, 3 g carbo., 2 g fiber, 1 g pro.

basil

Once upon a time, if a tall Italian lad came calling with a sprig of basil in his hair, young maidens blushed, for it meant that he had come to propose marriage. Happily, the thrill's not gone. This herb may not be as romantic as it once was, but basil—the most handsome brother of the mint family—still puts on the moves. Warm, robust, and sweet-smelling, basil infuses contemporary dishes with an unforgettable fresh and spicy flavor. While its favorite partners may be tomato-based pasta sauce, lasagna, and pizza, it also dances beautifully with zucchini, onions, eggplant, and other sunny, healthful Mediterranean vegetables. Match basil with shellfish—particularly crab and shrimp—or pair it with simple roasted chicken and pork. Use it with abandon: Toss its vibrant leaves into green salads, sliver them over soft cheeses, or stir them into simmering soups and stews. Basil pairs well with almost anything.

Homemade Salsa

Start to Finish: 15 minutes

3   small tomatoes, seeded and coarsely
    chopped (1⅓ cups)
1   small onion, chopped (⅓ cup)
1   to 2 fresh jalapeño peppers, seeded
    and finely chopped
2   tablespoons lime juice
1   to 2 tablespoons snipped fresh cilantro
¼   teaspoon salt

1. Combine tomato, onion, jalapeño, lime juice,
cilantro, and salt in a food processor. Cover and
pulse with several on/off turns until mixture is
evenly chopped. Season to taste with additional
salt, if needed. Store in covered container in
refrigerator up to 3 days. Makes 1 cup.

Per ¼ cup: 20 cal., 0 g fat (0 g sat. fat), 0 mg chol.,
150 mg sodium, 5 g carbo., 1 g fiber, 1 g pro.

Sausage-Chili Dip

Prep: 15 minutes   **Cook:** 3 hours (low)

    Nonstick cooking spray
8   ounces bulk mild or hot Italian
    sausage
2   15-ounce cans chili without beans
1   8-ounce package American cheese,
    cubed
1   cup salsa
    Sliced green onion tops (optional)
    Assorted dippers, such as scoop-
      shape corn chips and/or red,
      yellow, or green sweet
      pepper strips

1. Coat the inside of a 3½- or 4-quart slow
cooker with cooking spray; set aside. In a large
skillet, brown sausage over medium heat. Drain
off fat. Stir in chili, cheese, and salsa. Transfer
sausage mixture to prepared cooker.
2. Cover and cook on low-heat setting for 3 to
4 hours. Stir well. Serve immediately or keep
warm, covered, on low heat for up to 2 hours,
stirring occasionally. If desired, top with green
onion tops. Serve with desired dippers. Makes
5½ cups.

Per 2 tablespoons: 61 cal., 5 g fat (2 g sat. fat),
13 mg chol., 2 g carbo., 207 mg chol., 0 g fiber, 3 g pro.

Three-Pepper Pecans
Start to Finish: 25 minutes

½ cup sugar
3 tablespoons water
1 teaspoon garlic salt
½ teaspoon paprika
¼ teaspoon ground black pepper
¼ teaspoon cayenne pepper
3 cups pecan halves
    Nonstick cooking spray

1. Preheat oven to 325°F. In a large skillet, combine sugar, water, garlic salt, paprika, black pepper, and cayenne pepper. Bring to boiling over medium heat; boil gently, uncovered, for 2 minutes. Stir in pecan halves until well coated.

2. Line a 15×10×1-inch baking pan with foil; coat foil with cooking spray. Spread nuts on foil. Bake for 15 to 20 minutes or until browned, stirring occasionally. Cool; break apart large clusters. Makes 3 cups.

To Make Ahead: Prepare as directed. Store cooled nuts in an airtight container at room temperature for up to 1 week.

Per ¼ cup: 218 cal., 19 g fat (2 g sat. fat), 0 mg chol., 80 mg sodium, 12 g carbo., 3 g fiber, 3 g pro.

Creamy Mocha Tarts

Start to Finish: 20 minutes

1   cup semisweet chocolate pieces
¼   cup whipping cream
1   to 2 tablespoons instant coffee
     crystals
1   2.1-ounce package (15) baked
     miniature phyllo dough shells
     Frozen whipped dessert topping,
     thawed
     Grated semisweet chocolate
     (optional)

1. In a small saucepan, heat and stir chocolate, the cream, and coffee crystals over low heat until smooth. Remove from heat; let stand 10 minutes or until slightly thickened.
2. Spoon filling into phyllo shells. Top with whipped topping. If desired, top with grated chocolate. Makes 15 tarts.

Per tart: 104 cal., 7 g fat (2 g sat. fat), 11 mg chol., 13 mg sodium, 10 g carbo., 0 g fiber, 1 g pro.

Citrus-Raspberry Coolers

Start to Finish: 15 minutes

2   cups water
⅓   cup sugar
5   raspberry-flavor herbal tea bags
1   6-ounce can frozen orange
     juice concentrate, thawed
2   1-liter bottles red raspberry-flavor
     sparkling water, chilled
     Ice cubes
     Lemon slices (optional)

1. In a small saucepan, combine water and sugar. Bring to boiling, stirring to dissolve sugar. Remove from heat.
2. Add tea bags. Let steep for 5 minutes. Discard tea bags. Transfer mixture to a medium bowl. Stir in the orange juice concentrate.
3. To serve, pour the tea mixture into a large punch bowl. Slowly pour in sparkling water; stir gently. Serve in ice-filled glasses with lemon slices, if desired. Makes 12 servings.

Per serving: 38 cal., 0 g fat (0 g sat. fat), 0 mg chol., 32 mg sodium, 10 g carbo., 0 g fiber, 0 g pro.

something sweet

sugar
and spice

... and everything nice.
That's how every meal
should end!

Whether it's a little something
fruity you crave or a lot of
something chocolatey, you'll find
the perfect dessert to calm your
sweet tooth right here. Cookies,
brownies, sundaes—even an
irresistibly easy pie—can be made
at a moment's notice. No more
excuses—get baking! (If it's cakes
you're hungry for, check out the
next chapter.)

Shortcut Pecan Pie

Prep: 25 minutes   **Bake:** 35 minutes

½ of a 15-ounce package rolled
  refrigerated unbaked piecrust
  (1 crust)
3 eggs, slightly beaten
1 cup light-colored corn syrup
⅔ cup sugar
⅓ cup butter, melted
½ teaspoon salt
2 cups pecan halves

1. Preheat oven to 375° F. Bring piecrust to room temperature according to package directions. Unroll piecrust; transfer to a 9-inch pie plate. Trim; crimp edge as desired.

2. For filling, combine eggs, corn syrup, sugar, butter, and salt; mix well. Stir in the pecans.

3. Place the pastry-lined pie plate on the oven rack. Carefully pour the filling into pastry shell.

4. To prevent overbrowning, cover edge of the pie with foil. Bake for 25 minutes. Remove foil. Bake for 10 to 15 minutes more or until a knife inserted near the center comes out clean. Cool on a wire rack. Cover and refrigerate within 2 hours. Makes 8 servings.

Tip: If desired, prepare egg mixture as above, set aside 2 tablespoons of the mixture. Stir 1 cup of the pecans into the egg mixture and pour into prepared pie crust. Add remaining pecans to the reserved egg mixture; toss to coat. Arrange on top of the filling. Bake as above.

Per serving: 530 cal., 36 g fat (10 g sat. fat), 102 mg chol., 350 mg sodium, 51 g carbo., 3 g fiber, 5 g pro.

Banana Brownie Bars

Prep: 15 minutes   **Bake:** 20 minutes

Nonstick cooking spray
1   **8- to 10-ounce package brownie mix**
1   **cup quick-cooking rolled oats**
1   **egg**
2   **to 3 tablespoons water**
1   **cup coarsely crushed dried**
      banana chips
1   **cup milk chocolate pieces (6 ounces)**
1   **cup miniature marshmallows**
¾   **cup chopped walnuts**

1. Preheat oven to 325°F. Coat a 13×9×2-inch baking pan with cooking spray; set aside.

2. In a medium bowl, stir together brownie mix, oats, egg, and water. With floured hands, spread brownie mixture evenly in bottom of prepared pan. Bake for 5 minutes. Layer dried banana chips, chocolate pieces, marshmallows, and nuts over partially baked crust; press down gently. Bake for 15 minutes more. Cool in pan on a wire rack; cut into bars. Makes 24 bars.

Per brownie bar: 135 cal., 7 g fat (3 g sat. fat), 10 mg chol., 38 mg sodium, 17 g carbo., 1 g fiber, 2 g pro.

A Billow of
Berries 'n' Brownies

Start to Finish: 15 minutes

2 cups fresh red raspberries
2 tablespoons sugar
1 teaspoon finely shredded
    orange peel
2 cups whipped cream
2 to 3 three-inch squares
    bakery brownies (milk
    chocolate, blond, or
    marbled brownies),
    cut into irregular
    chunks

1. Set aside ⅓ cup of the berries. In a bowl, combine remaining berries, the sugar, and orange peel. Place berry mixture into a 4- or 5-cup serving bowl or divide among 6 dessert dishes.

2. Spoon whipped cream over raspberries. Top with brownie chunks and reserved raspberries. Makes 6 servings.

Per serving: 241 cal., 19 g fat (10 g sat. fat), 65 mg chol., 63 mg sodium, 17 g carbo., 3 g fiber, 3 g pro.

no pecans, no problem

Some brownies need a bunch of nutty toppings, but this one's perfect as is.

No-Nuts Zebra Brownies

Prep: 20 minutes   **Bake:** 25 minutes

Nonstick cooking spray
1   **15- to 22-ounce package brownie mix**
1   **8-ounce package cream cheese, softened**
¾   **cup milk**
¾   **cup powdered sugar**
1   **package 1-layer-size white cake mix**
2   **tablespoons water**

1. Preheat oven to 350°F. Coat a 15×10×1-inch baking pan with cooking spray; set aside. Prepare brownie mix according to package directions. Spread evenly in prepared pan.

2. In a medium mixing bowl, beat cream cheese with an electric mixer on medium speed for 30 seconds. Gradually beat in the milk and powdered sugar until well combined. Add the cake mix and water. Beat well. Spoon the cake mixture on top of brownie batter. Gently lift and fold brownie batter to marble into the white batter.

3. Bake for 25 to 30 minutes or until a wooden toothpick inserted near center comes out clean. Cool in pan on a wire rack. Using a wet knife, cut into bars. Store bars in refrigerator. Makes 48 brownies.

Per brownie: 109 cal., 4 g fat (1 g sat. fat), 6 mg chol., 115 mg sodium, 17 g carbo., 0 g fiber, 1 g pro.

nut allergies

easy nut substitutes

Seeds, seeds, seeds: Use sunflower, pumpkin, or sesame seeds on salads and in pesto. Poppy and flax seeds provide crunch and texture.

Jump for soy: Add chopped soy nuts to soy butter for a little crunch.

PB alternatives: Try cashew, almond, or macadamia butter if your child is allergic only to peanuts (since peanuts are actually in the legume family). Also consider apple butter, sweet potato butter, sesame paste, or sunflower butter.

read between the label lines

It seems the phrase "may be processed in a facility that manufactures nuts" is popping up on all kinds of labels. And sometimes on foods you wouldn't expect. That's because some nut allergies are so severe that manufacturers don't want to take any chances, even if the peanut-processing machine is a warehouse away.

Luckily a law went into place in January 2006 that required all sources of nuts and other common allergens to be listed on product labels. If you're specifically looking for an allergen, the first place to check is at the bottom of the ingredient list (they're often listed in bold). Always double check the ingredients by reading them slowly and carefully.

Keep these tips for nut allergies in mind when reading labels:

- Marzipan contains almonds
- Nougat has nuts
- European chocolate makers don't have to declare whether their products contain nuts or are processed with them
- Hydrolyzed vegetable proteins can be made from nuts
- Breakfast cereals, candy, and granola bars often include nuts (as do do ice creams, baked goods, and Thai food)
- Giaduja is a nut mixture found in some chocolates
- Pine nuts go by many different names, including pignoli, pignon, pinyan, and piñon

what you need to know

As with any health question, opinions vary, but there has been some consensus among experts in recent years. It seems the food allergies start when children are very small.

To lower the incidence of food allergies, here are a few tips: Don't start babies on solid foods until about 6 months of age, introduce one food at a time, and don't give nuts to kids under age 4.

Think your child might already be allergic to a certain food? Here are some common symptoms that occur after the child has consumed nuts or other common food allergens (such as milk, soy, shellfish, eggs, and wheat):

- difficulty breathing
- tingling mouth
- swelling tongue or throat
- stomach cramps
- drop in blood pressure
- vomiting
- diarrhea
- hives

Bad reactions to food can occur within minutes or hours after eating. If two or more of these symptoms occur, especially difficulty breathing, get your child immediate medical attention. They could be a sign of a severe anaphylactic reaction, which can be life-threatening. If you think your child has an allergy, cut suspect foods (such as nuts) from his or her diet and have a doctor conduct allergy tests as soon as possible.

Since there's no known cure for food allergies yet, the best way to cope is to completely avoid foods that cause reactions. Read labels carefully and introduce new off-the-shelf products slowly until you know they're safe. Also, ask questions at restaurants and tell servers up front that your child has a severe food allergy. Carry cards to give to servers listing all of the known foods that your child's specific allergens might be lurking in (see tip, left, for words to include for nut allergies). Accidents can happen, so ask your doctor what medicines, such as antihistamines and epinephrine pens, can be carried in case of emergencies. Above all, if your child exhibits any life-threatening symptoms, such as breathing problems, get to the hospital immediately!

Cinnamon Swirl Casserole

Prep: 20 minutes   **Chill:** 4 hours
Bake: 40 minutes   **Stand:** 15 minutes

1   **cup packed brown sugar**
½   **cup butter**
2   **tablespoons light-colored corn syrup**
1   **1-pound loaf unsliced cinnamon bread,
     sliced 1 inch thick**
8   **eggs, beaten**
3   **cups half-and-half or light cream**
2   **teaspoons vanilla**
1½ **teaspoons salt**

1. In a saucepan, combine brown sugar, butter, and corn syrup; cook and stir until mixture comes to a boil. Boil, uncovered, 1 minute. Pour into a 3-quart rectangular baking dish.

2. Arrange bread slices on top of brown sugar mixture. Combine eggs, half-and-half, vanilla, and salt; pour over bread slices. Cover and chill in the refrigerator for 4 to 24 hours.

3. Preheat oven to 350° F. Let baking dish stand at room temperature while oven preheats. Bake, uncovered, for 40 to 45 minutes or until top is browned and puffed and a knife inserted near center comes out clean. Let stand 15 minutes before serving. Makes 8 servings.

Per serving: 579 cal., 30 g fat (16 g sat. fat), 279 mg chol., 692 mg sodium, 65 g carbo., 1 g fiber, 14 g pro.

French Toast Dessert

French toast is so much more than just breakfast!
These slices have a decadent cream cheese mixture
stuffed in the center and a sweet orange-apricot
syrup drizzled on top.

Start to Finish: 35 minutes

1	**8-ounce package cream cheese, softened**
1	**cup apricot preserves**
1½	**teaspoons vanilla**
½	**cup chopped walnuts**
1	**1-pound loaf French bread**
4	**eggs**
1	**cup whipping cream**
½	**teaspoon ground nutmeg**
¼	**cup orange juice**
	Toasted walnuts, chopped (optional)

1. Preheat oven to 300°F. In a medium mixing bowl, combine cream cheese, 2 tablespoons of the apricot preserves, and the 1 teaspoon of the vanilla; beat with an electric mixer on medium speed until fluffy. Stir in nuts; set aside.

2. Cut bread into ten to twelve 1½-inch-thick slices; cut a pocket about 2 inches deep in the top of each bread slice, being careful not to cut all the way to the sides. Fill each pocket with a rounded tablespoon of the cream cheese mixture.

3. In a medium bowl, whisk together eggs, whipping cream, nutmeg, and remaining ½ teaspoon vanilla. Using tongs, quickly dip the filled bread slices in the egg mixture, allowing excess mixture to drip off (take care not to squeeze out the filling). Cook on a lightly greased griddle over medium heat about 4 minutes or until golden brown, turning once. Keep warm in the oven while cooking remaining slices.

4. Meanwhile, in a small saucepan, combine the remaining apricot preserves and the orange juice; heat and stir until mixture is melted. To serve, drizzle the apricot preserves mixture over the hot French toast. If desired, sprinkle with toasted walnuts. Makes 10 to 12 slices.

Per serving: 449 cal., 24 g fat (12 g sat. fat), 143 mg chol., 388 mg sodium, 49 g carbo., 2 g fiber, 10 g pro.

Banana-Apple Butter Bread

*Try serving this sweet bread kabob-style
with berries and whipped cream dip.*
Prep: 25 minutes **Bake:** 45 minutes

1½ cups all-purpose flour
1½ teaspoons baking powder
½ teaspoon ground cinnamon
¼ teaspoon baking soda
¼ teaspoon salt
⅛ teaspoon ground nutmeg
2 eggs, slightly beaten
¾ cup sugar
½ cup mashed ripe banana
½ cup apple butter
¼ cup cooking oil

1. Preheat oven to 350°F. Grease and flour the bottom and ½ inch up the sides of a 9×5-inch loaf pan; set aside.

2. In a large bowl, stir together flour, baking powder, cinnamon, baking soda, salt, and nutmeg. Make a well in the center of the flour mixture; set aside. In another bowl, stir together the eggs, sugar, banana, apple butter, and oil. Add egg mixture to flour mixture. Stir just until moistened. Spoon batter into prepared pan.

3. Bake about 45 minutes or until a wooden toothpick inserted near center comes out clean. Cool in pan on a wire rack for 10 minutes. Remove from pan; cool completely on a wire rack. Wrap and store overnight. Makes 1 loaf (16 servings).

Per serving: 168 cal., 4 g fat (1 g sat. fat), 26 mg chol., 92 mg sodium, 31 g carbo., 1 g fiber, 2 g pro.

Simple Lemon-Sugar Snaps

Prep: 25 minutes **Bake:** 9 minutes per batch

¾ **cup butter, softened**

1 **egg**

1 **package two-layer-size lemon cake mix
(with pudding in the mix)**

1 **cup yellow cornmeal**

2 **tablespoons finely shredded lemon peel
Granulated sugar or coarse sugar**

1. Preheat oven to 375°F. In a mixing bowl, beat butter and egg with an electric mixer on medium speed for 30 seconds. Gradually beat in cake mix until combined; stir in cornmeal and lemon peel. If necessary, knead dough until combined.

2. Using 1 tablespoon of dough for each cookie, roll into 1-inch balls. Roll balls in sugar. Arrange balls 2 inches apart on ungreased cookie sheets.

3. Bake for 9 to 10 minutes or until bottoms are lightly browned. Let cool on cookie sheet for 1 minute. Transfer to a wire rack; cool completely. Makes about 3½ dozen cookies.

Per cookie: 99 cal., 5 g fat (2 g sat. fat), 14 mg chol., 114 mg sodium, 14 g carbo., 0 g fiber, 1 g pro.

Raspberry Waffle Stacks

These teeny treats are perfect when you just
want something light to finish off the meal.
And they only take 15 minutes to make!
Start to Finish: 15 minutes

4   frozen square waffles
2   3.5-ounce (single-serving)
     containers lemon or vanilla
     pudding
1   cup fresh raspberries

1. Toast waffles as directed on package.
Cut waffles in half. Top four halves
evenly with pudding, reserving about
2 tablespoons of the pudding. Top
pudding-covered waffles with
raspberries. Top with remaining waffle
halves. Spoon remaining pudding on top
of waffle stacks and garnish each with
a raspberry. Makes 4 servings.

Per serving: 159 cal., 4 g fat (1 g sat. fat),
11 mg chol., 331 mg sodium, 28 g carbo.,
3 g fiber, 2 g pro.

Pudding Tartlets

Start to Finish: 15 minutes

2   individual oblong creme-filled
    sponge cakes or 15 cubes
    frozen pound cake, thawed
    (½-inch cubes)
1   2.1-ounce package baked
    miniature phyllo
    dough shells
    (15 shells)
½   cup desired-flavor
    pudding
    Whipped cream or
    frozen whipped
    dessert topping,
    thawed
    Unsweetened cocoa
    powder

1. Slice sponge cakes in half
lengthwise, then crosswise
into about 1-inch pieces. Place
cake pieces in phyllo shells (may
have a piece or two left over).
Spoon pudding over cake pieces.
Cover and chill for 5 minutes. Top
with whipped cream and sprinkle with
cocoa powder before serving. Makes
15 tartlets.

Per tartlet: 54 cal., 2 g fat (0 g sat. fat),
3 mg chol., 47 mg sodium, 8 g carbo., 0 g fiber,
1 g pro.

Saucepan Rice Pudding

Leaving the skin on the apple adds color and nutrients to this recipe. Choose a tart or sweet apple, depending on what you like.

Prep: 10 minutes   **Cook:** 30 minutes

- 3   cups milk or plain soy milk
- ⅔   cup uncooked long grain rice
- 1   cup chopped unpeeled apple
- ¼   cup granulated sugar
- 1   teaspoon vanilla
      Brown sugar (optional)
      Ground cinnamon (optional)

1. In a large heavy saucepan, bring milk just to boiling; stir in rice. Cook, covered, over low heat for 30 to 40 minutes or until most of the milk is absorbed, stirring occasionally. (Mixture may appear curdled.)

2. Remove saucepan from heat. Stir in apple, granulated sugar, and vanilla. Spoon into dessert dishes. If desired, sprinkle with brown sugar and cinnamon. Serve warm. Makes 6 servings.

Per serving: 179 cal., 3 g fat (2 g sat. fat), 10 mg chol., 51 mg sodium, 33 g carbo., 1 g fiber, 6 g pro.

Fresh Strawberry Fool

A traditional English fool is made with gooseberries, but this version features beautiful, juicy strawberries. Light, creamy, and simple to make, the fool highlights the fresh ripened flavor of the fruit.

Start to Finish: 15 minutes

- ½   cup whipping cream
- ⅓   cup powdered sugar
- ½   teaspoon vanilla
- 1   8-ounce carton low-fat lemon yogurt
- 3   cups sliced fresh strawberries or 2 cups fresh blueberries
- ½   cup coarsely crumbled shortbread cookies (5 cookies)

1. In a chilled medium mixing bowl, combine whipping cream, powdered sugar, and vanilla. Beat with chilled beaters of an electric mixer on medium speed or a chilled rotary beater until soft peaks form (tips curl). By hand, fold in the yogurt.

2. Spoon the whipped cream mixture into 4 dessert dishes. Top with berries. Sprinkle with the crumbled cookies. Makes 4 servings.

To Make Ahead: Prepare as directed except do not add crumbled cookies. Cover; chill for up to 2 hours. To serve, sprinkle with cookies.

Per serving: 272 cal., 15 g fat (8 g sat. fat), 47 mg chol., 98 mg sodium, 32 g carbo., 3 g fiber, 4 g pro.

Fruit Waffle Bowls

Start to Finish: 15 minutes

- 1 4-serving-size package instant lemon
     or white chocolate pudding mix
- 1⅓ cups fat-free milk
- 1 cup fresh fruit (such as blueberries,
     sliced kiwifruits, sliced strawberries,
     sliced bananas, or raspberries)
- 4 waffle ice cream bowls or large
     waffle ice cream cones

1. Prepare pudding according to the package directions except use the 1⅓ cups milk. Spoon fruit into waffle bowls. Top with pudding. Serve immediately. Makes 4 servings.

Per serving: 196 cal., 3 g fat (1 g sat. fat), 6 mg chol., 399 mg sodium, 40 g carbo., 1 g fiber, 3 g pro.

Sparkling Sorbet Floats
Start to Finish: 10 minutes

1   pint mango, peach, strawberry,
      or desired-flavor frozen sorbet
    Desired-flavor carbonated fruit juice*,
      chilled

1. Place two scoops of sorbet in the bottom
of each of four 6- or 8-ounce glasses. Fill each
glass with carbonated fruit juice. Makes
4 servings.
*Tip: Make your own carbonated fruit juice by
combining your favorite juice with club soda.

Per serving: 128 cal., 0 g fat (0 g sat. fat), 0 mg chol.,
23 mg sodium, 33 g carbo., 0 g fiber, 0 g pro.

Cookie Crunch Fruit Sundaes
This "sundae" uses fruit instead of ice cream.
Start to Finish: 15 minutes

½   cup whipping cream
3   tablespoons chocolate-flavor syrup
3   chocolate sandwich cookies, crushed
2   medium bananas
1   cup strawberries, sliced
      Shredded coconut, toasted (optional)

1. Chill a medium mixing bowl and the beaters of
an electric mixer. In the chilled bowl, beat
whipping cream with an electric mixer on medium
speed until soft peaks form (tips curl). By hand,
gradually fold chocolate syrup into whipped
cream until smooth. Fold in crushed cookies.
2. Cut bananas in half crosswise, then in half
lengthwise. To assemble, arrange bananas and
strawberries in dessert dishes. Top with chocolate
mixture. If desired, sprinkle with toasted coconut.
Serve immediately. Makes 4 servings.

Per sundae: 247 cal., 13 g fat (7 g sat. fat), 41 mg chol.,
75 mg sodium, 32 g carbo., 3 g fiber, 2 g pro.

Cereal-Coated Ice Cream Sundaes

You have lots of options with this dessert.
Use whatever ice cream and fruit you have on hand.
The cereal adds an unexpected crunch.

Start to Finish: 15 minutes

1   **10-ounce package frozen raspberries or strawberries in syrup**
2   **bananas, peeled**
2   **cups wheat cereal flakes, crushed**
½   **teaspoon ground cinnamon**
1   **pint ice cream (desired flavor)**

1. Thaw raspberries according to the quick-thaw directions on package; set aside. Meanwhile, cut bananas into ½-inch slices. Divide banana slices among 4 dessert dishes; set aside.

2. Place cereal in a shallow dish; stir in cinnamon. Using an ice cream scoop, place one scoop of ice cream in crumbs; roll the ice cream to coat with crumbs. Transfer to a dessert dish with bananas. Repeat with 3 more scoops of ice cream. Sprinkle any remaining cereal mixture over ice cream in dishes. Spoon raspberries and their syrup over each serving. Makes 4 servings.

Per serving: 410 cal., 13 g fat (8 g sat. fat), 68 mg chol., 174 mg sodium, 71 g carbo., 5 g fiber, 5 g pro.

Cherry-Chocolate Sauce

Need a last-minute dessert? Use this sweet-tart sauce over purchased cheesecake, pound cake, or ice cream. If desired, garnish with maraschino cherries.

Start to Finish: 15 minutes

½ cup dried cherries
6 tablespoons butter
½ cup semisweet chocolate pieces
1½ cups powdered sugar
½ cup milk
1½ teaspoons vanilla

1. In a bowl, cover cherries with boiling water; let stand for 5 minutes. Drain well.

2. Meanwhile, in a large saucepan, melt butter and chocolate pieces over medium-low heat, stirring constantly. Whisk in powdered sugar, milk, and vanilla until smooth. Stir in the cherries. Spoon over cheesecake or ice cream. Refrigerate leftovers in a covered container for up to 1 week. Makes 2 cups sauce.

Per 2-tablespoon serving: 61 cal., 3 g fat (2 g sat. fat), 6 mg chol.,17 mg sodium, 9 g carbo., 0 g fiber, 0 g pro.

Fruit Whip

Start to Finish: 10 minutes

2 **peaches or mangoes**
2 **ounces cream cheese, softened**
2 **tablespoons white grape juice
   or orange juice**
2 **tablespoons chopped pistachios**

1. Pit, peel, and cut peaches into wedges. Divide fruit between 2 chilled dessert bowls.
2. In a small mixing bowl, beat together cream cheese and juice. Spoon over peaches. Top with chopped pistachios. Makes 2 servings.

Per serving: 229 cal., 14 g fat (7 g sat. fat), 32 mg chol., 87 mg sodium, 24 g carbo., 4 g fiber, 5 g pro.

Almond Poached Pears

*Look for glazed sliced almonds in the produce
section of your supermarket.*
Start to Finish: 15 minutes

1   **29-ounce can pear halves in syrup**
2   **tablespoons packed brown sugar**
½   **teaspoon ground nutmeg**
½   **teaspoon almond extract**
⅓   **cup sliced almonds, toasted, or
    purchased glazed sliced almonds
    Vanilla yogurt or ice cream (optional)**

1. Drain pear halves; reserve liquid. In a large
skillet, stir together pear liquid, brown sugar, and
nutmeg. Bring to boiling; stir until sugar is
dissolved. Add pears and almond extract, turning
pears to coat. Remove from heat; cover and set
aside for 5 minutes.

2. Serve pears with some of the poaching liquid
and sprinkle with almonds. If desired, serve with
vanilla yogurt or ice cream. Makes 6 servings.

Per serving: 174 cal., 4 g fat (0 g sat. fat), 0 mg chol.,
13 mg sodium, 33 g carbo., 2 g fiber, 2 g pro.

Sweet Basil Peaches

When summer rolls around, basil is everywhere. But in dessert? It's actually fantastic! To make this dish kid-friendly, opt for apple juice instead of white wine.

Start to Finish: 20 minutes

5	medium peaches or nectarines
½	cup sweet white wine, such as Gewürztraminer or Riesling, or apple juice
⅓	cup fresh basil leaves
1	to 2 tablespoons sugar (optional)
	Snipped and/or whole fresh basil leaves

1. Remove pits from 2 unpeeled peaches; chop. Set remaining whole peaches aside.

2. In a medium saucepan, combine chopped peaches, wine, ⅓ cup basil, and sugar, if necessary, to sweeten. Bring to boiling; reduce heat. Simmer, uncovered, for 12 to 15 minutes or until sauce is slightly thickened.

3. Remove and discard the basil. Pour peach mixture into a food processor; cover and process until smooth.

4. Remove pits from whole peaches; cut into wedges. Serve with peach sauce and additional basil. Makes 4 servings.

Per serving: 73 cal., 0 g fat (0 g sat. fat), 0 mg chol., 0 mg sodium, 13 g carbo., 2 g fiber, 1 g pro.

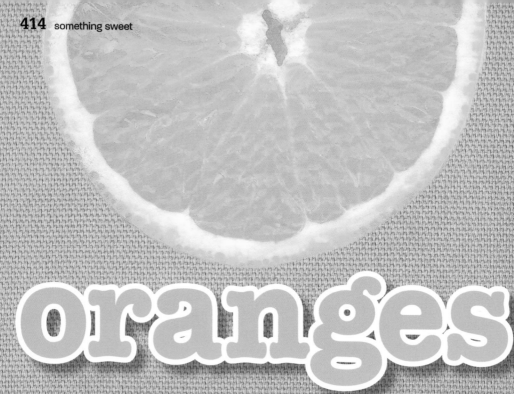

oranges

Sure, fresh, ripe oranges are terrific peeled and eaten plain, but they also taste great drizzled with sweet caramel sauce. Although oranges supply high levels of vitamin C, keep in mind that this vitamin begins to diminish as soon as the orange is cut. For highest levels, prepare this dessert right before you're ready to serve it.

Caramel Oranges

This elegant dish, laced with a distinct ginger flavor, is one of the quickest and easiest desserts you can make!

Start to Finish: 10 minutes

½	cup caramel ice cream topping
1	teaspoon finely shredded orange peel
4	medium oranges, peeled and sliced crosswise
1	tablespoon finely chopped crystallized ginger

1. In a small saucepan, combine caramel topping and orange peel. Cook over low heat until heated through.

2. To serve, arrange orange slices on 6 dessert plates. Drizzle with caramel mixture. Sprinkle each serving with ginger. Makes 6 servings.

Per serving: 133 cal., 0 g fat (0 g sat. fat), 0 mg chol., 74 mg sodium, 32 g carbo., 3 g fiber, 1 g pro.

Orange comes in third place as the world's **favorite flavor,** right after chocolate and vanilla.

apples

Can an apple a day really keep the doctor away? It's possible! Apples are packed with antioxidants and fiber, which can help in preventing certain ailments such as some cancers, memory loss, asthma, heart disease, and obesity. So grab your favorite apple variety and get a taste of healthful (and delicious) living. Or try one of the following apple recipes.

Choose-a-Flavor Caramel Apples

Jonathan apples have a nice size and flavor for this recipe. You can dip the caramel apples into other crunchy ingredients, such as crushed cookies, chopped peanuts, or assorted candies.
Prep: 25 minutes **Stand:** 30 minutes

- 10 small apples
- 10 wooden sticks
- 1 cup coarsely chopped toasted pecans, crushed pretzels, candy-coated milk chocolate pieces, and/or crunchy granola (optional)
- 21 ounces (about 75) vanilla caramels, unwrapped
- 3 tablespoons water
- 6 drops cinnamon oil, 1 cup semisweet chocolate pieces, or ½ cup creamy peanut butter

1. Wash and dry apples. Remove stems. Insert 1 wooden stick into the stem end of each apple.

Place apples on a buttered baking sheet. If desired, place chopped pecans, pretzels, candy-coated chocolate pieces, and/or granola in separate shallow dishes; set aside.

2. In a heavy medium saucepan, heat and stir the caramels and the water over medium-low heat just until caramels are melted. Remove saucepan from heat. Stir in cinnamon oil.

3. Working quickly, dip each apple into hot caramel mixture. (If necessary, add hot water, 1 teaspoon at a time, to caramel mixture to achieve dipping consistency.) To remove excess caramel, scrape off bottom of apple with a metal spatula. If desired, for extra crunch, dip bottoms of apples into pecans, pretzels, chocolate pieces, or granola. Set apples on prepared baking sheet and let stand 30 minutes or until firm. Makes 10 servings.

Per serving: 384 cal., 11 g fat (6 g sat. fat), 0 mg chol., 156 mg sodium, 67 g carbo., 7 g fiber, 2 g pro.

Hot Caramel Apple Pizza

Prep: 20 minutes **Bake:** 30 minutes
Cool: 30 minutes

½ of a 15-ounce package rolled
   refrigerated unbaked piecrust
   (1 crust)
¾ cup purchased caramel apple dip
¼ cup dairy sour cream
3 tablespoons all-purpose flour
1 medium apple, cored and
   thinly sliced
3 tablespoons packed brown sugar
½ teaspoon ground cinnamon
½ cup pecan halves
   Vanilla or cinnamon ice cream
   (optional)

1. Preheat oven to 375°F. Let piecrust stand
according to package directions. Unroll
piecrust onto a 12-inch round pizza pan; gently
press to edge of pan. Bake 12 to 15 minutes or
until crust is golden. Cool 15 minutes.
2. In a bowl, stir together ½ cup of the caramel
dip, sour cream, and flour. Spread caramel
mixture over cooled baked piecrust. Arrange
apple slices over caramel layer. In another
bowl, stir together brown sugar and cinnamon;
sprinkle over apple slices. Sprinkle pecan
halves over top.
3. Bake 15 minutes or until apples are tender.
Cool 15 minutes. In a saucepan, heat the
remaining ¼ cup caramel dip until warm;
spoon over pizza. Cut into wedges. If
desired, serve with ice cream. Makes 10 to
12 servings.

Per serving: 222 cal., 9 g fat (2 g sat. fat), 5 mg chol.,
211 mg sodium, 33 g carbo., 1 g fiber, 4 g pro.

Spiced Apple Drops

Prep: 20 minutes **Bake:** 10 minutes per batch

Cool: 1 minute per batch

- ½ cup butter, softened
- ⅔ cup granulated sugar
- ⅔ cup packed brown sugar
- 1 teaspoon ground cinnamon
- ½ teaspoon baking soda
- ½ teaspoon ground nutmeg
- ⅛ teaspoon ground cloves
- 1 egg
- ¼ cup apple juice or apple cider
- 2¼ cups all-purpose flour
- 1 cup finely chopped apple, peeled if desired
- 1 cup chopped walnuts
- 1 recipe Apple Frosting (recipe, below)

1. Preheat oven to 375°F. Lightly grease cookie sheets. In a bowl, beat butter with an electric mixer for 30 seconds.

2. Add the granulated sugar, brown sugar, cinnamon, baking soda, nutmeg, and cloves. Beat until combined. Beat in the egg and apple juice until combined. Beat in as much flour as you can with the mixer. Stir in remaining flour, apple, and walnuts.

3. Drop dough by rounded teaspoons 2 inches apart onto prepared cookie sheets. Bake for 10 to 12 minutes or until edges are lightly browned. Cool on cookie sheet for 1 minute. Transfer cookies to wire racks; cool completely. Spread with Apple Frosting. Makes about 40 cookies.

Per cookie: 152 cal., 6 g fat (2 g sat. fat), 14 mg chol., 44 mg sodium, 25 g carbo., 0 g fiber, 2 g pro.

Apple Frosting: In a medium mixing bowl, beat 4 cups powdered sugar, ¼ cup softened butter, 1 teaspoon vanilla, and 4 to 5 tablespoons apple juice to make a frosting of spreading consistency. Makes 1½ cups.

goin'

Just peel 'em and eat 'em.
Bananas are one of the fastest and
cheapest snacks around. Plus, they're
rich in fiber, potassium, and vitamin C,
and they provide a great energy boost
if eaten an hour before physical activity.
Next time you're hungry for something
light and fruity, grab a banana and whip
up one of these flavor-packed treats.

bananas

Sweet Banana Bruschetta

Start to Finish: 20 minutes

5 ½- to ¾-inch-thick slices sweet
   Hawaiian bread, egg bread,
   or raisin bread
1 medium banana, mashed (½ cup)
¼ cup cream cheese spread with
   pineapple
2 medium bananas, thinly sliced
1 tablespoon butter or margarine, melted
2 tablespoons packed brown sugar
   Chocolate-flavor syrup (optional)

1. Preheat broiler. Cut bread slices crosswise in halves or thirds. Lightly toast bread and let cool. Combine mashed banana and cream cheese in a medium bowl. Spread some of the mixture over each toasted bread slice. Place slices on a baking sheet. Arrange banana slices on top of cream cheese mixture. Brush bananas with melted butter. Sprinkle with brown sugar.

2. Broil bruschetta 4 to 5 inches from the heat for 30 to 60 seconds or until banana slices just begin to glaze (sugar will melt). If desired, drizzle with chocolate syrup. Serve warm. Makes 6 servings.

Per serving: 270 cal., 9 g fat (5 g sat. fat), 30 mg chol., 174 mg sodium, 43 g carbo., 3 g fiber, 5 g pro.

{ **Sweet Banana Bruschetta** is a surefire family pleaser with toasted sweet bread, bananas, and a gooey chocolate drizzle. }

Banana Split Trifles

Prep: 15 minutes **Freeze:** up to 1 hour

4 **soft-style chocolate chip or oatmeal
   cookies, crumbled**
2 **bananas, peeled and cut into chunks**
1 **quart tin roof sundae, chocolate chunk,
   or vanilla ice cream**
1 **12-ounce jar hot fudge sauce
   or strawberry preserves**
   Whipped cream

1. In each of 4 parfait glasses, layer cookies, bananas, scoops of ice cream, and fudge sauce (you may not use all of the ice cream or sauce). Top with whipped cream and additional crumbled cookies. Cover and freeze for up to 1 hour. Makes 4 servings.

Per serving: 524 cal., 23 g fat (12 g sat. fat), 48 mg chol., 161 mg sodium, 73 g carbo., 3 g fiber, 6 g pro.

Maple-Glazed Bananas

Choose bananas that are ripe but still firm. Overripe bananas will become mushy during cooking.

Start to Finish: 15 minutes

¼ cup butter
¼ cup packed brown sugar
¼ cup pure maple syrup or maple-flavor syrup
1 tablespoon lemon juice
½ teaspoon ground cinnamon
3 firm, ripe bananas, halved lengthwise and cut into 1-inch pieces
1 pint vanilla ice cream

1. In a skillet, melt butter over medium heat. Stir in brown sugar, syrup, lemon juice, and cinnamon. Bring to boiling; reduce heat. Simmer, uncovered, for 2 minutes. Add bananas; stir gently to coat with syrup mixture. Cook and stir 1 to 2 minutes or until heated through. Remove from heat. Serve over ice cream. Makes 4 servings.

Per serving: 471 cal., 24 g fat (15 g sat. fat), 99 mg chol., 135 mg sodium, 64 g carbo., 2 g fiber, 4 g pro.

DOUGH MUCH FUN

Let the grocery store do all the hard work for you!

Grab a package or roll of purchased dough and get ready to create some of the best desserts—in half the time of made-from-scratch! Cookies, bars, and dumplings make easy work of the once complicated kitchen task of baking. The hardest part is waiting for the oven timer to go off.

Quick Tip:
For easier handling, freeze the peanut butter balls for 30 minutes. Flatten the balls slightly to form disks, then press cookie dough around them.

Surprise Chocolate Bites

Prep: 30 minutes
Bake: 10 minutes per batch

- 1 **18-ounce roll refrigerated sugar cookie dough**
- ⅓ **cup unsweetened cocoa powder**
- ⅔ **cup creamy peanut butter**
- ⅔ **cup powdered sugar**
  Granulated sugar

1. Preheat oven to 350°F. Place cookie dough and cocoa in a large resealable plastic bag and knead to combine. In a bowl, stir together the peanut butter and powdered sugar until combined. With floured hands, roll the peanut butter mixture into 30 (1-inch) balls.

2. To shape cookies, take 1 tablespoon of cookie dough and make an indentation in the center. Press a peanut butter ball into indentation and form dough around ball to enclose it; roll ball gently in your hands to smooth it out. Repeat with remaining dough and peanut butter balls.

3. Place balls 2 inches apart on ungreased cookie sheets. Flatten the balls slightly with the bottom of a glass that has been dipped in granulated sugar. Bake for 10 to 12 minutes or until set. Transfer cookies to wire rack; let cool. Makes 30 cookies.

Per serving: 118 cal., 6 g fat (1 g sat. fat), 5 mg chol., 87 mg sodium, 15 g carbo., 0 g fiber, 2 g pro.

Peanut Butter Pretzel Pops

Prep: 25 minutes   **Bake:** 8 minutes per batch

- 1   18-ounce roll refrigerated peanut butter cookie dough or chocolate chip cookie dough
- 1   cup finely chopped dry-roasted peanuts or honey-roasted peanuts
- 10   to 12 pretzel rods, halved crosswise

1. Preheat oven to 375°F. Lightly grease cookie sheets; set aside. Roll dough into twenty to twenty-four 1¼-inch balls. Place peanuts in a small bowl or shallow dish. Roll dough balls in peanuts, pressing to coat dough balls evenly. Reshape dough into balls if necessary. Insert the cut end of a halved pretzel rod into each dough ball, pressing rod into, but not through, the end of the dough ball. Place 3 inches apart on prepared cookie sheets.

2. Bake for 8 to 10 minutes or until tops are lightly browned. Let cool for 1 minute on cookie sheets. Transfer to a wire rack and cool completely. Makes 20 to 24 cookies.

Per cookie: 178 cal., 10 g fat (2 g sat. fat), 7 mg chol., 222 mg sodium, 19 g carbo., 0 g fiber, 4 g pro.

Sunflower Chip Cookies

Prep: 20 minutes
Bake: 9 minutes per batch

1   **18-ounce roll refrigerated chocolate chip cookie dough**
½   **cup flaked coconut**
½   **cup dry-roasted sunflower kernels**

1. Preheat oven to 375°F. Place cookie dough and coconut in a large resealable plastic bag and knead to combine. Roll rounded teaspoons of dough in sunflower kernels to coat. Place balls 2 inches apart on ungreased cookie sheets.

2. Bake for 9 to 11 minutes or until golden brown. Cool for 1 minute on cookie sheets. Transfer cookies to wire rack; let cool. Makes about 2½ dozen cookies.

Per cookie: 101 cal., 5 g fat (2 g sat. fat), 2 mg chol., 6 mg sodium, 12 g carbo., 1 g fiber, 1 g pro.

How to store these treats

Layer cookies between waxed paper in an airtight container; cover. Store at room temperature up to 3 days or freeze up to 3 months.

Shortcut Chocolate Revel Bars

These all-time favorite bars can be made with a fraction of the effort using refrigerated oatmeal chocolate chip cookie dough.

Prep: 20 minutes   **Bake:** 25 minutes

1½ cups semisweet chocolate pieces
1 14-ounce can sweetened condensed milk (1¼ cups)
2 tablespoons butter
½ cup chopped walnuts or pecans
2 teaspoons vanilla
2 18-ounce rolls refrigerated oatmeal chocolate chip cookie dough

1. Preheat oven to 350°F. In a saucepan, combine chocolate pieces, condensed milk, and butter. Cook and stir over low heat until chocolate is melted. Remove from heat. Stir in nuts and vanilla.

2. Press two-thirds (1⅓ rolls) of the cookie dough into the bottom of an ungreased 15×10×1-inch baking pan. Spread chocolate mixture evenly over the cookie dough. Dot remaining cookie dough on top of chocolate mixture.

3. Bake about 25 minutes or until top is lightly browned (chocolate will still look moist). Cool on a wire rack. Cut into bars. Makes 30 bars.

Per bar: 255 cal., 13 g fat (5 g sat. fat), 13 mg chol., 136 mg sodium, 33 g carbo., 1 g fiber, 3 g pro.

Praline Crunch Bars

Toffee bits and pecans give this basic cookie dough a tasty twist with little effort.

Prep: 10 minutes **Bake:** 12 minutes

1   **18-ounce roll refrigerated sugar cookie dough**
½   **cup toffee pieces**
½   **cup finely chopped pecans**
1   **12-ounce package miniature semisweet chocolate pieces**
⅓   **cup toffee pieces**

1. Preheat oven to 350°F. Place cookie dough, the ½ cup toffee pieces, and the pecans in a large resealable plastic bag and knead to combine. Press dough evenly over the bottom of an ungreased 13×9×2-inch baking pan.

2. Bake for 12 to 15 minutes or until golden brown. Sprinkle with chocolate pieces immediately after baking; let stand for 5 to 10 minutes or until chocolate is softened, then spread evenly over the bars. Sprinkle with the ⅓ cup toffee pieces.

3. Chill for 10 to 15 minutes to set chocolate. Makes 28 bars.

Per bar: 191 cal., 11 g fat (4 g sat. fat), 8 mg chol., 105 mg sodium, 19 g carbo., 2 g fiber, 1 g pro.

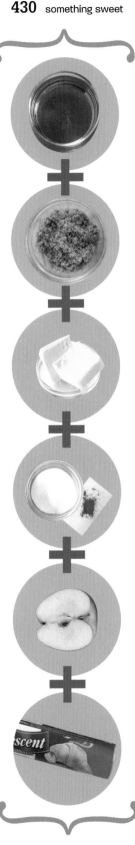

Easy Apple Dumplings

*Letting the dumplings cool for
30 minutes allows the syrup to
thicken slightly.*

Prep: 15 minutes   **Bake:** 25 minutes
Cool: 30 minutes

½   cup apple juice
⅓   cup packed brown sugar
2   tablespoons butter
2   tablespoons granulated
     sugar
1   teaspoon ground cinnamon
1   large cooking apple, peeled
     and cut into 8 wedges
1   8-ounce package (8)
     refrigerated crescent-roll
     dough
1   teaspoon coarse sugar
     Vanilla ice cream (optional)

1. Preheat oven to 375°F. Lightly grease a 2-quart square baking dish; set aside. In a saucepan, stir apple juice, brown sugar, and butter over medium-low heat until butter melts and sugar dissolves.

2. Meanwhile, in a bowl, stir together granulated sugar and cinnamon. Add apple wedges; toss to coat evenly. Unroll dough and separate at perforations. Place a coated apple wedge along the wide edge of each dough piece. Roll up dough around apple. Arrange in prepared baking dish. Slowly drizzle juice mixture over roll-ups to coat evenly. Sprinkle tops of roll-ups with coarse sugar.

3. Bake, uncovered, for 25 to 30 minutes or until golden and apples are tender. Cool for 30 minutes before serving. If desired, serve with ice cream. Makes 8 servings.

Per serving: 201 cal., 9 g fat (4 g sat. fat), 8 mg chol., 245 mg sodium, 28 g carbo., 1 g fiber, 2 g pro.

have your cake

(and eat it too!)

Doughnut Cakes

Prep: 25 minutes **Bake:** 20 minutes

Nonstick cooking spray
Flour
1 2-layer-size package yellow
    cake mix or your favorite-
    flavor cake mix
    Chocolate Glaze, Vanilla Glaze,
    and powdered sugar
    Nut topping, chocolate or
    multicolor sprinkles, or
    toasted coconut (optional)

1. Preheat oven to 350°F. Grease and flour three 8-inch round cake pans. Lightly coat the outside of three 6-ounce custard cups with cooking spray. Dust cups with flour; place upside down, in the center of the three pans; set aside.

2. Prepare cake mix according to package directions. Spoon batter into pans around custard cups, filling pans about half full. Bake for 20 to 30 minutes or until a wooden toothpick inserted in cakes comes out clean. Cool in pans on wire racks for 10 minutes. Run a knife around custard cup in each pan and around edges of pans. Invert cakes onto wire racks; carefully remove pans and custard cups. Invert cakes again onto another wire rack so top sides are up; let cool.

3. Top one cake with Chocolate Glaze, one with Vanilla Glaze, and sift powdered sugar over the remaining cake. If desired, top glazed cakes with nut topping, sprinkles, or coconut.

Chocolate Glaze: Stir together $2/3$ cup powdered sugar and $1/3$ cup unsweetened cocoa powder. Stir in $1/2$ teaspoon vanilla and enough milk (2 to 4 tablespoons) until smooth and of glazing consistency. Makes enough glaze for one 8-inch "doughnut."

Vanilla Glaze: Stir together 1 cup powdered sugar, $1/2$ teaspoon vanilla, and enough milk (1 to 2 tablespoons) until smooth and of glazing consistency. If desired, add 1 to 2 drops desired color food coloring. Makes enough glaze for one 8-inch "doughnut." Makes 18 servings.

Per serving: 220 cal., 8 g fat (1 g sat. fat), 37 mg chol., 195 mg sodium, 36 g carbo., 0 g fiber, 2 g pro.

These giant Doughnut Cakes are made in three 8-inch round cake pans; a custard cup placed in the center of each pan forms the hole. For bakery-style presentation, display the cakes in a large paper-lined box.

PB Swirl Ice Cream Cake

Prep: 45 minutes   **Freeze:** 6 hours or overnight

½   **gallon vanilla ice cream**
24   **chocolate sandwich cookies with**
       white filling
5   **tablespoons butter, melted**
30   **chocolate-covered wafer cookies**
       or your favorite chocolate-covered
       stick-shape candy bar
⅔   **cup peanut butter (not reduced-fat)**
¼   **cup honey**
2   **tablespoons cooking oil**
½   **of an 8-ounce container frozen whipped**
       dessert topping, thawed
½   **cup bottled hot fudge sauce**

1. Remove ice cream from freezer 30 minutes before using. Place chocolate sandwich cookies in food processor. Cover and process into fine crumbs. Add butter. Process to combine.

2. Line the sides of a 9-inch springform pan with wafer cookies. Reserve ¾ cup of chocolate crumb mixture. Spoon remaining crumb mixture into pan; press evenly over bottom.

3. In a small bowl, stir together peanut butter, honey, and oil until combined.

4. Spoon half of the ice cream into the prepared pan; spread evenly. Spoon half of the peanut butter mixture over ice cream and spread to edges. Sprinkle evenly with reserved chocolate crumb mixture, pressing mixture down with back of spoon.

5. Top with remaining ice cream; spread evenly. Top with the remaining peanut butter mixture, spreading to edges. Pipe whipped topping over cake. Place the cake on a baking sheet, cover loosely, and place in freezer. Freeze until cake is firm, at least 6 hours or overnight.

6. To serve, in a small saucepan, heat fudge sauce until warm. Drizzle over cake. Cut cake into wedges. Makes 16 servings.

Per serving: 539 cal., 33 g fat (17 g sat. fat), 78 mg chol., 269 mg sodium, 54 g carbo., 1 g fiber, 7 g pro.

Flower Power Cake

Prep: 30 minutes   **Bake:** per package directions

1   **2-layer-size package lemon cake mix**
1   **16-ounce can white frosting**
    Small gumdrops
    Candy-coated fruit-flavor pieces
    Sour fruit-flavor straw candy

1. Preheat oven to 350°F. Prepare and bake cake mix according to package directions using two 8- or 9-inch round baking pans. Cool on wire racks for 10 minutes. Remove from pans. Cool cakes completely.

2. Place one cake layer on a serving plate; spread with frosting. Top with remaining cake layer. Frost top and sides of cake with frosting.

3. To decorate cake with flowers, slice small gumdrops in half horizontally to form flower petals. Use candy-coated fruit-flavor pieces for flower centers. Flatten gumdrops and cut into leaf shapes for leaves. Snip sour straws to desired lengths and use for flower stems. Makes 12 to 16 servings.

Per serving: 448 cal., 17 g fat (4 g sat. fat), 55 mg chol., 371 mg sodium, 70 g carbo., 0 g fiber, 3 g pro.

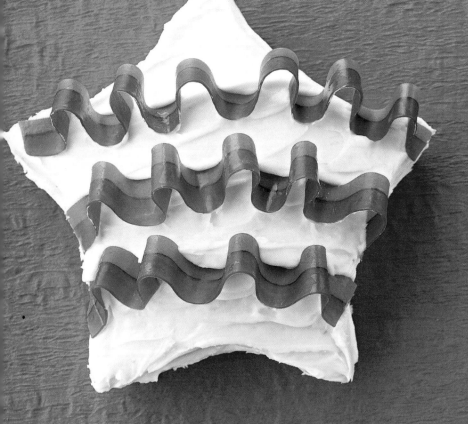

Shooting Star Cakes

Prep: 1 hour   **Bake:** 14 minutes

1   package 2-layer-size confetti
     or white cake mix
2   16-ounce cans white frosting
     Desired decorations, such as rolled fruit
       leather, red cinnamon candies,
       shoestring licorice, and/or nonpareils
       and colored sugars

1. Preheat oven to 350°F. Grease and flour 12 miniature star-shape baking pans.* Prepare cake mix according to package directions. Fill each about half full (about ⅓ cup batter). Bake for 14 to 16 minutes or until a toothpick inserted near the center of each comes out clean. Cool in pans on wire racks for 10 minutes. Remove from pans and cool completely.

2. Frost each cooled star with frosting and decorate as desired. Makes 12 star-shape cakes.

* Tip: Look for miniature star-shape pans in the cake decorating section of hobby stores, online, or at specialty cooking stores. If you can't find star-shape pans, bake the cake in a greased and floured 15×10×1-inch baking pan for 16 to 18 minutes or until a toothpick inserted near center comes out clean. Cool in pan on a wire rack. Use a 3- to 4-inch star-shape cutter to cut shapes from the cake. Frost tops only and decorate as desired. (The cakes' cut edges are very tender and will crumble if you attempt to frost.) Makes 8 to 10 star-shape cakes.

Per cake: 560 cal., 20 g fat (6 g sat. fat), 0 mg chol., 438 mg sodium, 88 g carbo., 0 g fiber, 3 g pro.

Watermelon Cake

Start to Finish: 45 minutes

1   **2-layer-size strawberry, cherry chip, or desired-flavor cake mix**
2   **16-ounce cans white frosting**
    Paste or liquid red and green food coloring
    Black jelly beans

1. Preheat oven to 350°F. Grease and flour two 9-inch round baking pans; set aside. Prepare cake mix according to package directions. Divide batter between prepared pans.

2. Bake according to package directions. Cool in pans on wire racks for 10 minutes. Remove cake from pans. Cool cakes completely on wire racks. Cut each cake layer in half to create 4 semicircles.

3. Tint one can of frosting with red food coloring until it reaches desired shade of watermelon red. Tint remaining frosting with green food coloring until it reaches desired shade of watermelon-rind green. Divide in half; add food coloring to one half to make a darker green frosting.

4. Frost top of one cake piece with red frosting. Top with another cake piece. Frost rounded side with darker green frosting. Make a 1-inch-thick stripe of lighter green frosting inside the darker green frosting on the top and straight side of cake. Frost remaining top portion and straight side with red frosting to resemble watermelon slice. Pipe vertical stripes of lighter frosting on rounded side. Top with black jelly beans to resemble seeds. Repeat with remaining cake pieces and frosting. Makes 2 watermelon cakes (16 to 18 servings).

Per serving: 436 cal., 17 g fat (4 g sat. fat), 41 mg chol., 330 mg sodium, 66 g carbo., 0 g fiber, 2 g pro.

Orange Pumpkin Cake

Prep: 30 minutes **Bake:** 40 minutes
Stand: 2 hours

- 1 2-layer-size white cake mix
- 1 3-ounce package orange-flavor gelatin
- 1½ cups water
- 2 eggs
- ⅓ cup cooking oil
- ¼ cup semisweet chocolate pieces
- 1 teaspoon shortening
- 3 cups powdered sugar
- 3 to 4 tablespoons pulp-free orange juice

  Orange food coloring
  Large green gumdrops

1. Preheat oven to 350°F. Grease and flour a 10-inch fluted tube pan* and two 2½-inch muffin cups. In a bowl, combine cake mix, gelatin, the water, eggs, and oil. Beat on low speed for 30 seconds; scrape bowl. Beat on medium speed for 2 minutes. Spoon batter into prepared muffin cups, filling each two-thirds full. Pour remaining batter into tube pan.

2. Bake 18 to 22 minutes for cupcakes, 40 to 45 minutes for cake, or until a wooden toothpick inserted in center comes out clean. Cool 10 minutes. Remove from pans; cool completely.

3. In a saucepan, melt chocolate pieces and shortening over low heat until smooth. Pour mixture over one inverted cupcake to coat completely; let stand until set. In a bowl, combine powdered sugar and enough orange juice to make an icing of pouring consistency. Tint with food coloring.

4. Place cake on serving plate. Place plain cupcake in center of cake. Pour icing over cake to coat completely; let stand until set. Place chocolate-covered cupcake in center of cake (on top of first cupcake) to resemble a stem.

5. On a lightly sugared surface, roll gumdrops flat with rolling pin. Cut into strips for vines; use a small leaf-shape cutter to cut out leaf shapes. Use leaves and vines to garnish cake. Serve cake within 12 hours. Makes 12 servings.

Lightly dust your work surface with granulated sugar to keep the rolled-out gumdrops from sticking. A double bonus: The sugar granules add a delicious bit of texture and help the leaf-shape cutter slice through the gumdrop.

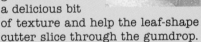

*Tip: Look for fluted tube pans in the cake decorating section of hobby stores, online, or at specialty cooking stores. Some fluted cake pans will create a more "classic" pumpkin shape, so be sure to look closely if you're purchasing a new one. However, any fluted cake pan will be sufficient in creating the general pumpkin shape.

Per serving: 408 cal., 12 g fat (3 g sat. fat), 35 mg chol., 329 mg sodium, 73 g carbo., 0 g fiber, 4 g pro.

Dutch Apple Cake

Serve this fall favorite as a dessert or a mid-morning snack.

Prep: 25 minutes   **Bake:** 60 minutes

1	**package 2-layer-size yellow cake mix**
1	**teaspoon ground cinnamon**
¼	**teaspoon ground cloves**
1	**cup applesauce**
2	**medium apples, cored, peeled and very finely chopped**
1	**cup raisins**
1	**cup chopped pecans**
1	**cup powdered sugar**
2	**tablespoons maple syrup**
	Milk

1. Preheat oven to 350°F. Grease and flour a 10-inch fluted tube pan. Prepare cake mix according to package directions, except stir cinnamon and cloves into dry cake mix and substitute 1 cup applesauce for the water. Stir in apples, raisins, and pecans. Spread in prepared pan.

2. Bake for 60 to 70 minutes or until a toothpick comes out clean when inserted near center and top springs back when pressed lightly. Cool 10 minutes in pan. Remove from pan and cool completely on wire rack.

3. In a small bowl, stir together powdered sugar and maple syrup. Add enough milk to make a drizzling consistency. Drizzle over cooled cake. Makes 12 to 16 servings.

Per serving: 352 cal., 17 g total fat (3 g sat. fat), 0 mg chol., 282 mg sodium, 54 g carbo., 2 fiber, 2 g pro.

Pumpkin Pear Cake

When you turn this cake upside down, a delicious caramel-pear topping appears.

Prep: 25 minutes **Bake:** 35 minutes
Cool: 35 minutes

- 1 **cup packed brown sugar**
- ⅓ **cup butter, melted**
- 1½ **teaspoons cornstarch**
- 2 **15-ounce cans pear halves in light syrup**
- ½ **cup coarsely chopped pecans**
- 1 **2-layer-size spice cake mix**
- 1 **cup canned pumpkin**

1. Preheat oven to 350°F. In a small bowl, combine brown sugar, butter, and cornstarch. Drain pears, reserving 3 tablespoons of the syrup. Stir reserved syrup into brown sugar mixture. Pour mixture into a 13×9×2-inch baking pan. If desired, cut pear halves into fans by making 3 or 4 lengthwise cuts ¼ inch from the stem end of each pear half to the bottom of the pear half. Arrange whole or fanned pear halves on top of syrup in pan, cored sides down. Sprinkle pecans evenly into pan.

2. Prepare cake mix according to package directions except decrease oil to 2 tablespoons and add pumpkin. Slowly pour cake batter into pan, spreading evenly.

3. Bake for 35 to 40 minutes or until a wooden toothpick inserted near center comes out clean. Cool in pan on a wire rack for 5 minutes. Run a thin metal spatula around edges of cake. Carefully invert cake into a 15×10×1-inch baking pan or onto a very large serving platter with slightly raised sides. Cool about 30 minutes before serving. Serve warm. Makes 16 servings.

Per serving: 337 cal., 15 g total fat (4 g sat. fat), 51 mg chol., 254 mg sodium, 51 g carbo., 2 g fiber, 3 g pro.

Easy Swirl Cheesecake

Prep: 20 minutes   **Chill:** 1 hour

1   **11.1-ounce package cheesecake mix**
2   **tablespoons dry-roasted sunflower kernels**
½   **teaspoon finely shredded orange peel**
¼   **cup semisweet chocolate pieces**
1½   **teaspoons shortening**
     Sliced strawberries

1. Prepare cheesecake crust according to package directions, except stir in sunflower kernels. Pat crust mixture firmly into bottom of an 8-inch springform pan; set aside.

2. Prepare cheesecake filling according to package directions, except increase milk to 1¾ cups and stir in orange peel. Spoon filling into crust-lined pan, spreading evenly. Place chocolate pieces and shortening in a small microwave-safe bowl. Microwave on 100-percent power (high) for 1 minute. Stir until melted and smooth. Pipe melted chocolate mixture onto cheesecake and create swirl pattern (see photo, below).

3. Cover and chill at least 1 hour or up to 24 hours. Run a knife around outside edge of cheesecake to loosen it from the sides. Remove sides of pan. Use a wide metal spatula to loosen and lift cheesecake from bottom of pan. Slide onto a serving plate. Arrange sliced strawberries around top edge of cheesecake just before serving. Makes 10 servings.

Per serving: 366 cal., 18 g fat (9 g sat. fat), 34 mg chol., 452 mg sodium, 46 g carbo., 3 g fiber, 7 g pro.

To make the swirl pattern, fill a resealable plastic bag with the melted chocolate mixture; snip a small hole in the corner. Pipe the mixture on top of cheesecake in a spiral. Starting at the center of the cheesecake, pull a toothpick through the spiral lines to create a swirl pattern on the top.

If you need a fast dessert, angel food should be your new go-to choice. It's light, easy-to-prepare (just purchase it), and melt-in-your-mouth-delicious! Could it be any more perfect?

Do you have 15 minutes? get dessert!

Chocolate-Drizzled Angel Food Cake

Start to Finish: 15 minutes

1	7- to 8-inch angel food cake
2	tablespoons orange liqueur or orange juice
2	tablespoons orange juice
6	ounces bittersweet or dark chocolate
½	cup butter
1½	cups powdered sugar
¼	cup whipping cream

1. Generously poke holes from the top of the cake all the way through using a long wooden skewer. Stir together orange liqueur and orange juice. Drizzle orange mixture over cake. For the chocolate glaze, in a small saucepan, combine bittersweet chocolate with butter over low heat, stirring frequently until melted. Remove from heat. Whisk in powdered sugar and whipping cream. Spoon evenly over cake. Makes 10 to 12 servings.

Per serving: 396 cal., 23 g fat (12 g sat. fat), 43 mg chol., 49 g carbo., 2 g fiber, 3 g pro.

French-Toasted Angel Food Cake

Start to Finish: 15 minutes

1   7- to 8-inch angel food cake
6   eggs, slightly beaten
1½   cups milk
3   tablespoons sugar
2   teaspoons vanilla
1   tablespoon butter
    Whipped cream
    Maple syrup
    Cut-up fresh strawberries

1. Slice the angel food cake into ten to twelve 1-inch-thick wedges. In a shallow dish, combine eggs, milk, sugar, and vanilla. Soak wedges in egg mixture for 1 minute per side.

2. In a nonstick skillet or on a nonstick griddle, melt butter over medium heat. Cook 4 wedges at a time for 1 to 2 minutes on each side or until golden. To serve, stand slices in cake formation. Top with whipped cream. Drizzle with maple syrup and top with strawberries. Serve immediately. Makes 10 to 12 servings.

Per toasted serving: 275 cal., 12 g fat (6 g sat. fat), 187 mg chol., 305 mg sodium, 33 g carbo., 1 g fiber, 8 g pro.

Honey-Rosemary Angel Food Cake

Start to Finish: 15 minutes

½ cup honey
8 ounces soft cream cheese
½ cup whipping cream
1 teaspoon lemon juice
1 teaspoon snipped fresh
   rosemary
1 7- to 8-inch angel food cake

1. In a saucepan, heat honey until thin enough to brush over cake. Beat together cream cheese, whipping cream, and 1 tablespoon of the honey until light and fluffy. Fold in lemon juice and rosemary.

2. Slice the cake in half horizontally. Brush tops of layers with remaining honey. Spread bottom layer with filling. Top with second layer. Serve immediately or cover and chill up to 2 hours. Makes 10 to 12 servings.

Per serving: 208 cal., 8 g fat (5 g sat. fat), 27 mg chol., 324 mg sodium, 32 g carbo., 0 g fiber, 4 g pro.

Tropical Angel Cake

For even more tropical flavor, sprinkle this refreshing, summery cake with toasted shredded coconut.

Start to Finish: 15 minutes

1   **8- to 9-inch angel food cake**
3   **cups desired fruit-flavor sherbet**
¼   **cup unsweetened pineapple juice**
1   **8-ounce container frozen whipped dessert topping or frozen light whipped dessert topping, thawed**
    Fresh raspberries (optional)

1. Slice cake in half horizontally. Hollow out insides, leaving two 1-inch-thick shells. Spoon sherbet into bottom shell. Set top half, hollow side down, over bottom. Poke holes in top using a long wooden skewer or the tines of a long fork. Drizzle pineapple juice over top of cake.

2. Frost top and sides of cake with whipped topping. Serve immediately or cover loosely with plastic wrap; freeze up to 1 week. If desired, garnish with raspberries. Makes 12 servings.

Per serving: 222 cal., 4 g fat (4 g sat. fat), 0 mg chol., 305 mg sodium, 41 g carbo., 2 g fiber, 3 g pro.

Angel Food Cake with Lemon Cream & Berries

If blueberries are too expensive, substitute whatever berries or other fresh fruit is in season for this easy, light dessert.

Start to Finish: 15 minutes

3   6-ounce cartons lemon yogurt
1   4-serving-size package instant vanilla pudding mix
1   8-ounce container frozen light whipped dessert topping, thawed
     Fresh blueberries
1   8- to 9-inch angel food cake, cubed

1. In a medium bowl, whisk together yogurt and one-fourth of the pudding mix until smooth. Gradually add remaining pudding mix to yogurt, whisking after each addition until smooth. Fold in whipped topping, half at a time. Serve lemon cream and berries over cubed cake. Makes 16 servings.

Tip: Any leftover lemon cream can be stored in the refrigerator up to 4 days.

Per serving with ½ cup berries: 172 cal., 2 g fat (2 g sat. fat), 2 mg chol., 269 mg sodium, 34 g carbo., 4 g fiber, 3 g pro.

Snow Angel Cake

Toasting the coconut gives it more flavor and a delightful light crunch—a nice contrast to the fluffy dessert topping and cake.

Start to Finish: 15 minutes

1   purchased angel food cake

2   ounces white baking chocolate or white baking pieces

1   8-ounce container frozen light whipped dessert topping, thawed

¼   cup flaked or shredded coconut, toasted if desired

1. Place cake on a serving plate; set aside.

2. In a small saucepan, melt white chocolate over low heat, stirring occasionally. Remove from heat.

3. Frost cake with whipped topping. Sprinkle with coconut. Drizzle with melted white chocolate. Makes 12 servings.

Per serving: 154 cal., 5 g fat (4 g sat. fat), 1 mg chol., 225 mg sodium, 24 g carbo., 1 g fiber, 2 g pro.

Kitty Cupcake Cones

Prep: 45 minutes   **Bake:** 20 minutes per batch

24   ice cream cones with flat bottoms
 1   2-layer-size package desired-flavor
       cake mix
 1   16-ounce can white frosting
12   to 15 drops desired food coloring
       Small jelly beans
       Candy corn
       Black shoestring licorice or pull-apart
         twist candy

1. Preheat oven to 350°F. Stand ice cream cones in 2½-inch muffin cups. Prepare cake mix according to package directions. Fill each cone with 2 to 3 level tablespoons of batter. Bake 20 to 25 minutes or until a toothpick inserted in centers comes out clean. Cool completely. (Use remaining batter to make 12 regular-size cupcakes and bake according to package directions.)

2. Combine frosting and food coloring for desired color. Frost tops of cupcakes. For kitty faces, use jelly beans for eyes and nose, use candy corn for ears, and cut licorice strands for whiskers and mouth. Serve the same day. Makes 24 kitty cupcake cones plus about 12 regular cupcakes.

Per cupcake cone: 180 cal., 7 g fat (2 g sat. fat), 18 mg chol., 140 mg sodium, 28 g carbo., 0 g fiber, 1 g pro.

For perfect cupcake cones, bake a few cones with each amount of batter (2 and 3 tablespoons) to see which quantity works best. The amount varies among cake-mix brands.

Lazy-Daisy Cupcakes

Prep: 25 minutes
Bake: 12 minutes per batch

Nonstick cooking spray
1 16-ounce package pound
   cake mix
1 egg
1 16-ounce can white frosting
   Small gumdrops
   Small oval or round candies
   Lollipop or popsicle sticks
   Jelly beans
   Bay leaves (optional)

1. Preheat oven to 350°F. Line 1¾-inch muffin cups with paper bake cups or lightly coat cups with cooking spray; set aside. Prepare cake mix according to package directions, except add 1 additional egg. Spoon about 1 tablespoon batter into prepared cups, filling each about two-thirds full. Bake in the preheated oven about 12 minutes or until a wooden toothpick inserted in centers comes out clean. Cool in pans on wire rack for 5 minutes. Remove from pans; cool completely. Repeat with remaining batter. (The batter makes 84 mini cupcakes. If desired, make as many mini cupcakes as you wish and use remaining batter to make regular-size cupcakes.)

2. Frost cupcakes. Cover and store any remaining frosting in the refrigerator for another use. On a sugared surface, flatten a small gumdrop using a rolling pin or your fingers; snip to resemble flower petals. Place on frosted cupcake with a small candy in the center to resemble a flower.

3. Using a small knife, cut a small slit into the bottom of each cupcake, cutting through paper liner, if using, and partway into bottoms of cupcakes. Insert a lollipop stick into bottom of each cupcake.

4. Fill a small pot with foam to hold the cupcake pops. Top with jelly beans. If desired, add bay leaves. Makes 84 mini cupcakes or 24 regular-size cupcakes.

Per mini cupcake: 49 cal., 2 g fat (1 g sat. fat), 8 mg chol., 31 mg sodium, 8 g carbo., 0 g fiber, 4 g pro.

Cut the colorful blooms out of flattened gumdrops. Push lollipop sticks into cakes and arrange in a flowerpot filled with foam. Add candies, then tuck in a few herb leaves—and you're done.

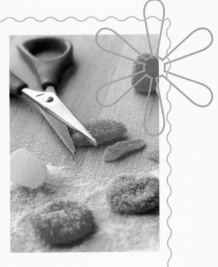

Caramel Gingerbread Cupcakes

To make this quicker, skip Step 1. Instead, use boxed ice cream and cut it into 1-inch slices, then quarter the slices. Sprinkle with toffee bits. Or, if you're really short on time, just top each cupcake with a scoop of ice cream and garnish!

Prep: 30 minutes **Bake:** 15 minutes
Freeze: 4 hours

½   gallon vanilla ice cream, softened
2   to 3 teaspoons grated fresh ginger or ½ to 1 teaspoon ground ginger
½   to ¾ cup toffee baking bits
1   14- or 14½-ounce package gingerbread mix or 9×9-inch purchased gingerbread
1¼ cups lukewarm water
1   egg
1   12-ounce jar caramel ice cream topping or 1 recipe Orange-Caramel Sauce
6   gingersnap cookies, broken in half

1. Line a 13×9×2-inch baking dish with plastic wrap or foil; set aside. In a medium bowl, combine softened ice cream with the ginger. Spread ice cream into prepared dish. Sprinkle with toffee bits, pressing lightly into ice cream. Cover and freeze at least 4 hours.

2. Preheat oven to 350°F. Grease or line twelve 2½-inch muffin cups with paper bake cups; set aside. Prepare gingerbread mix according to package directions, using the lukewarm water and egg. Divide batter evenly among muffin cups. Bake for 15 to 18 minutes or until a wooden toothpick inserted in centers comes out clean.

3. Just before serving, in a small saucepan, heat caramel topping over medium-low heat, stirring occasionally. Keep sauce warm.

4. To assemble, remove wrappers from cupcakes. Place cupcakes on plates or in shallow bowls; set aside. Lift ice cream from dish using plastic wrap; remove plastic wrap. Cut out twelve 2-inch squares of ice cream. (Reserve any leftover ice cream to eat later.) Top cupcakes with the ice cream squares. Top ice cream with cookie halves; drizzle with warm caramel topping or, if desired, Orange-Caramel Sauce. Makes 12 servings.

Orange-Caramel Sauce (optional): Prepare caramel sauce as directed, except stir ½ cup orange marmalade into caramel topping until marmalade melts.

To Make Ahead: Place cupcakes (without ice cream topping) in an airtight container. Cover and freeze for up to 4 months. Thaw at room temperature. Prepare ice cream topping as directed and garnish as directed.

Per serving: 585 cal., 28 g fat (13 g sat. fat), 111 mg chol., 370 mg sodium, 78 g carbo., 1 g fiber, 6 g pro.

Lemon-Spice Cupcakes

*If desired, top the cupcakes with crushed
gingersnaps, a twist of candied lemon peel,
or snipped spiced gumdrops.*

Prep: 25 minutes   **Bake:** per package directions

1   package 2-layer-size lemon cake mix
1   16-ounce can cream cheese frosting
1   teaspoon apple pie spice

1. Preheat oven to 350°F. Line twenty-four
2½-inch muffin cups with foil or paper bake cups;
set aside. Prepare cake mix according to package
directions for cupcakes. Spoon batter into prepared
cups, filling each about one-half to two-thirds full.
Bake according to package directions. Cool for
5 minutes. Remove from cups and cool completely
on a wire rack.

2. Stir together the cream cheese frosting and
apple pie spice. Spread frosting over each cupcake.
Makes 24 cupcakes.

Per cupcake: 183 cal., 5 g fat (2 g sat. fat), 0 mg chol.,
198 mg sodium, 33 g carbo., 0 g fiber, 1 g pro.

Coconut-Lemon Puffs

Prep: 35 minutes **Bake:** 25 minutes

¼ cup butter
¼ cup all-purpose flour
⅛ teaspoon salt
1 cup purchased unsweetened
    coconut milk or milk
5 egg yolks
⅓ cup sugar
⅓ cup shredded coconut
2 tablespoons finely shredded
    lemon peel
¼ cup lemon juice
5 egg whites
    Shredded coconut, toasted

1. Preheat oven to 350° F. Butter the sides of six 6-ounce soufflé dishes or custard cups.

2. In a saucepan, melt butter over medium heat. Stir in flour and salt; add milk. Cook and stir until very thick and bubbly around edges of pan; set aside. In a mixing bowl, beat yolks and sugar with electric mixer on high speed about 3 minutes or until light and lemon-colored. Stir in coconut, lemon peel, and lemon juice.

3. Stir in flour mixture. Wash beaters. In a separate bowl, beat egg whites with mixer on medium speed until stiff peaks form. Fold about 1 cup of the beaten egg whites into lemon mixture. Fold lemon mixture into the remaining beaten whites. Transfer to prepared dishes (dishes will be full).

4. Bake, uncovered, 25 to 30 minutes or until a knife inserted near the center comes out clean. Sprinkle with toasted coconut. Serve immediately. Makes 6 servings.

Per serving: 337 cal., 25 g fat (18 g sat. fat), 199 mg chol., 221 mg sodium, 23 g carbo., 2 g fiber, 8 g pro.

Tropical Fruit Shortcakes

Start to Finish: 15 minutes

1	cup chopped papaya
1	8-ounce can pineapple tidbits (juice pack), drained
2	kiwifruits, peeled and coarsely chopped
2	tablespoons honey
¼	cup orange juice
6	slices purchased pound cake or angel food cake
1½	cups frozen whipped dessert topping, thawed
	Toasted macadamia nuts (optional)

1. Stir together papaya, drained pineapple, kiwifruit, and honey. Drizzle orange juice over cake slices. Spoon fruit mixture over cake slices. Top with whipped topping. If desired, sprinkle with nuts. Makes 6 servings.

Per serving: 428 cal., 19 g fat (12 g sat. fat), 115 mg chol., 163 mg sodium, 30 g carbo., 2 g fiber, 5 g pro.

Crunchy Pound Cake Slices

Start to Finish: 15 minutes

4 ½-inch slices purchased pound cake, thawed
¼ cup chocolate-hazelnut spread
¼ cup chopped nut topping for ice cream
1 pint caramel or cinnamon ice cream

1. Preheat broiler. Place the pound cake slices on a baking sheet. Broil 3 to 4 inches from heat for 1 minute on each side or until lightly browned. Cool slightly. Spread one side of each slice with 1 tablespoon of the chocolate-hazelnut spread. Sprinkle with nut topping; pat gently to form an even layer. Transfer each slice to a dessert plate and serve with a scoop of ice cream. Serve immediately. Makes 4 servings.

Per serving: 387 cal., 22 g fat (8 g sat. fat), 62 mg chol., 193 mg sodium, 42 g carbo., 1 g fiber, 7 g pro.

{ mix-and-match menus }

What's for dinner? Here's an easy answer— just pick one of these quick-fix menu ideas composed of the recipes from this book. There's a perfect menu for everything!

Family Breakfast

Hash Brown Casserole,
page 183

Orange Dream Fruit Salad,
page 308

Easy Cinnamon Rolls,
page 35

A.M. Special

Ham Wafflewich,
page 22

Fruit Kabobs with Creamy
Dipping Sauce, page 329

Blend 'n' Go, page 40

Play-Date Lunch

Twisted Tuna Salad,
page 149

Down-to-Earth Granola,
page 57

Frozen Yogurt Pops,
page 72

Weekend Lunch

Apple Butter & Banana
Sandwiches, page 325

Cinnamon Bagel Fries,
page 32

Pretzel Pets, page 328

Kids' Sack Lunch

Carrot-Raisin Peanut Butter
Sandwiches, page 326

Bear-y Good Snack Mix,
page 343

Winter Salad, page 304

Kids' Choice Supper

Saucy Cheeseburger
Sandwiches, page 228

Carrots with Dried
Fruit Dip, page 55

Cookie Crunch Fruit
Sundaes, page 408

Finger Fare

Pulled Chicken
Sandwiches, page 155

Veggie Nuggets, page 334

Pudding Tartlets, page 405

Family Favorites

Shortcut Lasagna, page 256

Cheese Bread,
page 361

Sweet Banana
Bruschetta, page 421

Dinner in 30 Minutes

Fast Chicken & Rice,
page 151

Asian Appetizer Salad,
page 386

Ice Cream with Orange-
Praline Sauce, page 289

Comfort Foods

Ketchup-Glazed
Meat Loaves, page 252

Italian-Style
Macaroni Salad, page 188

A Billow of Berries
'n' Brownies, page 397

Down-Home Cooking

Salsa Swiss Steak, page 226

Bacon and Spinach Mashed Potatoes, page 193

Shortcut Malted Chocolate Cake, page 276

Make Mom Proud

Chicken & Noodles, page 250

Home Run Garlic Rolls, page 100

Stir 'n' Bake Strawberry Shortcakes, page 275

Warm Up

White & Green Chili, page 238

Corn Bread Mini Muffins, page 103

Praline Crunch Bars, page 429

Picnic on the Patio

Finger Lickin' BBQ Chicken, page 221

Speedy Potato Salad, page 265

Rhubarb Raspberry Pie, pages 270–271

Saturday Night Grill-Out

Sweet & Spicy BBQ Ribs, pages 262–263

Grilled Veggie Foil Packets, page 357

White Chocolate & Blackberry S'mores, page 69

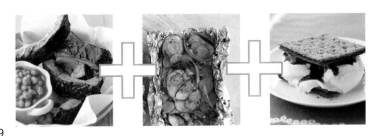

Pasta Perfect

Chicken Linguine
with Pesto Sauce, page 157

Parmesan
Twists, page 102

Crunchy Pound Cake
Slices, page 459

Catch of the Day

Lemony Cod with Asparagus,
page 216

Garden Pasta, page 95

Quick Fruit Crisp, page 273

Extra Flavor

Chili-Lime Chicken Salad,
page 84

Honey & Poppy Seed
Biscuits, page 300

Raspberry Waffle Stacks,
page 404

Special Occasion

Rosemary Chicken with
Vegetables, page 131

Grilled Asparagus with
Lemon, page 99

Angel Food Cake with Lemon
Cream & Berries, page 449

Company's Coming
for Supper

Apple-Pecan Pork Chops,
page 139

New Potato Bake, page 284

PB Swirl Ice Cream Cake,
page 434

Southern Favorite
Orange Sesame Ribs,
page 240

Boursin Mashed Potatoes,
page 192

Easy Fruit Cobbler, page 272

Mamma Mia
Chili Macaroni, page 169

Pesto Biscuits, page 194

Raspberry-Cranberry Sauce,
page 304

Go Greek
Greek-Style Chicken Skillet,
page 212

Garlic Bread, page 360

Honey-Rosemary Angel Food
Cake, page 447

Olé Yay
Southwest Chicken Wraps,
page 159

Cheesy Mexican-Style
Vegetable Soup, page 242

Lemon-Spice Cupcakes,
page 456

Asian Fusion
Glazed Teriyaki Pork Chops
with Potatoes, page 207

Golden Green Bean Crunch,
page 264

Caramel Oranges, page 415

{recipe index}

Metric Information

The charts on this page provide a guide for converting measurements from the U.S. customary system, used throughout this book, to the metric system.

Product Differences

Most of the ingredients called for in the recipes in this book are available in most countries. However, some are known by different names. Here are some common American ingredients and their possible counterparts:

Sugar (white) is granulated, fine granulated, or castor sugar.

Powdered sugar is icing sugar.

All-purpose flour is enriched, bleached or unbleached white household flour. When self-rising flour is used in place of all-purpose flour in a recipe that calls for leavening, omit the leavening agent (baking soda or baking powder) and salt.

Light-colored corn syrup is golden syrup.

Cornstarch is cornflour.

Baking soda is bicarbonate of soda.

Vanilla or vanilla extract is vanilla essence.

Bell peppers are capsicums.

Golden raisins are sultanas.

Volume & Weight

The United States traditionally uses cup measures for liquid and solid ingredients. The chart below shows the approximate imperial and metric equivalents. If you are accustomed to weighing solid ingredients, the following approximate equivalents will be helpful.

1 cup butter, castor sugar, or rice = 8 ounces = 1/2 pound = 250 grams

1 cup flour = 4 ounces = 1/4 pound = 125 grams

1 cup icing sugar = 5 ounces = 150 grams

Canadian and U.S. volume for a cup measure is 8 fluid ounces (237 ml), but the standard metric equivalent is 250 ml.

1 British imperial cup is 10 fluid ounces.

In Australia, 1 tablespoon equals 20 ml, and there are 4 teaspoons in the Australian tablespoon.

Spoon measures are used for smaller amounts of ingredients. Although the size of the tablespoon varies slightly in different countries, for practical purposes and for recipes in this book, a straight substitution is all that's necessary. Measurements made using cups or spoons should be level unless stated otherwise.

Common Weight Range Replacements

Imperial / U.S.	Metric
1/2 ounce	15 g
1 ounce	25 g or 30 g
4 ounces (1/4 pound)	115 g or 125 g
8 ounces (1/2 pound)	225 g or 250 g
16 ounces (1 pound)	450 g or 500 g
1 1/4 pounds	625 g
1 1/2 pounds	750 g
2 pounds or 2 1/4 pounds	1,000 g or 1 Kg

Oven Temperature Equivalents

Fahrenheit Setting	Celsius Setting*	Gas Setting
300°F	150°C	Gas Mark 2 (very low)
325°F	160°C	Gas Mark 3 (low)
350°F	180°C	Gas Mark 4 (moderate)
375°F	190°C	Gas Mark 5 (moderate)
400°F	200°C	Gas Mark 6 (hot)
425°F	220°C	Gas Mark 7 (hot)
450°F	230°C	Gas Mark 8 (very hot)
475°F	240°C	Gas Mark 9 (very hot)
500°F	260°C	Gas Mark 10 (extremely hot)
Broil	Broil	Grill

*Electric and gas ovens may be calibrated using celsius. However, for an electric oven, increase celsius setting 10 to 20 degrees when cooking above 160°C. For convection or forced air ovens (gas or electric), lower the temperature setting 25°F/10°C when cooking at all heat levels.

Baking Pan Sizes

Imperial / U.S.	Metric
9x1 1/2-inch round cake pan	22- or 23x4-cm (1.5 L)
9x1 1/2-inch pie plate	22- or 23x4-cm (1 L)
8x8x2-inch square cake pan	20x5-cm (2 L)
9x9x2-inch square cake pan	22- or 23x4.5-cm (2.5 L)
11x7x1 1/2-inch baking pan	28x17x4-cm (2 L)
2-quart rectangular baking pan	30x19x4.5-cm (3 L)
13x9x2-inch baking pan	34x22x4.5-cm (3.5 L)
15x10x1-inch jelly roll pan	40x25x2-cm
9x5x3-inch loaf pan	23x13x8-cm (2 L)
2-quart casserole	2 L

U.S. / Standard Metric Equivalents

1/8 teaspoon = 0.5 ml	
1/4 teaspoon = 1 ml	
1/2 teaspoon = 2 ml	
1 teaspoon = 5 ml	
1 tablespoon = 15 ml	
2 tablespoons = 25 ml	
1/4 cup = 2 fluid ounces = 50 ml	
1/3 cup = 3 fluid ounces = 75 ml	
1/2 cup = 4 fluid ounces = 125 ml	
2/3 cup = 5 fluid ounces = 150 ml	
3/4 cup = 6 fluid ounces = 175 ml	
1 cup = 8 fluid ounces = 250 ml	
2 cups = 1 pint = 500 ml	
1 quart = 1 litre	

From Better Homes and Gardens®

Cook Great
Food Fast
with these other favorites

Meredith® BOOKS